Bridging Engagement Gaps

Bridging Engagement Gaps

An Essential Resource Guide
to Strengthen Workplace Engagement

VINCENT MIHOLIC, PH.D.

BRIDGING ENGAGEMENT GAPS
AN ESSENTIAL RESOURCE GUIDE
TO STRENGTHEN WORKPLACE ENGAGEMENT

iUniverse books may be ordered through booksellers or by contacting:

iUniverse
1663 Liberty Drive
Bloomington, IN 47403
www.iuniverse.com
1-800-Authors (1-800-288-4677)

ISBN: 978-1-4917-9688-7 (sc)
ISBN: 978-1-4917-9687-0 (hc)
ISBN: 978-1-4917-9689-4 (e)

Library of Congress Control Number: 2016908003

Print information available on the last page.

iUniverse rev. date: 10/29/2016

To my dear wife, Michelle,
so engaged, we married;
To our brilliant daughter, Grace,
amazing, amusing, and cherished;
I am very grateful for your
love, humor, and tolerance!

Contents

Acknowledgements

The readers below toiled with messy stages of this manuscript. I am very appreciative of their considerable assistance to help me bring order to chaos. My wife, Michelle, a consummate English teacher and much more emotionally intelligent than I, remains my most patient first responder. My brother, Phil, a fantastic fiction writer, provided early, pertinent suggestions. Jeff Binder brought clarity and a discerning engagement perspective. Joseph Long nudged me further in the right direction. Jennifer Bullock's insights breathed more life into my ideas. I am grateful for their time and labor, and a special shout out to Scott Manguno.

To colleagues with whom I have served or advised on past and present engagement and recognition committees, and their understanding of ever-evolving and arduous work, as well as humor so important to the end results, thank you for the enjoyment brought to the process.

I thank each reader for choosing *Bridging Engagement Gaps* and forgiving any remaining confusion in my wording!

A special thank you is heartily extended to David Zinger for generosity of spirit and time dedicated to the opening words.

Throughout the book, I refer to leaders whose kindness encourages others to be free to explore, experiment and take chances, discover, be themselves, grow, change, and most of all model love and fun. I have encountered two such leaders in my work career. To Mel and Ned, I remain very grateful for the opportunities and support.

Foreword

by David Zi nger

I founded and host the 7000 member global Employee Engagement Network. I have seen almost every resource on employee engagement created over the past 8 years. Vincent Miholic's book is a very worthy, valuable, and helpful addition to the resources available on engagement. I applaud his unique and eclectic point of view laced with fresh insights and encouragement for the reader to reflect deeply on core engagement principles.

Bridging Engagement Gaps provides a cogent entry point for someone new to engagement while also offering a fine opportunity with those very familiar with the topic to refresh their thinking and perspective.

Vince offers us his expert guidance on the employee engagement journey as we bridge employee engagement gaps. He builds a multi-faceted bridge to span the disengagement gap so that our organizations and we are more fully engaged.

He avoids a prepackaged tour of guidance through engagement while setting the stage for us to explore both the superhighways of engagement while not neglecting the nooks and crannies of how we lead, manage, and work. After reading his exploration, you will arrive at your work with new insights and a better understanding of engagement.

I appreciated so many of his statements, such as, "for engagement to flourish, a disposition to build relationships must be present, accompanied by letting go of the security blanket of indispensability, status, and certainty. The expert must shift his or her priority from self-insurance to assuring on-going development of others, sharing, and creating reliance on many autonomous and fearless collaborators."

Vince also offers his unique voice to the engagement journey fused with extensive research and resources and provides full credit to the myriad of resources on engagement. And, perhaps, only Vince could talk about employee engagement and refer to Kim Kardashian and Mother Teresa in the same paragraph.

So pick up the book, dive right in and engage fully in both reading what Vince writes and taking action back in your workplace to make engagement better for all. He states, "Satisfaction is an example of complacency; engagement is an example of artistry." You won't finish reading this book being complacent, and you will be better equipped with the tools to develop your artistry of engagement.

Enjoy the following pages. Engage along with me– the best is yet to be.

David Zinger
www.davidzinger.com
Founder and Host– The Employee Engagement Network.

Introduction

Anyone who has held a few different jobs and has been in the workforce for decade or longer, can point to exemplary executives or influential colleagues who helped move work from being merely palatable to having more fun. I was fortunate to be influenced by one of my best bosses during my very first job as a hardware clerk during my high school and early college years. This great fortune, at minimum wage but with profit sharing, was a formative experience and remains a high benchmark against which I compare other experiences and bosses. What made it different? In part, what I experienced was being valued and respected, feeling like I was an integral part by being exactly deployed, by being reminded of what was important, and by being given the freedom to take on various responsibilities. I was surprised by being invited to join the owners as they trekked to the central warehouse on a stock run and when they offered unexpected opportunities. I was supported when I made mistakes and coached through errors with compassion and understanding rather than judgment, suspicion, or punishment.

Since that first job, where the priority was always attending to customer questions and needs, moving from unloading trucks and stocking shelves, ringing up sales, tracking inventory, to cutting glass and pipe, each motion encouraged and supported by a great boss, I have pitched gravel under a hot Arizona sun, maintained an apartment complex, painted and renovated houses, drove a panel truck delivering stacks of the morning news at 4:00 a.m., worked as a field representative for a major media research firm, and dedicated more than 25 years to a career in education. Along the way, few other owners or supervisors have lived up to that early formative experience. The difference, I believe, was that my first boss possessed an intuitive gift: an unconditional sense of what was right and a genuine concern for everyone. He understood, too, and never wavered from tapping into the unique and full reserves and promise within each individual.

Bridging Engagement Gaps explores those facets that nourish such a precious gift: realizing that by fully recognizing others, we recognize the untapped giftedness in ourselves. It also sheds light on flaws and failures that diminish us or hold us back from fully utilizing best practices associated with heightened engagement.

While reading an early draft of *Bridging Engagement Gaps*, my wife, Michelle, asked the tricky question, "Who's the intended audience?" Embedded in her question is "Who is responsible for uncovering gifts and nourishing talents at work?" The answer spans the organizational chart, and, of course, each person must map a course to realize personal horizons. Moreover, individual chapters in the book could have been specifically written for people in the board room or in the trenches, CEOs, or front-line managers and supervisors. In fact, the book is written for a collective us throughout the workforce.

I have made a concerted effort to frame "leadership" as everyone's stake in personal and organizational success, from an intern to a 30-year employee, from front line-workers to owners. Leadership, too, extends beyond title and position to basic decency and integrity. This concept of leadership insists upon widespread participation in critical decision-making, selfless motivation, and leading oneself through situations that result in maximum engagement for all.

With one exception: all engagement roads lead to the immediate supervisors whose conscious choices emphatically and empathetically orchestrate how others work together. While each person's role in an organization will influence degrees of results in responding to engagement needs, formal conductors[1]– namely those holding executive positions– possess greater sway in influencing others and shaping culture.

Therefore, the main intent of the book is to suggest principles and actions to help ourselves and each other to be the best we can be, whether in positions where we are still acclimating to new work, where we have obtained mastery, or in more challenging or successive positions. Because of the complexity of organizational contexts and interconnected, interactive roles (or in disengaged environments, feelings of disconnectedness and inactive roles) specific answers are complemented by exploratory questions to help navigate your specific engagement needs.

One of the goals of the book was to condense the most important aspects of engagement found in research, business articles, the arts, popular culture, philosophy, and in every day interactions. Intended as a starting point, each chapter provides tools, questions, and warnings for those who are arguing a case for and currently working at building stronger, longer lasting engagement. I use a variety of metaphors, hopefully not too mixed, pertaining to creating energy, being constructivists, and maintaining workplace clockworks (the cover art? See "Leader as Horologist" within this book or merely reexamine the nature of creativity and the young hero in Scorsese's film *Hugo*) to explore engagement in both abstract, concrete, and human terms. The more detailed engagement resources concentrate on readily accessible methods through associated web articles and sites.

Cultivating engagement is directly tied to learning more about engagement and altering behaviors toward more genuine caring for each other's success. Thus, Chapters 1 and 2, "Work" and

"Engagement Redefined" lay a cultural foundation for exploring the meaning of engagement.

In Chapter 3, engagement, in the abstract, could be considered both a value as well as an outcome, but our specific day-to-day, person-to-person actions to improve the workplace are our actual values. Thus, Chapter 3, "Active Values" asks to consider behaviors and explore how to translate definitions to actual lived values. The core value is what actions result in the demonstration of valuing others.

Chapter 4, "Disengagement and The Walking Dead," offers a metaphorical workplace barometer, and specific answers to the easiest part of the engagement puzzle, demonstrating appreciation through no cost/low cost acts of recognition. Offered here are universal engagement practices, employing the practices that work for everyone because they feel right and are intrinsically, morally, and ethically "good."

Chapter 5, "Derailed," visits variables that interfere with making engagement progress. Foremost, engagement entails complex interactions and requires everyone to draw out the best in each other. And when this does not happen, modeling and mutual respect are sacrificed. As everyone holds a share of responsibility in the engagement dance, modeling and coaching are not the exclusive terrain of someone who holds a managerial title. Everyone, in any position, brings influential attitudes and interactions (positive or negative) to the work product.

Chapter 6, "At What Price Engagement?" narrows the focus to unraveling the paradox of a significant derailer, misunderstandings about how we attend to workers' salaries and how we view value. Typing "employee engagement ROI" into a search engine quickly yields substantial commentary and research, much of which has been combed through and synthesized into the pages that follow, exposing the production, cultural, and monetary costs associated with disengagement[2] and, by extension, the benefits of engagement. Business articles are replete with scores of statistics exposing the negative effects of being dismissive of employees and hailing the dire state of disengagement in our early 21st century workforce.[3]

Obviously, companies are adjusting to transient employees and episodic employment trends; this shift to a more mobile workforce may explain part of an embedded reticence to "scale up" or marshal an engagement advantage. Others, however, stay relevant by blending creativity with pragmatics. Examples of long-term strategies that tend to understand engagement are Starbucks, whose top leaders continue to demonstrate their understanding of engagement ROI, as evidenced by distance education opportunity provided to its U.S. employees or housing allowances to those in China.[4] Or witness the U. S. military's 2016 acknowledgment of work-life balance benefits to recruit and retain women in the armed services.

Following that vein, Chapter 7, "A Taxonomy of Engagement," the book's core chapter, expands on the concrete realities of engagement in the context of moral and ethical prerequisites. In evaluating and assessing engagement initiatives, you may find the engagement taxonomy sheds light on unacknowledged or unresolved issues that confound progress. This chapter reaches beyond the paycheck, beyond survival, to refocus on motivators that stimulate workers so that they are encouraged to, invited to, and know how to thrive. Learning more about what autonomy means, and what sharing looks like, peels back an opaque curtain of control and silence.

Threads of all these pieces culminate in "Everyone Is a Leader," Chapter 8, which encourages more reflection about the roles we play. In addition to the vision of a pervasive and meaningful workplace education for all, including leadership development for all, the hard science of engagement is unequivocally tied to deficiencies in soft skills development. As all of the literature suggests in making headway with engagement, we have failed most at knowing and appreciating each other.

Given the moral, ethical, and psychological considerations outlined in the taxonomy, Chapter 9, "Transform Thyself," returns to personal and leadership considerations: particularly, the values exhibited from our formal leaders at the apex of the organizational hierarchy compounded by a heightened empowerment of everyone's share in leadership to make a difference.

Because actions modeled by our most immediate managers have a tremendous impact on an initiative's success, *Bridging Engagement Gaps* conveys a direct appeal to formal leaders. Executive teams set the tone as well as earmark and deploy the resources to navigate the engagement obstacle course. Thus, top leaders' commitment must be solid, long-lasting, and able to withstand naysayers, critics, their own shortcomings, and the often difficult journey that accompanies an honest and protracted venture into engagement territory.

Since managers, particularly, contribute to loss to the bottom line when people are not engaged, Chapter 10 is specifically written for "For Bosses Only," whose actions can be products of perceived competition and trappings of position. A consequence of unfounded or unproductive paranoia is that talented employees who welcome the right seat on the bus, scratching their heads about how to advance to more challenging work (and higher salary), become bored with or languish in unsatisfying jobs, or leave.

The closing chapter, "How Can I Help" returns us to thinking about where we are and asks, "Where do we begin" anew.

To complement the Chapter discussions, a basic library of the book's key words, articles, and related touchstones are found in the appendixes, some of which I hope are new to you and offer, beyond your current understanding, a trajectory to finding additional ideas, added perspective, and solutions to propel next steps.

An intent of *Bridging Engagement Gaps* is to fuel a personal understanding of engagement as well as drive discussions and team meetings toward more meaningful and fruitful conclusions.

In the final stages of production, I remembered Mortimer Adler's essay, "How to Mark a Book," in which he insists,

> There are two ways in which one can own a book. The first is the property right you establish by paying for it, just as you pay for clothes and furniture. But this act of purchase is only the prelude to possession. Full ownership comes only when you have made it a part of yourself, and the best way to make yourself a part of it is by writing in it. Reading, if it is active, is thinking…, [and] the marked book is usually the thought-through book. And that is exactly what reading a book should be: a conversation between you and the author.[5]

With Adler's "how" in mind, beyond the scores of exploratory questions that are posed throughout, I thought I should invite the reader to actively participate, so I chose to leave the Index incomplete and open-ended to invite you to bridge the gap between writer and reader. Use the empty space to map the page numbers that most touch on your current needs and issues. Over time, as some issues are resolved and others emerge, your marks should change.

Now, if you are "a die-hard anti-book-marker," that's ok, too. Just looking at the most recurrent words listed in the index, I hope, is interesting in and of itself.

Disengagement may well be the longest continuing human capital management issue facing business and industry, education, and public organizations. The debilitating effects of disengagement include unnecessary and costly failures and turnover, conscious and unconscious sabotage, lack of productivity, and declining health and well-being. This book alone cannot solve the idiosyncratic issues any particular workplace may be experiencing, but it does provide core strategies and probes deeper to unearth solutions to those problems.

I am thankful and gratified that this resource has reached your hands! Hearing about your progress and to initiate a conversation with you is perhaps the best measure of the book's intent. Please connect by sending your thoughts and stories to miholic@cox.net.

Chapter 1

WORK

"For constructivists, the moral response is a caring response.... The only good opinion is a humanistic one, one that shows an immense respect for the world and the people in it and for those you are going to affect." –Mary Field Belenky, et. al., *Women's Ways of Knowing.*

~

In the seminal 1974 oral history *Working: People Talk about What They Do All Day and How They Feel about What They Do,* author Studs Terkel's core conclusions foretold of the fundamental variables now touted as engagement "drivers." Compared now to 21st century definitions of engagement, Terkel presciently describes workers' desires as a "search for daily meaning as well as daily bread, for recognition as well as cash, for astonishment rather than torpor; in short, for a sort of life other than a Monday through Friday sort of dying."[1]

Core to satisfaction at work, beyond a paycheck, is meaningfulness of work. This includes consciously choosing pathways to challenge complacency and mediocrity. Despite systematic constraints that cause floundering, the responsibility in revealing meaning and unlocking passion, or escaping the common place, resides in each employee. Meaning is always a personal quest and derived by diving into growth and regulating self in relationship to tasks and contexts.

However, the organizational chart does exist, so leaders are responsible for "driving"[2] the processes and mitigating road blocks to help construct meaning within ourselves, our respective departments, units, and among the company of fellow travelers. Managers, supervisors, directors, and executives who serve others possess substantial influence in creating effective contexts and tasks which fuel worker passion and engagement.

Thus, formal leaders also possess a greater share of engagement responsibility, yet they often emblazon the scaffolding of their "construction" sites with the dubious motto "Manage to Avoid." This architecture of disengagement manages to breed indifference. Alternatively, the depth of design in making a difference resides in personal answers to two questions:

Am I allowed space to flourish?
Are my talents appreciated?

Responses to these questions imply joint responsibility, but for each person to progressively add value, we must also ask general organizational questions, such as "Am I provided the opportunity to make a difference and to bring my greatest assets? Are the values I bring valued by the company I keep? And more specific questions: Am I provided sufficient development and autonomy to make decisions, ask hard questions to fuel my initiative without threat, suspicion, or dismissal? Does the company or organization have purposeful and real, meaningful growth and development concretely built into my schedule and annual performance plan?"

Consumed by deadlines, attending to daily appreciation, acknowledgement, and recognition (valuations) may appear as superfluous considerations to some, but remains a necessary part of facile multi-tasking in the most engaged cultures. Yet, too often, the work day is overladen with tasks in which the employee fulfills the job description without earning the benefit of discretionary time. No time appears to be available to think beyond the immediate demands.

The "above and beyond" initiative engagement attracts can be easily ignored. Perhaps this is why many managers will argue during an annual performance review, "It's unrealistic to believe that you have earned a top rating." Actually, the standards are not so high; ironically, they are not high enough. For instance, an employee's efforts may have resulted in millions of dollars of recurring profits or savings. The employee may be recognized at a luncheon for the contribution but sometimes not a single high level executive is in attendance or takes the time to personally congratulate the person.

Or conversely, a team carries out an impossibly complex project without proper prep time nor resources. Against long odds, the outcome is moderately successful but more publically and privately criticized for its failings. Rather than leaders coaching and guiding the team members through regrouping and improvements, blame is ascribed. Some team members are pulled off the project rather than providing new or reinvigorating roles within the team to create greater collective opportunity and success.

Managers protect fragile distortions of what excellence means when they suggest that high marks are unattainable. For instance, in year-end evaluations, many of us have heard some form of this declaration, "If everyone earns a four out of four, there's no more to achieve!" Professing that only one or two employees are "Outstanding," thus maintaining a normal curve of mediocrity, is far easier than actually facing the obvious: that is, the failure to legitimately coach and dedicate ample time to help everyone excel and attain what is an outstanding level for them. What's missing is not a team member's skills and acumen, which should have been properly identified during hiring, but managerial accountability.

In the end, disengaged supervisors are likely not honest enough to talk to their disengaged employees, or equally destructive, not honest enough to acknowledge engaged employees, who by omission are being taught to be disengaged or mediocre. "Work," when managers ignore the obvious, lacks open, systematic means of fully attending to and understanding the interconnectivity of the person's direction, goal, participation, and fit within the company and its mission.

Above Board or Under Cover

And employees, perhaps after prior experiences of being disenfranchised or ignored, intrinsically feel unable to discuss their ambitions, concerns, or growth opportunities with their supervisors. Similarly, the opportunity for input or participation in decision-making are noticeably sparse. New leaders may lament, "I'm constrained by and limited to…," yet the truths are found in how we, in ourselves and in others, cultivate a universe of creative and questioning minds. We should not find ourselves captive to the ordinary. Time must expand to attend to neglected engagement needs.

While later in this book, the television show *The Walking Dead* is used as a workplace metaphor, another popular series, *Undercover Boss*, has generated a telling mixture of pertinent business lessons.[3] The most important lesson is the actual ability to slip undercover (and not be recognized) reveals the real problem of disconnectedness that cripples awareness, not being aware of employee concerns about problems they perceive to be at hand or their stories: "It shouldn't take an undercover executive or a reality TV production crew to shine a spotlight on outstanding employees."[4] Problems, from lack of appreciation to substandard customer service, are not reported nor accountability measures addressed as a result of the lack of employee or manager apathy. This may be compounded or produced by fear associated with patterns of retribution upon those who blow the whistle on questionable practices or overlooked needs. Therefore, we need to function above cover to aspire toward more:

- **Satisfaction**. Do what you can to put employees at ease and eliminate fear, gossip, manipulation, intimidation. Meeting basic needs requires moving beyond self and includes keeping promises and assuring fairness.

- **Empowerment**. Your role requires you to be an organizational coach. Step back, observe and adjust your approach by honestly including others. Remember, a great process is not the goal; a happy customer is, and happy customers are an effect of empowered, well equipped, and appropriately acknowledged and deployed employees.

- **Appreciation**. Colleagues thrive when acknowledgement for work product is *genuine*, appeals to individual preferences, and is pervasive and systematic (including discovering and recognizing outstanding people who made a difference). Acknowledgement is *reciprocal*.

- **Listening.** Leave your office, go the where the work is. Seek to understand employees' work experience viewpoints and follow-up with tangible, palpable actions after receiving feedback. But that listening must be other-centric, with clear intent to advance service, mission, and others, not self.

- **Empathy.** Leaders work harder to understand the personal stories of people carrying out the work; in so doing, they need to equitably extend the benefits and options that they enjoy to all, for example, extending the luxury of flex-time in order for all to responsibly cope with personal needs.

If we find, of our own volition, sanctity and comfort in complacency, then we should not find cause to complain about a regimented and monotonous work day, about salary, nor worry about fissures in workplace engagement. Our actions and inactions have helped shape and create the routine, the hum-drum. Predating the positive psychology teachings of today, James Allen suggested at the turn of the 20th century, "We gather in the sweet and bitter fruits of our own planting,"[5] so if the box in which we find ourselves is confining, too limiting, or too damaging to our well-being, the only healthy choice is to pursue engagement by breaking out. As good begets good, selfishness begets self, leaders (we) should be consciously and continuously helping each other to break through or break out. Hypocrisy and cynicism, therefore overall disengagement, feeds on leaders who succumb to choosing self over service or universal good.

This "sort of dying," status quo trap is usually constructed not from organizational rules but from worker and supervisor acquiescence to complacency. The trap is almost always accompanied by management's unresolved or ignored feedback, sometimes accompanied by control, ulterior motives, or sheer impoverished management skills. While some ambiguity is natural in dynamic organizations and some uncertainly is present while spurring innovation,[6] unambiguous and recurrent communication connecting individuals' meaning and purpose to institutional mission is constantly needed to maintain energy and push past impasse or conflict. Unfortunately, the by-product of complacency and undue compliance is worker frustration, meaninglessness, and disconnection.

A Reality or a Fantasy of Our Own Creation

But this trap is an illusion, akin to the symbolism captured in the 64 year-old mouse, Mr. Jingles, from Steven King's *The Green Mile*.[7] A central theme of the work is redemption. In one crucial scene, King' protagonist, prison guard Paul Edgecombe, consoles Eduard Delacroix, a distraught death row inmate as his execution date nears. The guards are entertained by Eduard's pet mouse, whose performances never cease to amuse. He worries about the fate of his cherished pet. To ease the prisoner's mind, Edgecombe fabricates the imaginary "Mouseville" and assures Eduard that his mouse would be a prime candidate for becoming a marquis performer in this imaginary mouse circus.

A fitting place to work and fitting into the workplace is not a fairytale, nor should it be a circus game where the participants run a mysterious obstacle course to win a prize or curry favor. Some leaders find solace in perpetuating control through misdirection, smoke and mirrors, micromanagement, or running employees through unnecessary myths and mazes. At worst, some leaders act like Edgecombe's fellow guard, the sadistic Percy Wetmore, who seated by nepotism, taunts Delacroix by stating that Mouseville does not exist.

Deep down, Delacroix admits the cards are stacked against him, but he would rather believe that the escape from confinement is perhaps as safe as the harbor promised for his mouse. Mr. Jingles is long-lived because someone cares enough to breathe more life into him.

Leaders can be more forthright and much more creative than spinning white lies to assuage worker dissatisfaction. Leaders need to be more deliberate and deliberative in cultivating others, building cultures where workers collaborate with each other to create joy at work, find fun in work, and shepherd learning and growth. We can have joy, fun, and grow at work without sacrificing excellence. In fact, without joy and fun, we cannot grow.

What the engagement research tells us is that we have not fared particularly well in understanding what fun and joy represent. We are better at perpetuating an illusion that we have adequately met workers' needs than we are at examining "why" we have not fully met the worker. And perhaps because it takes as much effort as any other critical part of a business plan, M. Scott Peck, author of *The Road Less Traveled*, reminds us that all of us foster disillusion when "settling for the maintenance of a miserable status quo in preference to the tremendous amount of effort they realize will be required to work their way out of their particular traps."[8]

We know, in fact, what a great company looks like and basic acts required to escape traps of an ineffective workplace. The "hows" to valuing others are not mysterious. General engagement strategies and practices have been ardently discussed for years, just as the effects of manipulation and dehumanizing abuses have revealed themselves for centuries. The first step is possessing sufficient fortitude, will, and commitment to respond to the needs. Even if a metric is not available or a measurement is not a viable option, the priorities of how we cultivate value and productivity in, with, and among others is far from a Mouseville fantasy.

Breadth of commitment tells us quite a lot about both our dominant behaviors and ourselves. Our responses tells us about resolve and integrity.

The politically expedient tact is to protect self and maintain image (particularly adopted by managers) than attend to others. The "tell" of the illusion is that the manager's image is unrelated to realizing the company's mission. The worst managers are most uncomfortable with the reality that fun and joy are probably among the best known cultural attributes and reliable measures of workplace engagement and excellence. As we explore engagement, employees are either obviously enjoying or not enjoying their work. The excitement of the culture reveals all. How we get to fun and enjoyment is the harder part.

The wherewithal to implement engagement strategies to harvest more pleasure in work rests on the shoulders of all leaders at every intersection, but particularly through the vision, tone, and commitment exhibited by management and upper leadership. One can hardly expect front-line employees to transcend complacency, status quo, mediocrity, or half-hearted performance if the scaffolding erected by management for greater accomplishment is missing, rickety, elusive, illusionary, or unscalable. As critic Robert Snow, aptly writes about the plot line in Terry Gilliam's dystopic film, *Brazil*, "No sooner does he move into his laughably tiny office that he's sent down a never-ending rabbit hole of euphemism, betrayal and torture, all because he tried to burst free from the status quo."[9] Of course, indifference by anyone is a conscious choice to disconnect, but sometimes, to great corporate misfortune, we are *led* there.

Heart Attack

On the other hand, celebrating and fostering our collective abilities to help overcome inertia and welcome initiative, are critical to success. Intrinsic to change is maximizing each employee's awareness of his or her importance. Identifying and utilizing each person's significant value are the key catalysts for self-improvement and reshaping work ethic. In engagement, we always return to highlighting productive interactions, and what we do should be valuing and making a difference in our co-workers' lives.

Simply, we have a moral obligation and the accompanying conscious choice to transcend the common place. The research findings from Jim Collins' *Good to Great*[10] suggest core ground rules that align well to engagement practices:

- **"If we have to ask the question 'Why should we try to make [our work] great,'...we're probably in the wrong line of work."**

- **"Get involved in something that you care so much about that you want to make it [including self] the greatest it can be, not because of what you will get, but just because it can be done."**

- **"We cannot manufacture passion or 'motivate' people to feel passionate."**

Ultimately, our effectiveness, our progress, our business culture, and our engagement are products of the expectations, good and bad, embedded in our values. In performance and in each interaction, we should endeavor to stimulate and value those who dare move beyond the job description. Further, we should recognize the legitimacy of equals. Humility secedes power in order to acknowledge others' lives, willingness, and potential contributions.

Perhaps the foremost challenge is loosening the restraints in which we think we are confined. In leadership, rationalization and justification can breed neglect and constrict service from the heart. We see the world, not as it is, but as we have been conditioned to see it. The more we move beyond a fixed mindset of how "work" is bound by distorted or imposed norms, the easier we can begin to tap into more meaningful reserves about who our coworkers are, what really works, and what work really is.

If we choose not to question the cultural traps imposed on interactions, we blindly sink into the quicksand of inferior or incorrect definitions and perceptions of work. To be more fully actualized and more engaged, we must constantly explore our roles and expand boundaries and roles of others. Of course, this requires risk, courage, and resolve. We must revisit our maps to find new ways to transport passengers to solid land.

Shared discovery is the only means to lessen the daunting obstacles, and barring this, we may be stuck at "average." No matter how much transparency is required nor how uncomfortable that shared discovery and response may be, that which we have very systematically and successfully avoided, those blocked arteries that have caused disengagement, we need to <u>fill in those blanks</u>. We should shift our energy to the "nuisances" that we have convinced ourselves do not warrant our time, that which we have "managed" to avoid. We need to be vulnerable, and we need to celebrate others' strengths because, collectively, they are greater than any one person's (or manager's) talents.

Work, as Terkel concludes, should invite creativity and sustenance, and through which workers want "to be remembered" for their calling, yet "most of us have jobs... too small for our spirit."[1]

Chapter 2

"His solution was simple and inexpensive. Using a blank legal pad, he wrote the names of all the employees down the left-hand side of the page. Across the top he listed the days of the workweek. His goal was to say something personal every day to each of these employees and enter a check mark by each name when he had done so." –Dottie Bruce Gandy, *30 Days to a Happy Employee: How a Simple Program of Acknowledgement Can Build Trust and Loyalty at Work.*

~

In order for a workforce to build engagement momentum, we must first share and understand what engagement means and what it looks like. The chapter digs deeper into foundational knowledge and formulas for success. To successfully groom the landscape on which we toil, engagement must be placed within the context of maximizing worker potential. This specific worker context is the crux of "Why" engagement should be a business focal point. A person's potential, and the resultant worker and organizational profits, is realized through sustained, *conscious* effort.

Many of the organizational leaders with whom I have worked have not concentrated enough on syncing the "what is it" and "what does it look like" to the "how" in order to sustain engagement, which is supported by *Modern Survey*'s finding that only 26 percent of the workforce can even adequately define engagement.[1]

A good starting point to till the soil is by building our own definition of engagement.

What does engagement means to me and collectively to everyone as a business practice? What does it feel like?

_____

_____

_____

The Core Comparative Definitions

William Kahn is credited with coining "engagement" as "varying degrees of physical, cognitive and emotional selves" brought into work performance.[2] Wilmar Schaufeli and Arnold Bakker from Utrecht University elaborate that a fulfilled state of mind is indicated by vigor, dedication, and absorption,[3] which ties engagement to three factors: equity, achievement, and camaraderie.[4]

A consensus of experts[5] agree that engagement is a reflection of an employee's **psychological state embodied in positive meaningful involvement at work (passion), a commitment to organizational goals, pride in work, and a feeling of meaningful organizational belonging as demonstrated through initiative (discretionary effort), purpose, energy, and persistence**.

Moreover, complex daily interactions, especially in the nature and degree of each person's investment, as well as the depth to which engagement is integrated into business practices, are bound by moral and practical imperatives.

Our sense of value, belonging and growth, impact, commitment, purpose, and energy follow from degree of regard we have for others inherent in our interactions. If the engine is fine-tuned, work related well-being is characterized by efficacy and involvement; if the engine has blown a gasket, the result is burn-out, characterized by toxic exhaustion and compromised performance.[5] How perceptions of worth and associated business practices affect work ethic, for instance, are explored more in Chapter 6, "At What Price Engagement?" and Chapter 7, "Taxonomy of Engagement."

The psychological and sociological implications of engagement are profound yet very simply encapsulated: we should feel we matter. This feeling, more important than and aside from any title we may hold or salary we earn, is a product of understanding of how we fit and that our fit matters to us and to the business vision and mission in which we have been invited to participate.

Therefore, immediacy and intimacy accentuate the quality of personal engagement investments. Fairness, too, in this interaction, is not an arbitrary or relative value but a fundamental prerequisite. If we feel excluded or less valued, total commitment is sacrificed, and energy is consumed, not created.

When experts talk about engagement, they speak of enablement (strategies or ways of getting us there) and drivers (the general factors related to producing more effective outcomes). "Communication" in the abstract, for instance, is considered a driver. The specific action that improves communication is an enabler: a specific change, for instance, open invitations to meetings could be enacted to allow employees to peer behind the curtain. A step further, the invitation implies that employees are able to express their concerns and allows opportunity for more active participation during or after meetings, where team members become more of a part of discussing strategy and improvement rather than merely being informed of strategy decisions.

Effective change moves participants from a passive cog in the wheel to actually moving the wheel, adding to progress. This active role is enabling. Not be confused with psychological co-dependency, as stated in the Towers Watson Global Workforce Study, "enablement is the structure of the investments we make, within our economic means, to identify and remove obstacles in order to make effective choices related to business productivity and to employee growth."[6]

Further, Lenny DeFranco warns in "The (New) Definition of Employee Engagement," we can also mistakenly slow down our engagement efforts by only attending to drivers. Engagement is not determined by satisfaction nor motivatation.[7] These are ends. Satisfaction, as Daniel Pink expresses in *Drive*, is derived from the actions taken to derive personal investment (purpose – give me something important to do), which contribute to a quality product, and flow to and from a confluence of empowerment (autonomy – give me the freedom to create and coach me to do the best that I can). Happiness and satisfaction are the dividends of the specific liberties, tools, and assistance given to employees to maximize productivity. How well supervisors develop talent and are able and open to "discover what ignites passion"[8] runs jointly to how willingly the supervised accelerate themselves to sustain passion.

Moreover, the very presence of surveys and inventories can be an attractive, but deceptive, quantitative definition of engagement. Engagement is better sensed qualitatively, a finger on the pulse of quality interactions. Behaviors are reflections of values and understanding of vision as well as degrees of satisfaction, trust, recognition, communication, organizational improvements, and, ultimately, meaningful contributions to productivity.

We focus on engagement to stimulate personal growth, pave avenues of belonging and involvement, institute higher standards, recognize productive behaviors, and incorporate full-fledged feedback loops. To move the needle of the engagement meter toward "optimum," each of us pushes a "what" and "how." These palpable, not intangible, personal and business investments, become woven into the fabric of complementary interpersonal dynamics.

Drawing a blueprint to heighten engagement requires abandoning tactics such as alienation, ignoring, or igniting an exodus in order to refill the "seats on the bus," that incidentally, we may have been complicit in emptying. The best leaders not only actively recognize and recruit passionate and *com*passionate people but also identify and equip those who feel displaced and help them flourish, rather than enable them to flounder. We learn how to drive each other to achieve, not drive each other away. Identifying the best in others creates energy. Fueling and lighting the fire in others requires refining raw materials in ourselves, raw materials such as time, self-doubt, trust, introspection, and caring.

Not surprisingly, then, according to the "2014 Report on Senior Executive Succession Planning and Talent Development" published by Institute of Executive Development and Stanford Business School, engagement also serves as a catalysts for successful succession planning.[9] Given that voluntary resignations occur as early as within the first six months of employment and the median employee tenure over the last thirty years has ranged from three years in 1983 to 4.6 years in 2014,[10] engagement strategies require integrated attention to employees' onboarding and acculturation, to recognizing milestones, and through long-term growth and development. Thus, a definition of engagement must be complemented by depth of commitment to employees' growth, leading to an understanding of contribution, success, and belonging. Engagement is an effect of being systematically plugged in. It is not an add-on.

What does a definition of engagement actually look and feel like in the workplace?[11] A suggested, representational range:

- **Fully, constructively engaged** employees bring passion, purpose and discretionary energy to their work. They feel secure in taking risks and knowing that their suggestions count, whether their input is supportive or constructively critical. They are emotionally attached and committed to the organization and serve the greater good. An example of a constructive employee is not the person who serves a loyal, subservient "go for" role, but who brings a solution along with a complaint.

- **Moderately, collaboratively engaged** employees are willing to go the extra mile to achieve common goals and objectives as long as they can also satisfy their basic needs and own goals and objectives. These are not individuals who are merely assigned tasks within a group, but interactive participants who are held accountable to look out for each other and seek to help each other, filling in unassigned details, filling in gaps. They constantly approach tasks by thinking "Why?" and offering or welcoming "What if...?"

- There is one paradoxical roadblock to clarifying the "Why": we easily avoid authentic self-assessment and manufacture distorted answers to how and why by discounting valid information. When someone stumbles, we naturally ask, "How could we have approached this differently?" Answering "Why did this happen?" by blaming others is a false start. As part of a team or as the team leader, if my conclusion is that someone else is at fault, I am obligated to drill deeper "Why am I blaming others? What's my role in this?" Extracting equally viable grains of truths from multiple points of view is the only means to level faulty cause-effect positions. We should pursue all glimmers of truth. Finding fault, rather than admitting failure, moves workers from being engaged to being disengaged.

- **Content, but moderately disengaged** employees do what they have to do to get through the day but are unwilling to exert any extra effort to meet deadlines or support their colleagues in difficult times. The most significant difference between constructive, collaborative members from content employees is passion and the enjoyment derived from it. Workers who find themselves in this position, are usually the product of indifference. Improvement, exploration, questioning, or growth are neither business nor personal priorities. Further, this mode is usually accompanied by a sense of entitlement, as suggested in "I've worked here for 30 years. They owe me," rather than "What more or what new can I bring to the enterprise given my standing?" If the answer is none, the worker has been conditioned to believe that his or her legacy has no importance.

- **Disengaged** employees are frustrated, anxious, and fearful about not being able to satisfy their needs. Often, these employees have fallen victim to having been repeatedly ignored, disregarded, or rejected even when they know their input adds tremendous value. They have been conditioned to keep their heads down, not to question, and merely be content with repetitive motions.

- **Destructively disengaged** employees are unhappy at their work and act out their unhappiness by actively undermining goals and efforts and denigrate those who want to succeed or disagree with their perspective. How workers arrive here is a complex spiritual, psychological, and cultural study, but managers have a moral obligation to ask, "How did I/we contribute to this fall from grace, dignity, and collective consciousness?" Pervasive denial and culpability abound; usually, however, because of inattentiveness, the most innocent suffer the consequences. While passively disengaged workers might be considered to exist in a negative state, employees may destructively act-out when all other authentic attempts to be heard or recognized have been met with disingenuous or failed response.

From Definition to Definitive Practice

Applicable models and research consensus on practices exist. I am unsure of the number of internet results that might appear if someone types in "worker engagement" into a search engine, probably an astounding number, but I do know that the first five pages of results will provide a wealth of knowns. Properly plugged in, they do not merely promise but assure return on investment. Most defy measurement and metrics and harken to long forgotten yet unrefuted principles.[12] The most readily accessible and applicable basic means and ideas are explored below.

Repeatedly, current workplace research confirms this enduring strategic foundation: pro-growth/pro-engagement behaviors must involve mastery, construct meaning, and require modeling, empathy, purpose and reflection, the sum of which results in a healthy culture, higher levels of satisfaction, and the fun derived from work. We might reduce all of what we know about driving and enabling forces into core engagement formula: **Engagement = Personal Productivity ÷ Manger Responsibility**.

Engagement and Disengagement Characteristics	
Constructive	Energetic, Passionate, Emotional Commitment to Organizational Goals ("Citizenship"), "Do the Right Thing," Actively Involved, Share Responsibly, Seek Opportunity, Belong, Typically Selfless
Collaborative	Willing, Thinking, Innovative, Growing, Interested Learners, Aspirational, Recognized
Content	Well intended but Disconnected, Mechanistic, Job is Means to a Paycheck, Prefer the Status Quo, Not Looking (for a Job but Would Entertain a Switch if Offered), Not interested in Growth Unless Compensated/Rewarded
Disengaged	Tend to be Complacent and Compliant, Checked-out, Feel Stuck and Unvalued or Undervalued, Dull, Bored, 8-5 Routine, Unwilling, May be Activity Seeking a New Job or Counting Down to Retirement, and Search the Internet for Personal Needs to Occupy Time
Destructive	Locked in, No Escape (usually Wage/Developmentally related), Practice Terror by Gossip, Act Out, Do Not Share Victories nor Recognize Others, Disassociate/Denigrate Others, Typically Selfish

As each of us builds values into the formula, at a *minimum*, to move from merely being a survivor to "thriver," we should foremost assign inputs according to best fit, greatest growth, potential, and ability, and allow people sufficient autonomy to personally invest and drive maximum meaning from their work. In addition, managers must remove hidden agendas, invite employee input, value talent, maintain high expectations through constant assessment, and generously recognize others.

Personal Productivity =

(Meaningful, Progressively Appropriate
Growth <u>T</u>asks – <u>H</u>idden Agendas)

÷

Manager's <u>R</u>elationship Building Responsibility =

(Employee <u>I</u>nput + <u>V</u>aluing Talent + Right <u>E</u>xpectations +
Universally Fair and Culturally Acceptable <u>R</u>ecognition)

Of course, the specific order and variables we fit into the Personal Productivity ÷ Manger Responsibility formula will vary depending on the organizational climate and functional parts; many of the relevant inputs or specific strategies to be considered are more fully discussed in accompanying chapters.

A brief example of the dynamic of disengagement resolves around how we also define "productive." We have all been surprised by resignation announcements from highly productive or potentially productive colleagues. They are actually sad to depart but leave out of sheer frustration. They "do more with less," not without complaint, but in good faith. Nonetheless, more than a few, very productive people leave because they are being over-worked (failures in task sharing) and/or over-looked, with little if any support (failure in expectations and respect). Further, they are criticized when something goes wrong, and are the first to say, "This failure in execution would not have happened if someone would have listened to me sooner" (failures in valuing and recognition). When "personal" is stripped from "productive," we fail to see workers as people; instead, we reduce workers to objects (or positons).

The Arbinger Foundation's *Leadership and Self-Deception*[13] offers a much more detailed narrative of how and why workplace relationship go awry and how to avoid the "boxes" in which we trap ourselves, particularly the loss of regard and respect we create by objectifying others. The institute's argument stresses that relationship building is much more than acquiring training to hone people skills. Doing the right thing, whatever situational behaviors we might exhibit as we interact with each other, must be done for the right reasons. Right reasoning discards blaming, finding fault in, retribution, and resisting others. Rather, relationship and trust building insists upon finding the highest value in people by maintaining the highest regard for people. Of course, this is not possible when others are ostracized or labeled as malcontents.

When high regard from others dominates, all people are maximized. When we disregard others as equal partners, we have a difficult time seeing the inherent deception within ourselves (although, ironically, others readily recognize deception in others when they see and feel it). Simply, we escape an engagement dead zone by accepting, rather than rejecting those around us. This dynamic is important because we often excuse ourselves from asking probing question of those who agree with us as well as discard the relevance of those who offer disagreement yet ardently share the same mission and pursue the same ends. The only result generated from exclusion is the proliferation of blind spots, and a proliferation of negative gossip.

For instance, managers who assign tasks to "favored" employees and deliberately exclude exploit prejudices that undercut the utility of others' similar, and sometimes superior, talents, promise, or abilities. This tendency to dishonestly devalue people telegraphs a lack of trust.

How to best transform such misgivings into giving is uniquely situational yet universally simple. The more abstract ends of engagement revolve around fostering trust, purposeful and meaningful communication, and growth. Daniel Pink's[8] research ultimately reduces the principles to applications to reach mastery and autonomy, which result in initiative and purposeful, meaningful, and challenging work. These aspects are also found in characteristics of "best" companies' cultures identified by Josh Bersin at Deloitte Consulting:[14] great managers provide coaching and invite mutually profitable feedback loops, fund growth opportunities within inclusive, flexible, and fun workplaces.

Obstacles to engagement could range from ego and elitism to hidden agendas…, of which the viability of possible recourse varies according to depth of needs. "Relationship Building," as a remedy, for instance, would require soft skills awareness and developmental practice if one has risen in rank from an independent, analytical, subject matter expert and moved into supervisory role that requires interpersonal, behavioral, and more empathetic diverse problem solving. If some of this development has not progressively occurred over time, before the individual has moved up into a people management role, that black hole, the absence of reverberating values, in the engagement enterprise requires attention.

Chapter 3

ACTIVE VALUES

"Collective fear stimulates herd instinct, and tends to produce ferocity towards those who are not regarded as members of the herd." –Bertrand Russell, *Unpopular Essays*

~

First, Examine Business Values and the Nature of Leadership

Engagement stems from the depth of an individual's participation in the context of the organization's direction (vision and mission). Because differences exist in engagement needs, ranging, for instance, from the need to share information and interact more to foster each individual's growth, each initiative requires subtle differences in practice, and increased, personal one-on-one exploration.

The specific challenges in many cases are difficult to resolve because they are nested in ethics, morals, and values. We can trace the resistance, push-back, or sheer apathy to antiquity. In *Meditations*, emperor Marcus Aurelius wrote "Never value anything as profitable that compels you to break your promise, to lose your self-respect, to hate any man, to suspect, to curse, to act the hypocrite, to desire anything that needs walls and curtains."[1]

The chief caveat is that some leaders, who have created (or inherited) highly dysfunctional cultures and lack the wherewithal to authentically receive feedback and assess their own impact on a team's or team member's well-being, are susceptible to retreating, regressing toward average, and may remain intractable in not only recognizing others but in recognizing the effect of cultural neglect. If leaders at the top levels of the organization are disconnected and disengaged from fellow workers, they merely will enable push-back and sustain the status quo as well as the disillusionment and disengagement of employees.

Why is change so hard? "Most people are reluctant to alter their habits. What worked in the past is good enough," state professors of business David Garvin and Michal Roberto." In "Reinforcing Good Habits," they emphasize, "Effective leaders explicitly reinforce organizational values on a constant basis, using actions to back up their words."[2]

Despite the complications of which we are aware or we anticipate, leadership behaviors must be those that build high levels of confidence. They continue to reinforce, "There will be mistakes, but will persevere through them. This looks insurmountable but we will continue forward and dedicate ourselves to assuring we have found answers to prevailing concerns."

This trust is initially gained by cultivating highly inclusive, non-threatening and genuinely collaborative dynamics gained by mutual respect. Particularly, in inclusive cultures, leaders champion knowledge/perspective/multiple points of view. Within this supportive culture, sharing and open, constructive criticism, free from fear or chastisement, is considered an asset, not a distraction. Inclusive leaders do not espouse a "don't ask; don't tell" policy, and they do not clothe objectives with secrecy; rather, they frequently share and tirelessly search for alternative truths.

For instance, formal leaders often tout loyalty as an operational prerequisite yet model and practice secrecy. Aside from truly confidential needs, like the abstraction or outcome "engagement," loyalty is a product of concrete values in action. Loyalty may, in fact, function as an engagement outcome, but is often sacrificed by the absence of congruent values.

Supportive, growth cultures allow individuals to question, explore, be included, and learn from mistakes rather than being banished or punished. Moreover, coworkers within these cultures understand that mistakes occur only when clarity is missing. Moreover, supportive cultures are able to overcome emergent crises by objectively framing mistakes and collectively solving problems as means to improve each other and processes. In fact, we should value and better coach people who do the right thing for the right reason even if sometimes the approach an employee takes is perceived as a wrong way.

If principal workers are excluded or lack the wherewithal or the skills to make a difference, leaders require more attention to their responsibility to assist, advise, and facilitate others whom do not immediately see themselves as playing key roles. This requires leaders to consider a Zen approach to everyday activities, constantly looking outward to peer inward, selflessly teaching and learning in each moment,[3] asking the right questions to anyone connected in the pressing tasks of the day; then, listening to everyone anywhere at any time, pause, rethink, renew, redirect, and guide. Effective leaders and coworkers do not recruit feedback to reinforce their own points of view but to clearly understand and impartially respond to others' alternative, sometimes contradictory, points of view.

Effective people in effective workplaces, therefore, talk about what they are doing and why they are doing it, how to best leverage each person's talent in achieving objectives, as well as what they are learning along the way. They openly, genuinely seek improvement and cut through judgment, error, and misperceptions.

When such healthy regard exists for each other, each employee feels like a valued player in the momentum and "flow states"[4] proliferate; i.e., we are so absorbed in what we are doing, we lose track of time and are more prone to realize important breakthroughs. Businesses continuously evolve through involvement, focus, concentration, and clarity when flow states dominate the cultural landscape. Meaningfulness created in and at work increases the flow and performance of every willing person in the pipeline.

How do we embrace such responsibility and resolve? Interestingly, the primary impediment has confounded K-12 education and corporate training since the late 20th century. The goal, simply and in most instances, is to provide each person's continual, experiential, and quality growth opportunities to help move beyond mere task expertise.

A compelling conclusion is drawn by Mackey and Sisodia in *Conscious Capitalism*. Mere subject matter knowledge is insufficient to lead people. The persons who aspire toward leadership by consistently surpassing sales goals or who exclusively possess critical expertise are not the typical examples of effective engagement leaders. Highly engaged businesses and individuals are guided not by competition but by inclusion, finding meaning through each other and creating value for each other rather than dependence on policies and procedures.[5]

Recalibrate Seeing (Vision)

Clearly, disengaged employees feel under-acknowledged, so the engagement strategy must generate from an authentic belief that each employee is a pivotal participant and contributor; the result in this belief is a psychological affirmation which positively affects each employee's intuitive sense of place and workplace well-being. Again, efforts to heighten engagement must be accompanied by unwavering will to empower, to capitalize on personal values that dove-tail into institutional values, vision, and passion.

Therefore, in addition to appreciating the value an individual brings to a task, providing the autonomy to perform is crucial, accompanied by an on-going triangulation of person and task to institutional values, vision, and mission. *When* and *how* groups are asked to help construct values and mission, and the means used by managers to reaffirm these makes a difference in the health of the culture. How often employees weigh in on organizational mission or purpose, and how often the mission is revisited in the context of work being conducted, is a fairly powerful barometer of shared vision and, by extension, engagement.

Of course, the functionality of the workforce across the organizational chart can differ widely from highly effective and organic collaboration to pockets of cynicism and toxicity. The collective will to fulfill vision can be sabotaged by any individual at any level. A common cause of disengagement often emanates from front-line employees rife with discontent and criticism because they are kept out of the loop, or receive little support or reassurance, and feel disenfranchised. Very likely, when these types of conditions occur, the managers and top echelon are self-sufficient but generally out of touch with workers and perhaps in denial when facing unrest.

Each work group's dynamics require uniquely tailored approaches to propel vision, cement commitment to goals, and, thus, cultivate more engagement. The fulfillment of values affects the depth of conviction and relevance of team members, or conversely, as social researcher Elizabeth Morrison warns, employee silence,[6] brought on by exclusion, feeds disengagement. Evidenced, for example, when a colleague superficially points to the un-memorized posting of the company's mission statement, but really cannot articulate a meaningful connection to it.

Draft Specific Engagement Values and Plans

Respond to these two starting points:

What are our engagement values?

_____

_____

_____

How do we plan to live them and live up to them?

(How do I actively remind myself and others why what we are doing is important as well reminding ourselves of the importance of those we are serving?)

_____

_____

_____

In exploring these questions, at minimum, we should collectively attend to the following aspects to accelerate the probability of success:

- **Hold sufficient ideation and strategy sessions with time to analyze, share, compare and think through input (the more person-to-person, the better).** Such efforts emphasize inclusive, guided problem solving, and agreement, which minimizes complaints erupting from disenfranchisement. This community process, as Lewis Garrad suggests, leads to a establishing a common, "Grammar of Employee Engagement,"[7] and it recognizes and utilizes every creative mind.

- **Require periodic developmental progress reports of the status of vision and values statements.** Kick off each year, quarter or project movement… by reemphasizing the importance of a common business purpose.

- **Empower and entrust others by readying and allowing individuals and teams to autonomously execute tasks and plans.** More specifically, welcome creativity and define acceptable risk by reviewing contexts and barriers; this trust in others demonstrates commitment. The best leaders fail. Leaders who lead other leaders do not punish failure but know how to reconstruct from it.

- **Assess developmental progress, what's working and what's not.** Work through impasse and conflict by agreeing to disagree but also agreeing to plot the best solutions or corrective actions possible, given for instance, any ethical concerns or compliance restraints.

- **Tie encouragement, check-ins, questions, and affirmative messaging whenever** possible through repeated statements of commitment from upper management.

Once general values and vision consensus has been reached, the engagement effort can move to developing specific strategies. Commitment is best reinforced when leaders require specific tasks to be directly written into performance plans. This is a key acknowledgement and supportive action of any engagement initiative. This does not translate to "and other duties as assigned" but as specific line items and expectations. Engagement goals are not ethereal principles but require explicit tasks and commitments. They should be embedded in our conduct, in mentoring, development, appreciating, and coaching of employees. All of these are, therefore, part of accountability.

Moreover, as Air Force veteran and behavioral scientist Sydeny Savion suggests, each individual leader makes a difference, but senior leadership must focus attention to create a shared future by building a corporate culture that is open to and supports doing things openly and differently.[8] For instance, if incentives are solely tied to annual evaluations, recognition will lack immediacy. We may hold annual banquets to publically celebrate successes, but we need to understand that individual performance gains are most effectively captured in the instant and during episodic, formative moments.

Importantly, while human resource offices or organizational training arms may aid in generating and facilitating values analysis and construction of specific engagement task recommendations, the impetus and follow-through depends upon the will, disposition, intimacy and immediacy demonstrated by individuals within each department. Engagement, culture, personal commitment, and communication are inextricably interconnected and, therefore, reflect a company's brand. Human resources or learning and development branches are not the marketers of company brand; the initiative and branding is not seen in a logo or by any particular department but by individuals living the collective cultural values through the personal choices they make.

Ultimately, an employee's work should embody a positive appraisal of how she or he feels about work. One's appraisal is usually affected by the modeling seen by supervisors, owners, and managers. As author Susan Fowler suggests in *Why Motivating*

People Doesn't Work, well-being[9] and belonging within a collective enterprise determines intentionality, commitment, and the associated behaviors that generate "engagement." Managers, for example, can incubate disengagement by not embodying values, by exerting position and power to control information, or relegating workers to tasks without themselves being involved in learning about and discussing processes related to those tasks.

Engagement First Steps and Key Concerns

Given agreement on what engagement means, the generation of an engagement value statement should precede identifying needs. These values may change, and should be revisited annually, once more specific needs are identified and some actions have been taken. Furthermore, a values conversation may likely yield your first round of needs assessment. Remember, the pervasive engagement goal is to find ways to connect with each employee, which requires hearty communication and transparency. To cut through some of the issues that complicate engagement, below are the initial techniques to consider:

1) Should we employ a formal engagement survey instrument? The ways and means organizations choose to measure engagement, if engagement variables are measured at all, will vary. Remember, resounding agreement exists on what drivers and actions positively and negatively influence engagement. From instrument to instrument, the operational wording of variables may be slightly different, but common elements rise to the top, such as effective communication, stake-holding and sharing, recognition, valuing, respect, and transparency which assures trust-building. Realistically and intuitively, we can feel the pulse without being bound by a quantitative metric. The best measure is merely looking at and feeling changes in office climate and tone. Engagement is accompanied by obvious, palpable productive energy (not always positive, but always stimulating).

We do need systematic processes to address engagement needs, however. Ken Blanchard[10] emphasizes three key necessities in his *Ignite* newsletter:

- **Start with a frank evaluation (negotiating** *perceived* **obstacles to engagement as openly and objectively as possible).** Again, we can conduct an evaluation of effectiveness and implement specific action plans based on the results of fact finding without depending on an outsourced engagement survey. Alternative methods, such as internally conducted focus groups, can be used to collect information and identify needs as long as those efforts are perceived to be objective, impartial, and *follow-through* occurs, is perceptible, and is part of an on-going conversation about engagement. Such internal listening is useful to building trust if the input generates specific commitment to change and follow-up from the information gathering. Engaging in face-to-face conversations is recommended rather than depending on electronic surveys.

- **Tie assessment of project initiatives to specific, desired outcomes.** Know what you want to achieve, and be honest about the ground gained after experimenting with the means.

- **Devote resources to implementation,** particularly deployment of people to conduct various administrative and practical efforts as well as the resources necessary to carry out related training needs.

We must openly discuss and honestly receive input collected across the company, question the effectiveness of our current culture, and examine how engagement manifests itself within effective organizations. Among the other variables discussed in these chapters, talent management firm Harrison Assessments International[11] reduces the scope of crucial change areas (manager behaviors, communication, etc.) to these aspects:

- **Now: work toward job fit that result in sustained interest and enjoyment.**

- **Always: maintain high performance expectations, grounded in realistic work-life balance.**

- **Next: help employees get where they want to be or should be.**

Furthermore, engagement does not require a strict adherence to one way of thinking or doing to realize goals. If we are smart about how we move forward, we understand sociologist Bruce Cameron's adage, "not everything that can be counted counts, and not everything that counts can be counted."[12]

This is an especially prudent reminder in deciding if an engagement survey is to be used. If an instrument is being considered to help identify and narrow priorities, several factors, cautions, and options should be considered. Further, employing an engagement survey can be a tricky proposition, especially warding against seeing what we want to see. With respect to interpretations of data, it usually reflects what we already suspect, so considerable consideration should be given to possible hypothetical, gut impressions (before or after distributing a survey).

If a survey is to be deployed, leaders must message the importance, continue to be seriously and objectively involved, not use retributive action, and not abandon or reverse course because of caustic critics. If long-term commitment, disposition, and will (actions and words) to face the challenges and implement changes are lacking, stop reading here. Without these, any effort rightfully will be viewed as insincere, superficial, and meaningless.

If yours is a first attempt at approaching engagement, one of the questions to ask is whether a case exists for outsourcing, or for gradually equipping internal personnel and their toolkits, acquiring the materials and the skillset to do it ourselves? The decision to use or develop an internal instrument or employ an outside vendor should be based on concrete variables, such as revenue, expertise, and economies of scale, as well as emotional variables such as manager effectiveness and levels of trust. We should also give some foresight to what is to be done with the information we obtain (it should be carefully considered yet widely and completely shared, or trust is broken).

If trust is seen as an issue (typical of political and top-down organizations with very rigid control of information flow and, thus, wide ranging pockets of disconnectedness), the engagement endeavors should begin with institutional-wide assessment of awareness of vision and mission. If building or rebuilding trust is a concern, gathering the baseline data is best obtained through an outside source to assure confidentiality and perceptions of integrity. The more dysfunctional the culture appears to be, the greater need to outsource the collection of employee impressions and to adequately prepare employees (particularly supervisors and highest leaders) by discussing what engagement means, clearly communicating expectations and solid commitment, and orientating key players to conducting engagement work.

If, on the other hand, organizational structure tends toward more servant-oriented, situational, and democratic, where interdependence, mutual respect, and mutual influence are more prominent (and in which engagement confidence is usually higher), these metrics can be mined internally if accompanied by highly transparent actions and sharing. As suggested above, focus groups can be formed to identify needs, similar to conducting an internal SWOT analysis to generate recommendations (a process to identify Strengths, turn Weaknesses into Opportunities, and better understand and mitigate obstacles and Threats).

Nonetheless, a valid assessment includes maintaining respondents' confidentiality by using a collection means to assure non-threatening collection of survey data. No one should feel at risk by completing a survey (responding should be optional— low response rate, for instance, is itself indicative of diminished trust.) or participating in a focus group. Because trust is often a crucial engagement concern, employees should trust that the initiative is accompanied by immediate follow-up and carefully rendered follow-through in responding to results. Commitment means always moving forward.

Does an engagement survey, if deployed, need to be repeated? This depends. The short answer is no if the structural organization is stable (no major downsizing, hiring, or consolidation is underway or projected). Once you have the initial results, you'll know the lay of the land, and need to plot a solution.

An adage commonly attributed to Peter Drucker, "culture eats strategy for breakfast," applies to engagement. Responding to engagement requires years of purposeful planning and action, where even the best plans can go awry and require steady assessment and periodic crisis triage. Leaders must be willing to face and grapple with set-backs and corrections. Most initiatives gradually yield upward results but require constant attention, assessment, evolution as a conscious consequence of feeling the pulse of and listing to individuals as well as contingent groups.

Therefore, engagement embedded in the culture is a reflection of goals and values genuinely embedded in annual planning. To create a culture that inspires and enables others to succeed, long-term top-tier support and commitment is essential. Hardy-Vallee,[13] for instance, in interpreting Kenexa's results, recommends a five-year commitment from initial entry into exploring engagement variables to actually realizing culturally embedded results. Given a one-year start-up, design, planning, and implementation, if a survey is to be repeated, the third year may offer the most useful next look.

Finally, we do not want to be bound by a statistical number. From the time a survey is deployed to planning and strategy implementation, many strategic factors may naturally change (just deploying a survey, conducting focus groups will have a short term effect), so by the time a follow-up survey is conducted, various variables change, rendering a comparison of the numbers worthless. We should be much more bound to what appeals to our common sense and well-being than to measuring success with quantitative metrics.

2) As emphasized by David Lee, founder of HumanNature@ Work, **the quality of follow-through and need for survey transparency is imperative.**[14] If a survey is used, results must be reported to all in a timely manner, changes must be implemented, and if some areas appear to remain unattended, a need remains to explain why issues important to the rank and file were not seen as a priority. The method should assure integrity, sound organizational values, and shared successes/wins.

3) Engagement practice may begin as an add on or incidental effort, but **a full-throated response will require an in-depth**

plan for responding to engagement needs, ranging from basic appreciation milestones (collection and updating of information for celebrating years of service) to attending to comprehensive worker growth and development. Depending on the size of the work group and expertise, the number of people directly involved in orchestrating engagement efforts may range from the CEO to designated subject matter expert(s) to a team dedicated to orchestrating and carrying out the work. Distinct engagement personnel or team representatives should help to embody an engagement philosophy across related company initiatives, and be a partners in related process and planning discussions across core initiatives, for example:

- **Hiring** – Tim Leberect, author of *The Business Romantic*, reminds us that culture is co-owned. For example, to help build a more progressive and optimistic culture, Adam Grant in the "Ten-Step Guide to Working More Human" suggests building a culture of givers by screening out takers, those whose primary motivation is constantly trying to get more for themselves. To do this, interview questions might include, "How have you improved the lives of others?"[15] As with multiple interviews that screen for competence and welcome all hiring staff member's votes; interviews for management positions should ask "Demonstrate how you have welcomed and supported other people's ideas?"

- **Nurturing** – onboarding employees needs to be carefully and systematically integrated; beyond filling out forms and attending to rules and compliance orientation, the core of onboarding should be building belonging; robust 30-60-90-365th day check-ins and check-ups to gauge employee needs and acculturation should be incorporated into routines; leaders should be monitoring selves (360), climate, ascertaining work enjoyment, maintaining high expectations. This initiative involves all employees across the culture from colleagues and top management to mentors and related learning opportunities.

• **Inspiring** – retaining talent means supporting employees, assuring effective communication, and fully incorporating recognition (informal/peer-ownership, formal manager growth and development). This includes periodic, honest conversations about enrichment, conversations about aspirations and advancement options. Pragmatically, it requires embracing a pay for performance philosophy and constantly assessing job fit and satisfaction. Particularly, inspiring includes sustaining employee positive self-appraisals about how each person makes a difference and building confidence in others, but not side-lining nor inundating a select few with frustrating tasks; conducting periodic "stay interviews" in addition to exit interviews helps management remain proactive. An inspirational culture requires investment by top management. To compare your recognition efforts to general norms, see the World at Work's most recent "Trends in Employee Recognition" report.[16]

• **Retiring** – leaving an enduring legacy requires managers to move from high-task to high touch, including constructing relevant development for all, articulating and including everyone in fulfilling goals, challenges, and broadcasting achievements, and affirming all but investing differently in each person is a function of modeling, coaching and/or mentoring required from top management. *Fistful of Talent* author and HR executive Dawn Burke states a win-win philosophy invites inclusion, unconditional candor, and honesty, particularly coaching sessions that cut through the fog of mistrust. A second engagement formula falls into the legacy component of engagement: "Intimacy + Access = Trust."[17] Legacy is not tied to ambition but to inspiring others by being an agent who actively and honestly helps others identify, define, and realize career pathways and destinations.

Therefore, if individuals or teams are working, for instance, on improving hiring or onboarding, their efforts should be connected to the person or persons working on engagement initiatives. If these initiatives occur in isolation, full synergy in realizing mission and purpose is compromised. The more these efforts symbiotically overlap, the more likely engagement will be perceptually adopted as a pervasive cultural exercise and integrated strategic goal rather than isolated gimmicks or pigeon-holed to holiday parties, birthday celebrations, or exclusively to recognition.

4) *Growth* **management is a key driver beyond** *performance* **management**: aside from annual performance evaluations, ambitiously promoting informal coaching and implementing formal coaching mechanisms heighten engagement. At the very least, annual plans should explicitly include a directive that keeps supervisors accountable by requiring regular, formative discussions about growth and development, and more importantly add in time for conversations that focus on knowing the person. Progressive, meaningful formative interchange builds trust and is a crucial enabler of engagement. In *First, Break All the Rules*, Marcus Buckingham advises that a manager who cannot carve out one hour per quarter with each employee to discuss personal rather than work related items either has too many direct reports, or they should not be a manager, in essence have reached a level of incompetence.[18]

5) Recognize people skills, including emotional intelligence, as a core growth priority. On-going leadership training for all, starting as soon as entry, should be a benchmark: support associated curricular development and facilitate/encourage senior executives, managers, and supervisors to incorporate meaningful communication, recognition, and build genuine interest in employees.

6) Improve means of interactions specific to decision-making, problem solving, and transmitting new information; encourage greater employee participation by vigorously valuing stake-holding. This should not be confused with belaboring employees with admonishments or holding standing meetings that serve no productive purpose. To drive peak performance, the emphasis should be providing useful information to employees, bringing clarity to context, brainstorming, problem-solving, airing questions, fostering connectivity and possible collaboration, and wide-spread communication, not only with a select few, but with all stakeholders, at all stages (initiative brainstorming, formative problem-solving, implementation, and summative moments).

The need to continually update on progress cannot be understated. If only to convey "nothing more to report" the assurance should be uttered as frequently as each person's role dictates the need. For instance, if my project manager asks, "How much reassurance do you need?" My appeal, especially if that projected timeline is repeatedly pushed back, is "Weekly, until whatever's supposed to happen happens." I'm expecting as a matter of trust, a specific explanation of the cause of the delay, complications, and recommendations, or alternative steps, as well as predictions. Am I paranoid or insecure? Do I need my hand held? These types of questions imply unnecessary judgments. No. I am a human who deserves respect and trust is derived from clarity. Timely and frequent communication parallels the late Zig Ziglar's personal development adage on how often we should affirm others, "People often say that motivation does not last. Well,

41

neither does bathing – that's why we recommend it daily."[19] For everyone to thrive, optimum communication and recognition requires constant attention and refreshing.

7) Very simply, new starts require immersion and information loading. **Encourage informal development** by key engagement personnel through subscription to and exploration and discussion of at least one related recognition or engagement website/blog (see the "Tools" appendix), e.g.:

(a) David Zinger's Employee Engagement Network: http://employeeengagement.ning.com/;

(b) Bob Nelson's Blog: http://www.drbobnelson.com/blog/;

(c) Globoforce: http://www.globoforce.com/resources/.

8) Improve Attention to Recognition

Again, each work group's culture (section, department, unit, and team) requires uniquely tailored approaches to ignite and fuel passion. Thus, the main stage is to, first, "inspire a shared vision." Part of that vision must enable synergy and defeat division. The chief means, according to Kouzes and Posner in *The Leadership Challenge*, is to "model the way."[20] Leaders must enable (empower and grow) employees. High levels of disengagement is accompanied by employees' very keen understanding of false leadership practice: deception, manipulation, distortion, exclusion, blame, punishment, and insincerity.

Nonetheless, the best modeling is very simply demonstrated through frequent and pervasive appreciation and recognition, interactions that must be unconditionally individualized. Some workers desire infrequent recognition from their managers, owners, or chief executives. Some prefer the limelight; others desire private praise. Thus, some events are intuitively public and others private. For instance, recognition of work anniversaries should be a culturally shared experience and should always be public; equally affirming yet corrective coaching is private. In all cases, a robust response entails knowing each other, complemented by robust recognition activities.

Assess current recognition methodologies, and, if absent, create mechanisms to employ both peer-to-peer and also formal mechanisms, and continue monitoring: make adjustments when something is not clicking. Engagement requires teaching, and teachers' toolkits are always evolving; we employ perennial winning lessons, tweak those that need adjustment depending on the audience and purpose, and we throw out the debris that just does not make a difference. The next chapter, *Disengagement and The Walking Dead*, and appendixes offer more specific means.

Engagement could be considered both a value as well as an outcome. But we live specific actions and behaviors in the workplace; these are our values, and engagement is the outcome or penultimate value. Thus, narrow the focus, and explores how to translate definitions of engagement into actual lived values.

A Very Realistic Caution

Ted Bauer's article, "Employee Engagement Ideas: Cut the B.S.,"[21] offers a frank commentary about why engagement works or not. He points to indifference, buzzwords, and this admonition: "If you want real results from employee engagement, your decision-makers have to care." Indicative of red flags and foreboding obstacles, he offers a few tell-tale signs, one, speaking of managers at meetings, "One dude was on Facebook on his phone under the table...." If engagement is to be taken seriously, Bauer's article is an essential read.

Chapter 4

DISENGAGEMET AND *THE WALKING DEAD*

"My stories are about humans and how they react, or fail to react, or react stupidly. I'm pointing the finger at us, not at the zombies. I try to respect and sympathize with the zombies as much as possible." –George A. Romero

~

When our family hosted an 8th grade foreign exchange student, we scheduled a variety of South Louisiana activities, the obligatory swamp tour, local festivals, and sampling local cuisine. But the discovery process actually began with learning about what our guest liked. We learned of our visitor's love for football, soccer to be precise. When asked about American television shows broadcast in her country, she excitedly expressed that she was a fan of *The Walking Dead,* a television show that we had never watched, that is, not until we were assailed with her rave reviews.

Why did we start with our visiting learner's interests? For most of the 20th century, education was built upon a medical model (much of it still is): diagnose a problem and prescribe a cure. The learner, not the teacher, was seen as deficient, an empty vessel. Despite historical advocates from Montessori to Vygotsky,[1] only recently have educators focused more intimately on the learner (employee) to foster successes by acknowledging interests, connections, and building upon strengths and desires.

Learning about our visitor's likes and dislikes, and capitalizing on meaningful connections rather than imposing our own predilections, was pivotal to cultivating a positive, meaningful experience for all. A fulfilling experience depends on what motivates others, revealing and supplementing our know-how with the talents of others, not being blinded by the differences in our attributes and approaches. Similarly, crucial to workplace engagement is what motivates each employee, valuing what they know and what more they would like to know in order to work better and smarter.

Our guest helped us discover how to shape her engagement and create a psychological state embodied in positive, meaningful involvement, where potential is maximized and where pride of membership is demonstrated through initiative, purpose, energy, and discretionary effort. With her exchange experience, our household aimed for better than the one in three engagement success rate[2] commonly found in workplaces. *The Walking Dead* became part of our collective experience (and we have become fans, too).

Unfortunately, the disengaged, walking dead also populate our work-a-day worlds; disengagement is a virus that has infected the majority among us! In fact, since we (in the business/government service worlds) have been relatively unsuccessful at improving engagement at work, apart from work, we have been quite successful in launching a virtual cottage industry of engagement consulting subcontractors (even this book!).

Reading Culture

Our family's immersion efforts, like workplace dynamics, are a cultural enterprise. Some say culture is defined by gossip- what individuals or members of subgroups utter behind another's back- the worst of its foundation through ill-intended words, actions, or purposeful inactions, or through hushed conversations at the water cooler. Others suggest culture is reflected in how managers treat their employees.[3] In fact, the classical definition by sociologist Edward Hall emphasizes that culture is "revealed in what people do,"[4] and as Henry Trueba emphasizes "transmitted by communication."[5] Not surprisingly, communication, one of the universal and reciprocal descriptors of culture, also significantly moves engagement forward if frequently and transparently incorporated into business practices. This ranges, for example, from Friday debriefings and assessments to regular sharing of new information to foster understanding, to cross-training and shadowing, to having the most reluctant, high-task/low-touch introverted manager dare walk beyond his or her threshold and stand in someone else's doorway.

The basis of communication relies on "received standards," that is, how well, contextually and over time, words work and details are conveyed through formal (for instance, in productive meetings) or informal discourse (around the water-cooler). For example, likely at some point in your career, you have heard or spoken these laments, "I'm involved in the a, b, y, and z of it, but they didn't ask me," or "Yes, I was invited to a strategy session, but I'm not sure what became of that. I haven't heard anything in months."

Often top decision-makers assume employees know details in the process, or assume the flow in the chain of command is working, but leaders can overlook nuance by excluding employees, and dismissing informal network chatter, or overlook the obvious by ignoring the specific complications and frustration brought forward by engaged and disengaged employees alike. Timely solicitations for ideas from all and carefully listening to the feedback is pivotal to effect wider ownership and better executed initiatives. Follow-up and connection to closure is equally empowering and pivotal.

Similarly, in carrying out personal objectives, employees weigh potentially negative consequences even when the choice is ethically correct.[6] Often workers hedge on voicing opinions, knowing that they might likely suffer repercussions from management, such as being labeled negative or being dismissed with "stay in your own lane." Supervisors forget most employees are trying to do the right thing, that is, best advance and serve the institutional mission and values. And an employee takes a risk, a leap of faith and trust, in sharing a point of view. As the IBM Smarter Workforce Institute and others remind us, "When employees voluntarily communicate suggestions, concerns, and information about problems, or work-related opinions to someone in a higher organizational position, they engage in upward voice."[7] Thus, shared ownership, power, and leadership only arises when accompanied by the removal of fear, retribution, cronyism, and private, or worse, public rebukes.

Engaged cultures require increased awareness of active roles as they pertain to goals and decision-making. We would not now have to be preparing for the engagement zombie apocalypse if everyone at work had been properly recognized as valuable contributors and included earlier! New workplace scripts can turn the cultural wave of our "walking dead" away from the disengaged hordes merely on a quest to devouring a paycheck. To be sure, disengagement is not a disease to be cured. The zombies have a heartbeat. The question is: "Are we feeling the pulse?" Why are so many workers disengaged (upwards of 70 percent depending on what "fully engaged" means and how it's measured)?[8]

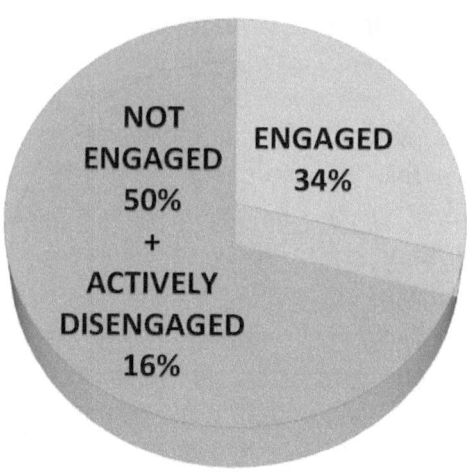

Officevibe, a commercial engagement company, published an infographic painting the disengaged employee as a complainer, lacking enthusiasm, a gossip, a knows-it-all, excuse maker, unhelpful, a liar and loner, who has no initiative and is irresponsible. Leadership development company Sonoma Leadership Systems suggests these traits form from a debilitating loop of disregard initiated by management. Rather than labeling the employee, we need to drill down to the conditions and decisions that created the discontent. Sonoma specifically points to "a lack of leadership and culture or a lack of management and accountability."[9]

Disenfranchised, ignored, or devalued employees both know what it is to be and how it feels to be under-acknowledged, so engagement strategies must first generate from an authentic commitment to the employee's participation and well-being.

Some of the systematic breakdowns have been often discussed in business literature. For instance, we know that annual performance reviews alone, which tend to be subjective and typically incomplete or raise questions about false reflections, are obsolete and substandard measures.[10] Annual evaluations become a ranking tool rather than a vehicle for growth and improvement. Impressively, after 23 years, the *Hollywood Reporter* magazine recognized this shift and changed its reporting policy. Its annual list of most powerful women in the industry no longer ranks the selections in order to thwart the distortions, unjustified comparisons, and possible paranoia that might arise by associating rank with worth.[11]

Moreover, even the most ardent champions of any initiative can be easily disenfranchised by a leader who favors unflagging and unconditional loyalty over candor and participation. We can concede one caveat: If distrust or control is culturally embedded, employees will be reticent to reveal their needs. Consequently, when conditional and controlling managerial philosophy is practiced, heightening engagement is more difficult, practically impossible. Similarly, cynicism is a by-product of dysfunctional workplaces, yet the cynics are often the castaways (a little like sideways management having its cake and eating it, too). More debilitating? Some cynics actually ascended to leadership by acquiescing to authoritarian, conditional, and compromised workplaces. Some argue, "If I'm more vulnerable and open to actually creating a legacy based on the growth and advancement of others, and capitalizing on the intrinsic motivations, I'll look weak or noncompliant!"

Nonetheless, we can find certain salvation by practicing an "other-centered" ethic.

Cultural Instincts

The fundamental question is what is dominant in each person's brain stem? Fight or flight? Transact or transform? (What do these mean? See Michael Zigarelli's "Ten Leadership Theories in Five Minutes."[12]) Agree to rewards and punishment as a quid pro quo exchange or encourage and care for others? Selfless servant leaders or selfishness? Are we driven by pure ambition or aspiration and inspiration? Engagement depends on building enduring relationships. Again, revealed in what people do and say, culture matters.

In our home, during our guest's first cross-cultural dinner with us, delicately avoiding the topic of eating brains, our conversation centered around the social implications of the *Walking Dead,* specifically, how individuals and groups act under extreme circumstances, a construct which Gallup[8], among others, suggests also applies to workplace engagement. Collaboration is so utterly effective, yet teams disintegrate when members resort to survival of the fittest, which is usually precipitated by latent aspects of ambition, status, distrust and/or ego.

Since disengagement is a product of exclusion, devaluing, complacency, interactions and actions that breed mistrust, and a wide variety of secretive decision-making and manipulative behaviors, one can easily understand worker paranoia and surrender to absurdity and meaninglessness.

Many workers find themselves grappling with the moral and ethical decisions that arise from being cast into a survival mode: do we join the dark side, or do we act ethically? Often self-preservation devolves into a lose-lose choice created by management, pitting an acquiescence to mediocrity against being branded as counter-productive or non-compliant.

Given historically consistent disengagement, at some point during each of our careers, we may have likely felt, or will feel, like a lost soul in a dystopic novel. Imagine, for instance, from your or your child's high school reading lists, stories such as *1984, Fahrenheit 451, Hunger Games*, and *Divergent.* Unfortunately, these fiction plot lines reflect oppression and defeat in dark and dreary worlds that far too much remind many of us of the real impediments we face at work, in which we have hungrily, yet too often hopelessly, run to the beach like Ralph, running for his life in *Lord of the Flies*, yet we find no rescue.

Curiously, the 20th and 21st centuries have revealed a common thread when we find ourselves feeling like we are part of a dystopic workplace story line: the zombie. From Romero's 1968 film, *Night of the Living Dead*, to the 2010 premiere of the cult classic television series based on *The Walking Dead* comic book series, we sometimes find ourselves struggling with the irony of "deadness," either in the tasks we are assigned, or not assigned, in poor communication, or related to simple pragmatics. We sometimes ask if our work-world leadership can actually distinguish between the dead, the selfishly opportunistic, and those of us humbly eking out a living. At least within highly disengaged work spaces, the behaviors that you may have witnessed from your colleagues may be hauntingly similar to the *The Walking Dead's* core characters' dispositions and interactions.

Here and throughout the book, of course, the names used as examples, names of characters, businesses, places, or comparisons, events, or incidents are fictitious. Any resemblance to actual persons, living or dead, or actual events are purely coincidental!

For instance, many of the workplace "living" exist in survival mode. Thus, grateful to have jobs with benefits, we mostly agree with the managerial flavor of the day in order to preserve those jobs. This acquiescence to being agreeable is a reluctant compromise. Many of these survivors consciously struggle with doing the right thing, being constructive, taking initiative, or a productive risk, but in the absence of reciprocal "good," they yield to specious modeling. In *The Walking Dead* plot line, many characters stumble on the path to finding refuge from the decay; for example, Gabriel Stokes, the minister who locks out his congregation, or Eugene Porter, whose cowardice results in weaving lies to protect himself by misleading others to believe he is an expert who is able to save the world.

Most of us would rather see ourselves in the company of heroes, such as in the shoes of Rick Grimes, the show's protagonist. Rick constantly struggles with salvaging some remaining visage of humanity or a return to a vestige of life, where liberty and the pursuit of happiness are not beset by abnormality. He is joined by a few other core team members: Darrel, the self-sufficient survivalist, possesses a strong allegiance with honest people. Because he is surrounded by dishonesty, zombies, and self-serving tactics, he is always suspicious and looking over his shoulders for folks who are not so honest, and he is indifferent to team spirit, taking or leaving it as the situation dictates. Like a decent scientist, however, he's trained himself to be skeptical. Fortunately, two more apparently noble characters include Morgan Jones, who concludes all lives, even the zombies', are precious, and Michonne, who deeply cares about protecting those in her core group. For all intents and purposes, Rick, Morgan, and Michonne, even with their suspicions and flaws, and perhaps even Darrel could be considered the show's engagement experts.

All are imperfect, human, but the choices they make are grounded not merely in survival. Given the circumstances and the urgency to make a decision, ultimately, they attempt to preserve truth and trust. A situation may be in flux, but good people are not relative, not conditional. In retrospect, would they possibly make a different decision? Yes. They are fallible, but they try to make the best decision that can be made at the moment in which it must be made. They assess, change, adapt, and move forward, or reverse course, in order to preserve the general well-being, not only to increase the odds of survival but to create a more perfect union. Unfortunately, in dysfunctional and toxic settings, even the good guys can be labeled "the enemy" and seen as dispensable.

But danger lurks. For other characters in the television show, and perhaps akin to sobering behaviors that inflict us at work, the moral and ethical struggle is less pronounced or absent. For instance, Carol is an interesting character study. On one hand, she is kind and matriarchal, and on the other, has mastered false faces, expressed sweetly or pitiable, just before she disposes of her next victim. Terminus, the population hub promising safety, is, as its name foreshadows, a subculture populated by fear, hostility, heartlessness, and doom. Its members stop at nothing, including laying traps to win. In fact, savage cannibals such as these are more common than not, see also the Wolves, who possess a similar pathology, or the utterly evil, despicable, and corrupt Negan, who cares for nothing but reinforcing his position and enforcing his point of view. And similarly, the Governor, a leader who veers off the righteous path, turns to lies, manipulation, and control to justify protecting others, but in reality uses and abuses others to solidify his own self-interests.

Moreover, in the series, these characters are engaged in a fight for survival (as are many employees in the workforce). George Romero, who created the genre's archetype, suggests this rhetorical question: are the worst of these survivalists, particularly the leaders, any better or worse than the walking dead? We wonder at work, why some leaders are so dead to emotion and people that they find a need to control and impose particularly maniacal rules, usually starting with the word "No." "No talking, pets, jeans, children, perfume," no joy. "No" to your input, or disingenuous, mean spirited leaders who insult, berate, criticize, find fault, or ridicule in one breath, yet effuse concern and salvation in the next.

We begin by facing facts and righting wrongs if we are equipped to impartially digest and confront our contributions or lack of them. The qualities of our workplace interactions have the greatest impact on results, even if we are hamstrung (leaders often inherit the living of our workplace landscapes), and did not, as Jim Collins explores in *Good to Great*, flawlessly identify and hire the right people, [13] or fail to provide challenging and meaningful work. When we choose to subjectively dismiss, or when we choose to passively rather than actively listen, some of our best workers are likely to move to a different employer because:

- **Lack of trust pervades from disingenuous words and/ or patronizing actions.**

- **Control, exclusion, blacklists, or sabotage prevails.**

- **"Thank you" is not heard enough about how an employee's work has aided progress, productivity, or profit, or more simply is daily valued.**

- **Growth opportunity does not accompany demonstrated acumen; employees feel stuck in dead-end jobs. Even worse, task completion supplants growth, development, cooperation, and process improvement.**

- **Invitations are seldom extended to occupy any given seat at various tables ("buses") even though the employee knows they could serve well or even have expressed an interest, but the overture is left unattended; a feeling of devaluing and disenfranchisement results, accompanied by performance decrease.**

- **People look busy but are not on task (and other, busier people, know this, as evidenced by whispering** out-groups who halt or break apart when in-group members walk in); disparity breeds discontent and mediocre effort.

- **Complaints are discounted, dismissed, or unaccompanied by solutions (from the complainer or by objective fact-finding and expedient response by management).**

- **Perfection, not excellence, is sought.**

- **Service is punctuated by complaint by the employee or lack of initiative as a result of lack of autonomy (interacting with distrust or lack of training) or excessive adherence to compliance.**

Perhaps your workplace is not this desperate, but how is an employee to stay alive and flourish when confronted by any one of these conditions?

Engagement and the Power of Negative Capability

Poet John Keats originated the term "negative capability" to describe that which interferes with finding alternative answers when confronted with rigid conventions. This notion is complemented by another artistic term "negative space," which pertains to not only apprehending the details of the structure but also attending to the space surrounding the structure.

Some leaders target negative people as interfering with sacred realities. Negativity, however, is part of the landscape and should be seen a means to getting at the truth, sometimes as a canary in the coal mine, not as the antithesis of being positive. The threat, to appropriate Spiro Agnew's famous phrase, is not the "nattering nabobs of negativism." The threat, rather, is not correctly apprehending the negativity.

Precious energy and time can be wasted placating destructive bullies or hostile critics whose agendas are more self-serving than constructive. However, rejecting obstructionists, saboteurs, or gossips should not be confused with resolving disagreements that may surface during genuine, transparent, and open avenues of constructive dialogue and ownership.

Adjusting Sight to Accommodate Negativity

Toxic others must be carefully navigated, yet isolating, labeling, and disconnecting from them is far easier, yet poor cultural modeling, than genuinely taking the time to understand their motivations, their fears, and the skepticism or cynicism that fear produces. Unconditional hearing helps address deep seated issues and plot corrective actions that benefit all.

Prejudicial conclusions and labeling or alienating detractors only indicates energy consumed, not energy created. The absence of listening, sharing, and collectively building consensus and relationships alienates employees from being good corporate citizens, drives them away from shared purpose and toward another employer, or toward unproductive habits. Additionally, leaders who do not have the courage to bring people together or do not invite questions tend to traffic in secrecy, compromise integrity, shun open communication, and defend ambiguity, and in so doing, cultivate distrust. Inaction is a sign of disrespect for others. If anything, exclusion reveals failings not in others but in those keeping the secrets.

In fact, senior leaders often unwittingly create the negativity they so arduously denounce. Labeling employees as "negative," often denigrating the disengaged as the enemy, or chastising them for not being on the bus, is itself wasteful. As American biographer Doris Kearns Goodwin, author of *Team of Rivals*, states of Abraham Lincoln's prowess in seeing that every person's position and perceptions are valuable:

> "His extraordinary array of personal qualities enabled him to form friendships with men who had previously opposed him; to repair injured feelings that, left untended, might have escalated into permanent hostility; to assume responsibility for the failures of subordinates; to share credit with ease; and to learn from mistakes.... A less confident man might have surrounded himself with personal supporters who would never question his authority.... While it was possible that his team of rivals would devour one another, Lincoln determined that 'he must risk the dangers of faction to overcome the dangers of rebellion."[14]

Fortunately, the blueprint for building a healthy culture is not mysterious nor elusive, and not nearly as foreboding as the crisis awaiting someone waking from a coma, surrounded by zombies and carnage. Anyone who has built or renovated homes knows, for instance, that demolishing a structure is far easier than building it. So, yes, negative voices that are destructive, rather than constructive, are counter-productive and add noise to problem solving or vision and value building. But those who constantly rile against authority, often caught up in an avalanche of negativity are no worse than negligent leaders who blindly triggered the mess.

We have a need to remember the insistence and persistence of these ardent voices is a result of not productively attending to their concerns, and their utterance is far more productive than those who choose not to aggressively question worrisome details in processes or decision making.

Allowing Negative Space

Our will and disposition should whole-heartedly embrace building upon inclusiveness, growth, strength, challenges, innovation, and improvement. Research by leadership consulting firm McKinsey & Company supports this thesis. Surveying 189,000 people across 81 organizations, three of four behaviors found to account for 89 percent of leadership effectiveness were solving problems effectively, seeking different perspectives, and supporting others.[15]

Front-line employees expect all leaders to continually drill down to the truth, as uncomfortable as that might be, and model inclusiveness and trust. If leaders are unwilling to model transparency, they should expect to see obfuscation and negativity reflected back by their employees. Inclusion is anchored to trust by hearing more, resistance to summarily discount others, and always attempting to fully see. This precise construction of truth allows seeing each other whole, not just seeing what we want to see. If this trust is secure, no employee need fear or question the intentions of others because we mutually look out for the best outcome for others.

As reiterated in Profiles International's "The Ultimate Guide to Employee Engagement," the most productive workforce is built through authentic shared values and vision by opening networked communication accompanied by clearly broadcasted expectations; listening to all (regardless of preconceived agendas) to help refine values and vision; ascertaining what motivates each individual.[16]

We should attend to constructive, progressive dialogue to support, update, and build better relationships, generating the best job matches and striving to invite as wide participation as possible in decision-making and problem solving. In stimulating workplaces, the only ambition is not ambition itself, but how ambitiously one sows initiative, how ably we recognize needs, and how frequently and freely we honor exemplary work. In other words, the negative or positive we reap, is the negative or positive we sow.

We all have blind spots in seeing ourselves and others, and can be susceptible to projecting misperceptions upon others to reinforce our prejudices. Sometimes our blindness is an inability to clearly listen to feedback, and we sometimes recoil from the insights others have the courage to share with us. To justify preconceived judgments and unmovable positions, we seek second-hand retellings and opinions, rather than distilling facts. And in reality, we should be as unwilling to readily dismiss the opinions of those who frequently agree with us or curry favor.

To build the power plant that generates discretionary energy, if we want to reenergize the zombies, we need the right tools, the know how to use them, the right hardware and materials, the right blade, and the exact measurements in hand. No matter how sharp the saw (as preached by leadership thought leader Steven Covey: body, mind, heart, soul[17]), the tines are likely to kick up some debris, so protecting sightedness is imperative. We should "measure twice and cut once." The more we know, the more time we need to eliminate false conclusions, evaluate the merit of "mistakes," and create space to break out of old habits.

Reforming the Curve:
Responding to Embedded Neglect

Most in business are familiar with Roger's Diffusion of Innovations Curve (see adaptation, below[18]).

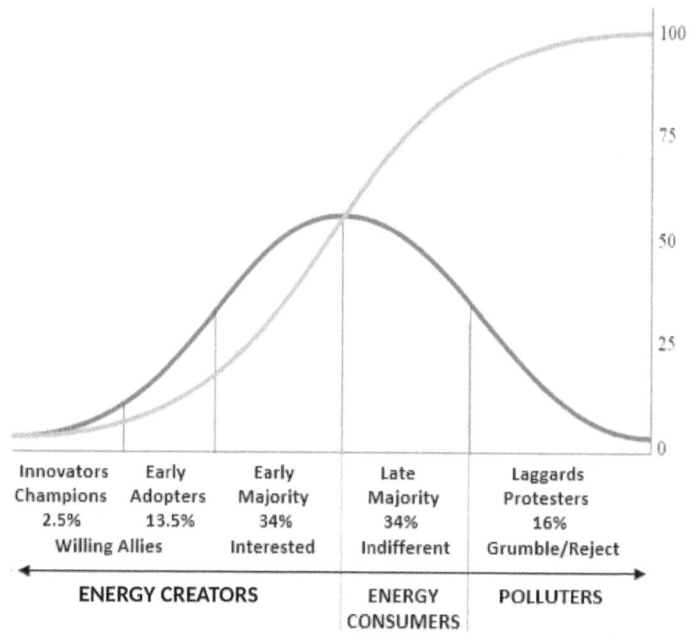

Innovators Champions 2.5%	Early Adopters 13.5%	Early Majority 34%	Late Majority 34%	Laggards Protesters 16%
Willing Allies		Interested	Indifferent	Grumble/Reject

ENERGY CREATORS   ENERGY CONSUMERS   POLLUTERS

Interestingly, engagement statistics inversely align with a normal distribution curve. The first year of employment, generally speaking, employees are typically highly engaged, which gradually drops off as soon as the end of the first year of employment, then arcs back up only after an employee logs progressive wins and reaches full maturity. The employee starts off eager, followed by a gradual drop off lasting years, then picks up nearer retirement.

On the innovation curve, on the other hand, the engaged are the innovators, early adopters, and some of the early majority. They start off strong, and if unabated by leaders, their engagement is sustained or progressively climbs. If engagement is preserved beyond the novelty of the first years of work, the curve shifts toward maintained excellence rather than dropping off and regressing toward "average." Highly engaged workplaces are centers for innovators and risk-takers. Laggards beware.

Respectively, then, enclaves of innovation and self-direction are characterized by the possibility of salvation, hope, equals, shapers, reparation and recreation. Enclaves of dysfunctional mistrust are characterized by reaction, fear, elitism, control, authoritarianism, crisis, and cannibals, and a "What's in it for me?" approach.

Negative and positive reactors reside between the two camps. We can choose to be distrustful and suspicious of all (as witnessing or experiencing counter-productive machinations makes us all weary). We can merely hang on to survival and languish, or we can choose to transcend the obvious inhibitors by dedicating ourselves to caring, developing, and responding to the people we neglect.

In this framework, some management thought suggests that the disenfranchised ultimately self-select or decay out. The accepted natural order is that those who choose to stand by the side-lines or criticize rather than offer new ideas and solutions should either retire, find a better fit, or be fired. This type of philosophy, however, is surrender to a sort of Machiavellian benign neglect.

Whether embedded neglect is structural or personal, and particularly if the culture is dysfunctional, toxic, or is beset by disproportionate power distribution, each person may still safely choose a fulfilling path. Two more hopeful messages lend perspective to facing obstacles that deter us from being innovators and part of a progressive leadership team. In *Man's Search for Meaning*, having survived four Nazi concentration camps Victor

Frankl reminds us, "Man can preserve a vestige of spiritual freedom, of independence of mind, even in such terrible conditions of psychic and physical stress," or prevailing over insurmountable odds to rise above disability, from Hellen Keller, "Everything has its wonders, even darkness and silence, and I learned, whatever state I may be in, therein to be content.... I must zigzag it in my own way. I slip back many times, I fall, I stand still, I run against the edge of hidden obstacles, I lose my temper and find it again and keep it better, I trudge on, I gain a little, I feel encouraged, I get more eager and climb higher and begin to see the widening horizon. Every struggle is a victory."[19]

At work or away from work, we can combat the voids created by disengagement by taking modest actions or incremental steps to make my job easier, less complicated, more enjoyable, and less stressful.

To make work more enjoyable, I will

_____.

How we make use of time remains a personal choice; that is, we can choose to approach tumult with a new ethic of vulnerability, then, adapt, experiment, and bring out the best in people during these reconstructive periods of time. Ultimately, the chief independent variable that can shift the curve is time. We have time to adapt. Of course, each person's decision and particularly the desired outcome of doing something differently, ranging from restoring sanity to escaping abuse, is a personal choice.

In my life, this is worth my time:

_____.

Not surprisingly, the challenge, when dysfunction is pervasive, is carving out sufficient time to address engagement. Appealing to the most willing allies is attractive and satisfies immediate needs, but the greater challenge is attending to those who choose to stay entrenched in ingrained habits.

Appealing to the Most Resistant or Indifferent

In 1970, Alvin Toffler first wrote about the "shock"[20] that may impede rapid or unexpected change. New workplaces require individuals to embrace their opportunities in order to move beyond survival and to fully thrive. The cold controls that preserve shock and a keep-your-head-down mentality, organizational philosopher Chris Argyris reiterates, is caused by "people themselves making the status quo so resistant to change. We are trapped by our own behavior."[21]

As growth and change are bedfellows and change is inevitable, ultimately only those who want to be moved can be moved. To identify the most willing and able, flexible, and critical thinkers, all employees, at the beginning and the end of the day, must feel empowered and know that they serve a significant part of the synergistic whole.

A first response usually heard by engaged and disengaged alike if asked to begin an engagement initiative is "I'm already overloaded." A second, similar response usually follows. In many institutions, employees often advance up the ranks by the virtue of technical knowledge, sales, or some other performance metric; however, if this talent is not accompanied by moving from task-oriented to people/positive regard-oriented behaviors, engagement is likely to derail (examined more deeply in the next chapters). "Engagement," whatever that means, makes sense to people-oriented leaders. Task-oriented individuals who lack a complementary people-orientation might protest, "I cannot waste my time," or ironically, "my people's time on this."

Therefore, positioning engagement within an on-going learning context is important. Foremost, engagement is a product of how well one can authentically help grow and develop others, not how we act to dismiss them. For engagement to flourish, a disposition to build relationships must be present, accompanied by letting go of the authoritarian security blanket of indispensability, status, and certainty. For instance, an expert-micromanager must shift his or her priority of detecting errors in others' work to assuring the best on-going developmental options for others. Constructive, non-threatening sharing and mutual caring creates not one micromanager but many autonomous experts and fearless collaborators.

Given the obstacles, one can forgive the errant choices employees make to navigate mixed or non-existent messaging. In any case, whether employees invoke leadership voices, or leaders truly lead, how each reacts and responds to needs, tweaking the variables can reform the curve if the tweaks (time, the method of how we interact, content, how we measure performance, etc.), represent a movement to honesty, excellence, and engagement. Again, of all these variables, creating the time is the most crucial. *Outliers* author Malcom Gladwell reasserts that 10,000 hours (give or take, 5-10 years) of evolving practice is necessary to accommodate the other variables and reach maximum potential,[22] so we can conclude that dedicated, intensive engagement efforts should take at least as long.

Business leaders, particularly, should lean on foresight to construct structural scaffolding to identify prerequisite needs, stop gaps, and the perseverance to construct developmental pieces to help people adapt to transitions and, thus, empower the engagement process that leads to each individual's pursuit of excellence.

Reversing the Horde: To See the Human Is to Repel the Zombie

In *The Walking Dead*, survivors who disguise themselves in Zombie decay live to see another day. In the workforce, faking it is not a useful tactic. If all of this "engagement," "passion," and "empowerment" jargon sound like an idealist walking on lunar-lit, zombie-free fields, we need to constantly remind ourselves that our everyday life—a great deal of which is conducted at work—is for the *living*. Everyone would rather thrive in flow than be held in suspended animation.

Our drivers remain remarkably similar; emotion moves us; making a difference reinforces the meaning we derive from our work. At work, we desire and deserve freedom from obstacles to succeed as well as availability of resources. We desire mutual trust and respect. We thrive on empowerment, opportunity, and the ability to develop our talents and assets. We want to be a part of "all hands," from janitors to engineers, *serving* as indispensable co-contributors to "put a man on the moon."[23]

Even in a zombie ridden landscape of defeatists, egos, and selfish agendas, positive stimuli can be introduced by those not side-tracked by power and control to shift the cultural normal curve closer and faster to innovative shareholding.

Therefore, negative and positive reconcile each other. To apprehend the full engagement picture, we are best served by attending to the negative space that may surround workplace interactions. As to positive space and the science of workplace engagement, once pretense is removed, there is a place, too, for the thing itself (see Henry James' "The Real Thing"[24]), particularly the reoccurring research and commentary pointing to specific applications demonstrated to heighten engagement.

We should, for instance, attend to the messaging of positive psychology researchers and pundits, such as Lisa Aspinwall, Shawn Achor, Michelle Gielan, Teresa Amabile, Dale Carnegie, and Jon Gordon, etc. We should be very careful in identifying corrupted versions of "being positive." Manipulative leaders cannot distinguish between "My way or the highway positive bus" (coaching that insists on maintaining a positive attitude despite hypocritical and contradictory actions) as opposed to an open dialogue, e.g., "Question and challenge everything I say" (which is inclusive, engaged, and cultivates truth and trust).

Taking more heart than brains, our emotional abilities applied to freely and purposefully recognizing others can transform the workplace. Action resides between idealism and pragmatism; neither should be ignored. With respect to the human art, see for instance Peter Hart and David Zinger's *People Artistry at Work*.[25] One illustration of clarity of response includes appreciation of work-life balance as seen demonstrated in the 2016 decision to provide greater opportunity and relative benefits for women in the U.S. military. Another is Starbucks providing a college education to its employees. Sure, these are bottom line recruitment and retention tools, good for the bottom line, but they are also good for the employee.

These types of choices are examples of win-win strategies that demonstrate supportive valuing of people. Some, for instance allowing employees to work from home, demonstrate a trust in people. For detailed examples of ways people and the bottom line reap profits, see Employment New Zealand's case studies.[26]

Obviously, given historic disengagement statistical trends, management has not yet mastered core aspects of workplace belonging and membership. Foremost, as seen throughout engagement literature, but most clearly summarized by Josh Bersin from Deloitte Consulting, exemplary human capital management resides in authentic appreciation and through simple acts of recognition.[27]

While obtaining some sort of engagement metric to gain a bearing is useful, even without conducting an engagement survey, some universal recognition principles apply, the foremost being recognizing excellence of the work product and potentialities in others.

Resounding convergence exists on recognition practices to improve engagement. These recognition suggestions are general but necessary—top soil for a cultural harvest that inspires and motivates others to succeed. Core engagement initiatives incorporate social celebrations (birthdays, years of service, etc.) but go much further:

- **Seek fresh and different ideas.** Some may have been around for years, but new to, and perhaps a fitting recipe for your group. Most importantly, being social is vastly and distinctly different from specific, purposeful recognition. Remember, **birthdays and holiday parties may enhance but are not substitutes for how people are engaged in their work.** Most work groups have perennial activities that we incorporate into our year. Participation in activities might be one of those periodic measurements to provide a metric of climate change, but assessing and adjusting variables affecting engagement should be continual.

- Particularly, consider these factors: specific appreciations should be immediate and frequent. All employees should be a part and <u>feel</u> like they are an integral part of the whole.

Reinforce solution-centered, not problem-centered expectations: We celebrate people when we include them in daily business, so assessing and improving formal and informal communication should focus on building inclusion, such as transmitting new information and encouraging and inviting greater employee participation in decision-making.

- **Commit to robust internal communication**, such as (a) publishing quarterly newsletters, (b) holding annual/semi-annual general meetings dedicated to recognition purposes; these can be electronic, and (c) continuously connecting values and mission to work product and weekly goals. Remember, communication by itself does not reflect engagement nor assure trust building. Communication must be accompanied by reinforcement of mission, be purposeful to employees (supportive and productive), and accompanied by genuine regard for the well-being of people.

- **Blend formal and informal means of recognition** (for specific low cost/no cost starting points, see the on-line library appendix for specific tools). Incorporate a wide variety of means to recognize or reward, but not solely locked into cash incentives (see Chapter 5, "At What Price Engagement" and an animated translation of Daniel Pink's *Drive*[28]). Publicly share successes and wins. It's not the pin, the watch, nor the gift card that counts—it's the story! Why am I, the person who is being recognized, important to the company? While each section should have its own means of recognizing specific mileposts, recognition should be public. Even better, on significant anniversaries, invite family. Read and reread Roy

Saunderson's "Top 10 Differences between Rewards and Recognition." [29]

- **Assess and evolve methodologies**, and, if absent, create mechanisms to employ peer-to-peer informal means of recognition. For more see Forbes Leadership article, "5 Ways Leaders Rock Employee Recognition."[30] If your workplace is more competitive, establish, for instance, a peer-to-peer nominated traveling trophy (create a creative title and trophy). Being mindful to apply procedures that eschew favoritism, this an informal bi-weekly award for attitude or esprit de corps (presented by the nominator and last recipient, but must always move to a new person). If your workplace is more collaborative, establish a conduit for frequent verbal affirmations. Peer-to-peer eclipses top-down methods and should primarily function as a vehicle to build camaraderie and have fun.

- Consider, in addition to informal recognition, less frequent but more formal, yet low cost performance-driven awards. A formal award should also be also peer nominated based on clear criteria, but presented by the highest ranking department head (see samples, appendix E, "Awards Templates"). **Focus on recognition based on increased quality performance, not simply quantity of effort**. Link recognition to specific business milestones, achievements, services, and production, as well as desired cultural values. Each presentation should be accompanied by a public acknowledgement, everyone gathers around during a formal meeting and the presentation is published in a newsletter or group email. A meaningful, personally written accolade, if properly executed, lasts much longer in the employee's mind than any monetary award.

- Create avenues for each employee to explore new areas while not sacrificing immediate needs. **The greatest recognition incentive, returns us to the power that growth, opportunity, and progressive development yield.** This includes, but is not limited to, capitalizing on the now, supported by coaching; targeting quality job growth as an on-going expectation woven into the culture and organizational values, either for cross-training efficiencies, upward mobility, or continual updating and newest job specific mastery. Even if someone has not followed the traditional educational track and has not graduated with an advanced degree, or has not been mentored to be a life-long learner, we all desire to learn more. Moreover, endeavor to know your employees and how you ascertain and assure an individual's growth. Examine your core competency design for leadership: Are coaching, development, and succession plans in place and regularly practiced? Most importantly, support curricular development and facilitate/encourage senior executives, managers, and supervisors to incorporate meaningful communication, recognition, and demonstrated interest (work and personal) in employees.

On these final, but most important growth-related needs, even if we agree that one of the goals to running an effective workplace is to retain and advance employees, often the job does not permit rapid upward mobility. Whatever the impediments to advancement, employees should always know that their potential is always not only highly valued but always appreciated. Whether employees grow in and up within their current jobs or grow out by accepting greater challenges with other employers, one of a manager's foremost concerns should be advancement of every employee's well-being and opportunity.

The Difference between Metaphorical Plot Lines and Reality

For a moment, let's return to wearing Rick Grime's shoes, *The Walking Dead*'s protagonist and reluctant, struggling hero. He is highly motivated to remain among the living, without himself turning monstrous. In the world of the walking dead, where mistakes are usually very costly, Rick is a forgiving but unrelenting coach. In both the graphic novel and the television series, he is highly trusted and valued by the group he shepherds. He earned that trust by trusting the power and the talents that others possess and by inviting differences. Part of his coaching is modeling; he's no hypocrite. Rick not only emphasizes the basic rules, not only what to do but <u>why</u> (a focus on compliance aspects that assure effectiveness is complemented by context), but he also allows his compatriots to improvise and gives group members sufficient room and multiple opportunities to learn, recover, and do better, given the attendant risks (allows improvisation within acceptable risk and fully articulated "why" parameters).

Characters in *The Walking Dead* who ignore the lessons soon join the zombies. Workplaces, hopefully, do not follow the predictability of this dystopic plot line. Sufficient autonomy and mastery should flourish, yet if mistakes do occur, the repercussions should not be as dire or ominous. If the leader is concerned about the well-being and growth of others, and contains the capacity to selflessly coach, we are able to absorb constructive criticism and grow through mistakes, not autopsied because of them.

Growth embedded in a supportive company culture depends on these basic interdependent concepts:

- Generally speaking, **work should be fun and joyous**. If work is not fun, the leader has an obligation to ferret out those who are offended by fun. If the offended insist that

71

fun is not professional, they need to be reminded that fun is relative to the situation (and those who are offended by fun probably require a lesson on relaxation techniques!).

- According to the *Harvard Business Review*, friendships should exist at work.[31] We should be able to rely on a confidant at work who aids our well-being— whether an immediate supervisor, near-by coworker, or just someone different at lunch table— someone who understands that **you are defined by more than your work role**. (One generally accepted caution to this make friends at work principle is "...but do not hire friends" if you want to remain as objective, if the pillars of engagement, fairness and equity, are valued.)

- Writing teachers know this: writing "good job" on a paper is meaningless. **Be specific with praise when providing formative feedback.**

- According to the Ross Center for Positive Organizations, **little things create big ripples**.[32] For leaders/for ourselves, ignoring or trivializing the small things is almost always indicative of larger, lurking problems. Not to be confused, the "little things" concept does not refer to mistakes that result in someone being banished from the kingdom. Rather it speaks to simple acts of kindness. Here's a personal example. One day, as I was chatting with the director of our section, he handed me a juice drink. I thanked him for the refreshment and jokingly added, "What I need is protein." A few days later, he stopped by my office and handed me a bag of beef jerky.

- Whether providing a particular service, expertise, or product, the little things require attention to make the biggest differences. How we act determines how we nourish others' engagement and our own. If everyone shares in successes and feels like a significant contributor, if we are more compassionate rather than preoccupied with judging others, we are more prone to fuel passion.

A great deal of engagement success can be harvested by applying the "Every Day in Every Way" appreciation practice. The ultimate way to reach this goal is with an abundance of affirming messages. Indeed, as confirmed by a former Campbell's soup executive, increased frequency of saying "thank you"[33] may well be another valid indication of engagement effectiveness. "Thank you" is scarce? Gratitude is forgotten? You can bet disengagement is an effect. See Globoforce's "The Power of Workplace Gratitude" for the research behind gratefulness.[34] Too task consumed to be human? How many of the emails that you receive begin or end with something personal, jovial, or uplifting (see have fun at work above)? How many of your emails, excluding the auto signature line, actually contain a personal salutation, including your name or unique complimentary closing for your specific audience?

Moreover, an authentic intent is necessary to know and grow another individual and improve the workplace. We have become accustomed to accepting a status quo I'm-too-busy engagement strategy. Does getting out of the lobotomizing habit of emailing rather than actually walking into a colleague's office make a difference? Substantially, yes.

The regular in/ex-clusion of these effortless, timeless courtesies are probably an accurate reflection of a coworker who is an affirming and engaged person.

Take note: generous, selfless actions are indicators of your real leaders. Affirmation means we are not caught in an artificial construct of "survival of the fittest, "not enough time," or "not worth my time." Simple, kind gestures, as effortless as they are to incorporate into every day actions, appear to be largely ignored. Consumed by daily pressures, some would argue, such acts are superfluous, but taking time to affirm others is our chief resource and asset. Thus, time can be made abundant by choice. If time is literally not available, it's time to reorganize and reprioritize the humans at work, including yourself.

Again, while executives in the organization have a particularly vested interest, engagement is everyone's business. We need to listen carefully to complainers who constantly harp about what is wrong. If the complaint is shared, supported, validated, we need to take a step back and reassess our biases and problem-solve. If it appears altogether non-productive, we need to turn to opposing beliefs and positions which are also accompanied by initiatives, ideas, perspectives, options. While the old adage is true, don't come with a complaint, unless you also bring a solution, we need to remember that "energy vampires" are as much a part of the status quo as those who create the status quo. Executives, particularly, should focus on what's really important, specifically: Incorporate emotional intelligence (EI) as a core competency for managers, supervisors, and leaders. As organizational and applied psychologist Cary Cherniss notes, EI is notably a stronger indicator of overall success than tenure, technical ability, or personal ambition.[35]

Finally, our vision of expectations and enactment of vision should be higher. At the core of meaningful work, mindful that everyone has a share of responsibility in a recovery from the apocalypse (the zombies too), the drive must begin to evolve intrinsically within each person and collectively in each office.

The chapter opened with George Romero's quotation, "My stories are about humans and how they react, or fail to react, or react stupidly. I'm pointing the finger at us, not at the zombies. I try to respect and sympathize with the zombies as much as possible." At the very least, with respect to engagement, decades of dismal track records suggest we have generally failed to seriously and conscientiously act. Warren Bennis joins Studs Terkel (from Chapter 1) among the prescient engagement thinkers, stating in 1989, "Only when we are fully deployed are we capable of that triumphant expression [of talent]. Full deployment, engagement, hone and sharpen all of one's gifts, and ensures that one will be an original, not a copy."[36] Leaders who are too prone to say, "Away with you!" have accepted the zombie in themselves, which makes accepting the zombie in others much more palatable.

Funny, the effects simple catalysts have on engagement. If our foreign exchange student had not introduced our family to the television show, I probably would have never seriously thought about this book. At the core of engagement is a more conscious resolve to acknowledge the presence and actualize the importance of others. If writers of *The Walking Dead* television series and workplace leaders initiate and support simple behavioral changes listed throughout, the tide will turn in the living's favor.

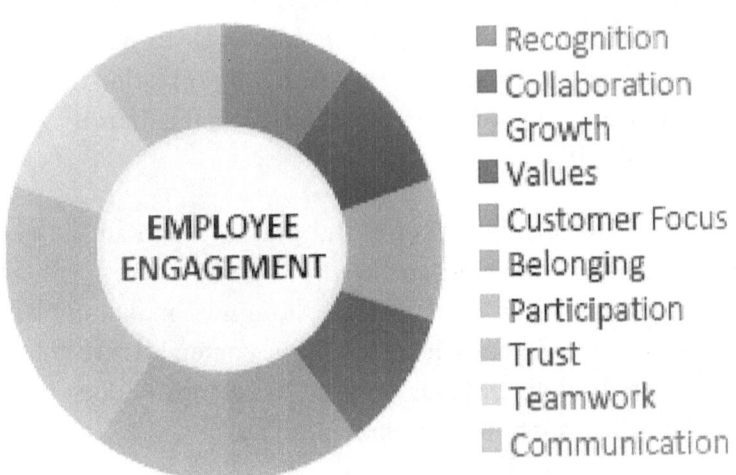

Recognition
Collaboration
Growth
Values
Customer Focus
Belonging
Participation
Trust
Teamwork
Communication

EMPLOYEE ENGAGEMENT

Chapter 5

"And then they want the person to change. If someone isn't what others want them to be, the others become angry. Everyone seems to have a clear idea of how other people should lead their lives, but none about his or her own.... The Soul of the World is nourished by people's happiness. And also by unhappiness, envy, and jealousy. To realize one's destiny is a person's only real obligation." –Paulo Coelho, *The Alchemist*

~

The interactions that interfere with the art and science of engagement refocus our attention to a fundamental question: How difficult is it to move from routine to progressive, from average to great? Jim Collin's research,[1] as chronicled in *Good to Great*, insists that for long-term successes to be achieved, those who lead well and infuse enduring organizational impact must possess a paradoxical blend of personal humility and professional will.

Further, hiring the right people and placing them in the right places nourishes an employee's well-being and, therefore, his or her engagement. In fact, without these, he argues, maintaining any enduring success is impossible. Finally, he contends that retaining faith with a disciplined focus on what the company does best is essential..., but not blind faith, nor blindness.

Structurally, Collins' conclusions appear largely applicable and irrefutable. Particularly reemphasized in this chapter, core constituents must brutally face facts by regularly questioning effectiveness and processes to maintain an engaged workforce.

As *The 8 Dimensions of Leadership* assessment exercise cautions, a main derailer is that "we remain captive to our own beliefs, attitudes, which can all too often blind us to the reality of a situation and the needs of our organization."[2] Particularly, what counts most on driving engagement is exploring unexplored routes.

However, what transforms a dark alley (fear and isolation) is well placed lighting (clarity) and a well-trodden path (inclusion, belonging). Different from a road paved with potholes is a road paved with good deeds, particularly acts that generate conversations, honest discourse, dissent, discussion, tough questioning, and planning that involves actual ownership, and input by anyone with a functional role (no matter how minute the connection).

Because engagement is grounded in both ethical and moral behavior, in "Defining Moral Leadership" researchers Nancy Maldonado and Candace Lacey reassert an underpinning engagement philosophy: leadership is reciprocal.[3] The power or energy created by any individual is an effect of giving, which produces trust. This requires letting go of power and control, particularly by those ensconced in the top positions. They must learn to trust that others possess a genuine, good intent to integrate and assert their autonomous skills, talents, and gifts within a team ethic. Creating this ethic and championing common purpose is no small feat.

Birds of a Feather

Ironically, we still struggle to shrug off remnants of 19th and 20th century captains of industry who believed that they were not paying people to be happy nor cared about common share in ownership nor leadership or the lives of others for that matter. While our 21ˢᵗ century living conditions and standards have improved, we may be too prone to lament our lots at work, rather than be grateful for the relative, albeit imperfect, comforts now present in our work.

One graphic, historic illustration reaches back to the turn of the 20ᵗʰ century, Alfred Lansing's *Endurance*, which chronicles explorer Sir Ernest Shackleton's team's maiden, uncharted trek to the South Pole:

> Daring to sail alone across the world's most tempestuous sea, her rigging festooned with a threadbare collection of clothing and half-rotten sleeping bags. Her crew consisted of six men whose faces were black with caked soot and half-hidden by matted beards, whose bodies were dead white from constant soaking in salt water. In addition, their faces, and particularly their fingers were marked with ugly round patches of missing skin where frostbites had eaten into their flesh. Their legs from the knees down were chafed and raw from the countless punishing trips crawling across the rocks [for ballast in the bottom of the boat]. And all of them were afflicted with salt water boils on their wrists, ankles, and buttocks. But had someone unexpectedly come upon this bizarre scene, undoubtedly the most striking thing would have been the attitude of men... relaxed, even faintly jovial almost as if they were on an outing of some sort.[4]

Some might think this retelling is a barbaric or hyperbolic comparison of today's engagement challenges, but Lansing's retelling demonstrates that engagement eclipses conditions. Regardless of our current situation or conditions, engaged individuals bring others on board, help others work through adversity. They sacrifice and are constructive contributors in reaching shared goals and purpose.

Do our present human foibles appear too foreboding to even fathom a trek across disengagement's arctic tundra? Rather than leaving others out in the cold, cultural formation depends on supporting one another, such as the ingenuity, perseverance, and team work common in the animal kingdom, see "Remarkable Workplace Lessons from Bird Flight Patterns," below.[5]

Beyond Decoys and Duck Calls

The initial conflict for most employees, often with some justification, is the threat of being punished for doing the right thing. Too regularly, we hear repeated stories of disregard or retribution against 20th through 21st century whistle blowers, recently allegations of retribution by Transportation Security Administration employees who pointed out lapses in airport screening. From financial sectors – Bernard Madoff, to public sectors – Flint water crisis, to environmental disasters – Deepwater Horizon, to our own workplaces, many wary employees witness not only process, but ethical and moral lapses, yet remain silent in order to preserve their own fragile standings. To survive in the workplace, a corrupt culture insists that silence is tantamount to maintaining trust. Fairness insists on caution, protective means to air concerns. However, we are reminded, beyond repercussions visited upon whistleblowers, as reported in *The Washington Post* article, "Beware the Rule-Following Co-Worker," "unethical workers have longer tenures at companies than ethical ones."[6]

Remarkable Workplace Lessons from Bird Flight Patterns

1. **As each bird flaps its wings, it creates an UPLIFT for others behind it. A 71% greater flying range is achieved In V-formation than in flying alone.** Lesson: People who share a common direction and sense of purpose (lift and lift up) arrive at their goal more quickly.

2. **Whenever a bird flies out of formation, it feels drag and tries to get back into position.** Lesson: The bird doesn't drag the group down, but endeavors to find a productive position. The individual constructive contribution assures collaborative success.

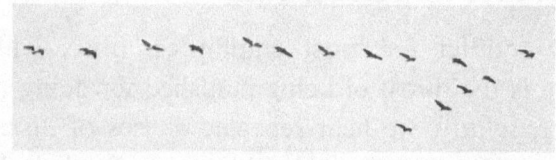

3. **When the head bird tires, it rotates back into formation and another in the flock takes the lead.** Lesson: The flock does not function as a rigid hierarchy but embraces shared leadership and interdependence. Each enjoys empowerment in decision-making as well as opportunity to rest.

4. **Birds flying in the rear of the formation call to encourage those up front to keep up their speed.** Lesson: Encouragement is motivating.

5. **When a member falters, is sick or wounded and falls, others fall out and stay with it until it revives or dies. Then, they catch up or join another flock.** Lesson: Since everyone needs help from time to time, standing by our colleagues in difficult times is admirable.

--Adapted from Arrien Angeles, Milton Olson, and Robert McNeish

Distrust is compounded by disconnected, top-down control, position, or expertise by dominating leaders, which easily creates a "dogmatic effect."[7] Social psychologist Victor Ottati explains that we are not only enamored by our own designs but are unmoved by compelling arguments, and close our minds to valid feedback. When this effect is present in leaders, full ownership and collaboration is corrupted or compromised, and achieving pervasive engagement is unlikely.

Part of a compromised dynamic is rooted in dependence on compliance and authority. Another part stems from deficiencies in relationship building, which defeats trust. We want to build relationships that welcome and appreciate different points of view, regardless of political or personal agenda. In fact, multiple points of view, if carefully heard, may help us see our own political and personal positions much differently.

Preserving trust, on the other hand, requires a combination of will and humility. Humility, as defined by the Thrive Center's developmental psychologist Justin Barrett, "is full ownership constituted by a state of openness to new ideas, receptivity to new sources of evidence and the implication of that evidence, and willingness to revise even deeply held beliefs in the face of compelling reasons."[8]

We are far from being "great" mentors, coaches, or colleagues when we have not comprehended the differences between a "good soldier" and the effective inclusion of a team member who, as Collins argues, does not "blindly acquiesce to authority and is a strong leader in her own right."[9] In dysfunctional cultures, leaders convolute "the right seat on the bus," rather than actively listen. Some may resort to ferreting out and minimizing or ostracizing the transgressing[10] party, relying on retributive action for those who have the courage to be transparent and honest. Fitting the right people into the right seats requires moral tools and ethical conviction, not hammer and pry bar.

For instance, labeling someone as "negative" is far easier than being open to dissent in open debate. Cognitive dissonance is always good; dissonance should always be valued as virtuous, not a hindrance. It helps us to identify our own biases, distortions, and possible failings. Finding the center of truth, and thus trust, can only be derived from honest airing and, as objectively as possible, distilling all first-person interpretations by filtering out conflict and focusing on why we reached a point of conflict, receiving all points of view, and eliminating disruptive or unproductive personal agendas.

The Volkswagen auto emission scandal is the perfect example of ends (pressure to increase sales numbers) justifying the means (cheating brought on by a chain of mistakes and illegal actions, precipitated by turning away from transparency). The fear of the status quo, followed by cover-up, demonstrates how difficult it is to police internally. Because *outside, independent* scientists found discrepancies (creating irrefutable cognitive dissonance), the auto maker was compelled to analyze verifiable evidence and moved toward developing new processes and systems to avoid future lapses. Aside from fines and penalties associated with law violations, following a precipitous stock decline after the scandal broke, stock futures began to rise only after the company announced an assertive, corrective course including an auto buy-back program and compensation to consumers. The intervention was instrumented by another *third party*, the Environmental Protection Agency.

Of course, those responsible for Volkswagen's woes, by direct action or by negligence, were destructive, and, therefore, brought about as a product of disengagement. Volkswagen's woes were probably not a product of trusting too much, but likely a product of fear and a bunker mentality. A moral, ethical, and or political ambiguity should breed uncertainty, caution and skepticism. Dissonance, not fear or acquiescence to cultural pressure, should occur in response to deficient standards and practices.

One of the best illustrations of why dissonance does not prevail is explained in The Arbinger Institute's *Anatomy of Peace*:

> Workers recruit colleagues and others with the tales they tell, leading to organizations that are divided into warring silos, one group complaining incessantly about another, and the other returning the same. Until finally, organizations are filled with people whose energies are largely spent on sustaining conflict— what we call collusion—and who therefore are not fully focused on achieving the productive goals of the organization (54). Seeing an equal person as an inferior is an act of violence (34). When our hearts are at war, we not only invite failure, we invest in it (40).[11]

Moreover, because some critics consider engagement no more than a social trend or passing fad,[12] responding to disengagement augmented by dysfunction is foreboding. Effective progress is nearly impossible if leaders adopt war footings by discounting the legitimacy of others or by discounting the validity of engagement drivers.

Overcoming Bunker Mentality

Being aligned with mission and purpose is not at odds with being happy and finding meaning at work or with those who, sometimes unwittingly, make work miserable. Engagement, mission, and purpose are mutually supportive. We must consider, therefore, those intersections in organizational structure that, if left unattended, can contribute to disengagement and disconnection. Certainly, hierarchical dynamics influence the engagement picture. How managers assert authority, keep chains of communication clear and open, build trust, rather than rationalize distrust, reflect not only personal qualities but organizational values.

Assessing the willingness to collaboratively share and collectively commit should be part of engagement exploration. Larger organizations may feel bound to a relatively top-down structural hierarchy to exert control (typically driven by position and authority and by rewarding loyalty and compliance). Even within these strictures, however, pockets of innovation, which cultivate diverse influence and trusted independence, can abound. Learning and growth, as well as independence in cross-functional connectivity can be dynamic levers within overarching chain of command.

The Center for Creative Leadership explains the benefits of such fluid organizational interactions. Dependent, rigid top-down organization is exclusively driven by compliance, unconditional loyalty, and authority. Interdependent structures are less rigid and invite more interactive discussion and influence without excessive demarcated lines of communication. Interdependent cultures invite shared, flexible leadership and are based on growth and best situational alignments.[13] Not surprisingly, interdependent cultures contain more fulfilled and productive employees.

The graphic below captures a portion of Informal Networks, Ltd.'s, example of "making employee engagement natural":[14]

Promoting Structural Improvisation

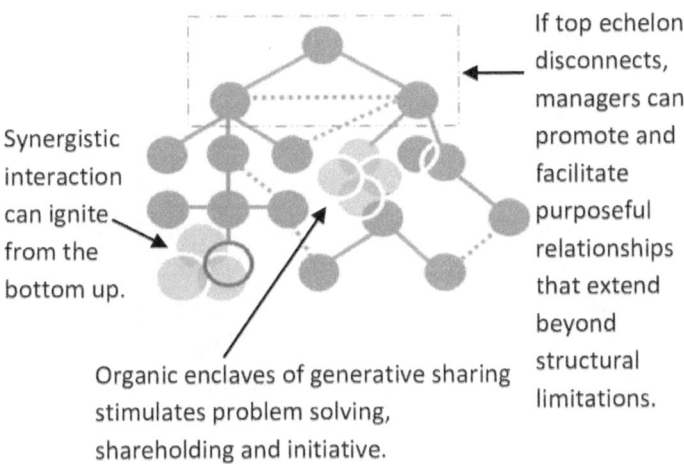

Synergistic interaction can ignite from the bottom up.

If top echelon disconnects, managers can promote and facilitate purposeful relationships that extend beyond structural limitations.

Organic enclaves of generative sharing stimulates problem solving, shareholding and initiative.

When hierarchical interactions flatten, that is, move from dependency to interdependency, even when top level administration remains more dictatorial or relatively disconnected, autonomous pockets of innovation and interrelatedness create greater local trust and synergistic engines that transcend the ordinary. If recognition programs are not in proper place, these incubators are often lauded but the lessons learned are rarely explored nor shared as models to replicate. Of course, if you have been in the workforce for any length of time, it's likely you have been part of a very special collective, unique to the time and place. We could speculate on the "magic" of it, but usually one attribute is shared purpose, complemented by members who supported, respected, and learned from each other.

Each person within these subcultures can be a catalyst to shape synergy. However, "flattening" does not suggest totally abandoning structure; it's not a call for a laissez-faire approach. The Zappos experiment provides sufficient caution. Having tested the feasibility of a flattened hierarchy, a more democratic (perhaps "holacratic") administration, which eliminated hierarchical bosses, the on-line company's restructuring resulted in confusion, no clear structural authority, and debilitating turn-over.[15]

Perhaps the lesson is that leaders and managers must find the happy medium, yet move to abandon counter-productive, rigid structures and vestiges of behavioral pitfalls once touted in *Walden Two*.[16] In *Walden* Henry David Thoreau's (1854) walk in the woods was an autobiographic sojourn to transcend the ordinary. A century later, in *Walden Two* (1948), B. F. Skinner perilously tacked from personal introspection to behavioral science, speculating that authoritarian leaders could simply manipulate a better world into existence.

Near 2020, we appear to have closed the circle by returning to introspection, reminded that what matters is what is human. Individuals who are tireless innovators and contributors require emotional satisfaction, not social experiment. We need merely appeal to the human desire for virtuous, constructive acts. Self should be attended to by introspection (not selfish acts) and community should be attended to by selfless acts. We seek outward, coalescing multiple points of view, to more clearly peer inward.

Leaders who require absolute loyalty merely impose subservience through opaque subjectivity. The misuse of unquestioned loyalty deepens mistrust. This is evidenced by leaders who label dissent as disloyal, or, for instance, why ineffective meetings lack thinking, forward movement, trust, and are dominated by ego or image.

Engagement means that employees are fully equals, participating in the process, and focus on what works, what doesn't, what's missing, embrace alternative points of view and the next best action, and seek multiple answers to hard questions, particularly boundless input to "How do all of us contribute to make this better?"

Subscribing to a power posture worsens the conditions for cultivating engagement. For example, the invitation,

1) "Let's have lunch!" is communal, a social invitation that promotes relationship building. Similarly, a heart grounded in well-being and service is apparent in,

2) "May I bring you some lunch?" Since the heart of engagement is encouraging others, the best leaders are, in fact, servant leaders and frequently seeing, knowing, and understanding how they can help others, not how others can help them.

The third alternative, reflects a stance and actions that are out of touch with cultivating engagement, for instance, when a manager issues this request to a subordinate,

3) "Would you please run to _____ (ex., the cafeteria) and bring **me** _____ (ex., lunch)?"

Regardless of the courteous "please," the difference between scenario three and examples one and two, above, is the third reinforces authoritarian posture, rather than communal act. If a leader is too preoccupied to attend to her or his own basic needs, for instance stepping out to grab one's own cup of coffee, or ream of paper, and cannot arrange time to actually schedule something as simple as a lunch break, the evidence suggests that the leader may have succumbed to the Peter Principle, or an ego disrupts seeing others as co-equals in the organizational partnership.

Until the late 20th century, culturally accepted perks of the personal assistant smacked of sexism, bullying, subordination, disrespect, and were, essentially, demeaning. Certainly, in the 21st century, this sort of act, unless "wait on me hand and foot" literally appears in the job description, is not setting the stage for engagement. In fact, the victims of such questionable modeling are being groomed from corrupt misinterpretations of engagement and leadership.

Engagement grows from inculcating the values and practicing the behaviors that uplift and challenge all. From CEO to newcomers, selfless actions inspire, model the way, challenge processes, enable others, and as touted by Kouzes and Posner throughout their book *The Leadership Challenge*, most of all, encourage the heart.[17]

The goal of a hybrid, humane dynamic is to ensure more meaningful communication, creative thinking, and open problem solving, not model subservience. The result of constriction and control, the lack of hybrid constructive interconnections and relationships, may result in laments such as, "Our department is responsible for providing clients this information, yet my customer knew that this was happening before we did!"

Engagement/disengagement, culture, and communication are inextricably interconnected. To heighten engagement, our psychological make-up must possess these two variables: the **will** to do something differently, demonstrated by unwavering commitment to experiment and employ refreshed means to build empowerment and to capitalize on values, vision, and passion, and **disposition**, demonstrated in personal and interpersonal actions, appreciation of the abilities, skills, dimensions, and respect for each other's personal characteristics.

Not only our employees but our corporate nature need nurturing. What type of work culture do we want to design? Organizational structure requires scaffolding of opportunity and experiences, not merely position. Cervantes had it right, "The journey is better than the inn."[18] The paths we take, our stellar successes and rough drafts, are more important than the title on a business card. Valuing others and the positions in which they find themselves, all others' perspectives provide better depth of field than any singular perch upon which any one person sits or the platforms of any special or political interests. If these voices and experiences are not attended, if we choose, rather, to ignore or constrict them, we ignore progressive science and construct no more than a Skinner Box of workplace disengagement.

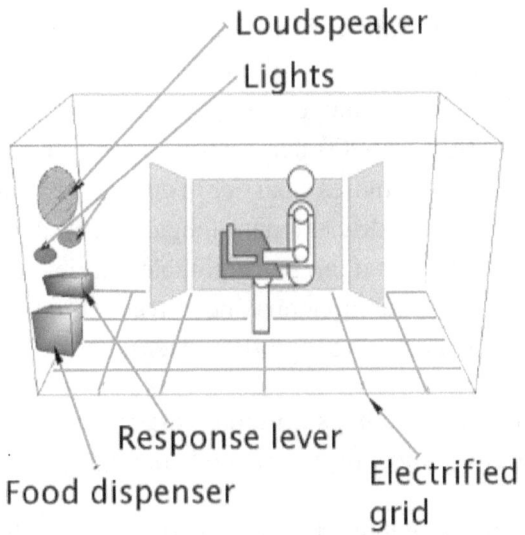

Loudspeaker

Lights

Response lever

Food dispenser

Electrified grid

"Between stimulus and response, people have the power of choice."[19] – Steven R. Covey, *The 8th Habit: From Effectiveness to Greatness*

Chapter 6

At What Price Engagement?

"It's not about the money, money, money…"
– Jessica, "Jessie J.," Ellen Cornish, *Price Tag* lyric.

~

This chapter is not about how disengaged workers contribute to approximately $300-400 billion per year in lost productivity, $2,246-$3,400 per employee in potential liabilities, nor the estimated $12,000-$50,000 per employee rehire costs.[1] "At what price" more deeply explores a barrier to engagement, and suggests the best investment of discretionary (engagement) dollars. Finally, this chapter asserts that if fair and equitable salaries are earned, the paycheck and any other monetary incentives should be eliminated from the engagement or recognition discussion.

Advancement (and perhaps a higher salary) should follow from validated performance; performance is not a product of money.

To move from disengaged to engaged cultures, discretionary investment is required, but the investment needs to be much more personal, emotional, and psychological than budgetary.

The chapter asks to consider the conditioning to which we have become accustomed about how value is defined, and how the workplace answers when an employee asks, "Am I valued?"

How an employer demonstrates appreciation of its workers is certainly embedded in engagement but remains a conviction that is sometimes based in rewards and punishments rather than any other, more effective actions that build and preserve engagement.

I would like you to suspend your thinking for a moment of any personal beliefs or biases you might hold about the allure of money as an effective incentive. Eliminating the amount printed on the paycheck, if we then think about what employees desire from work or at work, what specific actions do you believe will prime performance and yield the greatest ROI?

Business articles, for instance, have focused on flex-time as a motivator. Take as many vacation days as you would like? Increased maternity or paternity leave? A shorter work week? What stimulates employees: uncompromising, stressful demands or generous time off? On the last question, except perhaps for very few people at either end of the spectrum, neither really.

Does paying everyone the same salary solve the engagement puzzle? *Gravity Payments* creator Dan Price tested the hypothesis of the influence salary has on motivation, that is, after earning a respectful salary, somewhere between conspicuous consumption and minimum wage, does more money affect performance? Price pegged that number at $70,000 for all employees. As the taxonomy of engagement suggests (discussed in depth in the next chapter), Price's intent to establish equitable stakes had an admirable and noble aim, but additional sustainability needs, such as recognition, must be part of the engagement fabric after salary fairness and equity have been realized.[2]

Engagement actually resides beyond pay and requires not only understanding but a substantial intrinsic response to personal aspiration and professional validation.

The answers to discovering the best incentives to foster engagement are dependent upon the nature of the workers, geographic needs, and local, institutional variables. However, generally speaking, when companies approach engagement consciously, profit flows from the fundamentally right things rather than an obsessive focus on profit or compliance. If engagement is high and workplace dynamics are highly functional, profit and compliance are effects, not drivers or regulators or engagement.

Two counter-productive manager-employee refrains often confound true employee engagement efforts. From the employee (ironically heard loudest from the highest wage earners) is an expectation of a raise or bonus ("I'm entitled to"). The size of the raise, we are conditioned to believe, validates importance and our value at work. A similarly telling and occasional refrain heard from managers, "Some people are perfectly content doing..." is sometimes used to justify "I'm entitled to." These types of embedded institutional values unwittingly perpetuate low expectations of a salary as the prime motivator and drown out championing an expectation of excellence.

Very few people will turn down more money. And in a capitalistic society, money serves as a status symbol and a measure of success. Thus, salary remains an effective lure;[3] however, while money may entice workers to sign on, it does not assure continued retention. Once employees have joined a company and have experienced the interworking, culture trumps salary.[4] In fact, if we do not leverage employees' strengths and talents, their motivation to leave is not a larger paycheck; they may even entertain a pay cut. With greater passion and purpose, they leave to best match self-perceptions and untapped potential levels of contribution. And if they do not leave, they can be held captive by salary or lack of accountability. The percentage of "tenant, captives, or disconnected,"[5] employees who intend to stay, according to PWC Consulting, falls somewhere between 48 percent and 75 percent.[6]

While we may still number salary among the variables that typically prompt employees to leave for greener pastures, its influence is eclipsed by quality of supervision and fewer growth opportunities being available. A survey by software company PayScale found a vast perceptual disagreement in employee/employer on fair pay (37 percentage points), employee valuing (33), and pay transparency (19). In addition, while it found pay was not a factor in recruiting but in retention, manager impact and growth experiences appeared to have a stronger relationship to retention.[7]

Particularly in the context of nested workers, we should prudently reexamine salary, especially in the context of a fair market and the function of the pay raise in relationship to well-being.

For instance, the raise or bonus is often seen as the primary transactional (the carrot part of "carrot and stick" approach to motivation) means to demonstrate value. The increase is a fair and earned reward acknowledging a worker's productivity. But answer honestly, when you received your last pay raise, how much of your work ethic, habits, and behaviors substantially changed? The answer is probably very little. The type of work may change by the virtue new learning and challenges associated with a promotion, cross-training, etc., and this may stimulate greater enthusiasm and result in greater well-being, but probably will not result in long-term changes in work habits, unless the changes continue to challenge, better capitalize, and optimally capture each worker's talents and strengths. In reality, a raise results in a short-lived response to perceived entitlements. A pay raise may reinforce or confirm "we deserve" rather than function to positively alter any behaviors.

Thus, one of the less attractive outcomes of using pay as a motivator (since we are conditioned to think that pay is equivalent to personal value) is the unhappy career nested in complaints, feeling of powerlessness, and dissatisfaction followed by the happily disingenuous countdown to the sweet release of retirement. Consider this engagement quiz:

> **Away from your desk, in the hallway or by the water cooler, what do you most often hear other employees talking about: <u>breakthroughs on a new project</u> or counting the number of years/days remaining until someone's retirement? <u>A recent business victory</u>, a lament about a pay freeze, or countdown to the weekend? A want for more information about some change at work, character assassination, or <u>a compliment about a fellow co-worker</u>?**

If you selected anything but the underlined options in the quiz above, blind spots probably exist and require reflection. If you circled the pay freeze option, read on. Even when financial bonuses are part of the compensation picture, focusing on the person rather than the paycheck yields higher performance dividends.

The unproductive stuff and misconstrued values have another unfortunate outcome: the disgruntled worker who does leave or is fired and finds true engagement and passion elsewhere or by filling the blogosphere, or hallways when the supervisors are out of earshot, with more havoc than a demolition derby. Prohibited from breaking through artificial barriers and out of the status quo, some find a measure of solace by throwing stones at the glass door.

The research and commentary is resounding. Bersin at Deloitte, business psychologist Tomas Charmorro-Premuzic at Hogan

Associates, and Juliana Schroeder at Haas Business School[8] conclude that beyond fair, equitable compensation (meeting survival and safety needs), money does not substantially impact or alter behavior or levels of engagement. Further, rewards and recognition should not be tied to a single responsibility, behavior, nor compliance.

And even if monetary awards are introduced, as they tend to merely reward normal performance, workers learn to "game" the system, or as Dina Gerbeman reports from Harvard, after reaching a certain level, money, relative to your perceptions of what others are worth, does not motivate much, and it may even demotivate. [9] The *Energy Project* comments on the degree to which the perception of wages skews an effect on productivity:

> Since the dawn of capitalism, time for money has been the core value exchanged between employees and their employers. It no longer serves either party well. Paying for people's time is no guarantee you'll also get their energy, engagement, focus, or passion. Conversely, no amount of money people get paid is sufficient to meet their core needs.[10]

And again, in *Outliers*, Gladwell echoes Daniel Pink's conclusions on valuing, meaning, purpose:

> Autonomy, complexity, and a connection between effort and reward are, most people agree, the three qualities that work has to have if it is to be satisfying. It is not how much money we make that ultimately makes us happy between nine and five. It's whether our work fulfills us.... Work that fulfills those three criteria is meaningful.[11]

Of course, in a capitalistic society, money remains a potent stimulant. Over repeated experiments, psychologist Kathleen Vohs found "people reminded of money shift into professional, business, and work mentality. They exert effort on challenging tasks, demonstrate good performance and feel efficacious." However, salary should not be confused with meaning, value, or appreciation. In fact, her study also found a disconcerting correlate: "people reminded of money are less interpersonally attuned, less caring and warm, and eschew interdependence."[12]

This finding supports one of the most significant engagement disconnects. The central argument to deepen the playing field of administrator growth is that engaging and engaged managers must be interpersonally warm, caring, and champion interdependence.

Elegant Actions Are Priceless

Each work culture has idiosyncratic dynamics, so each requires an authentic audit to make headway in determining a reasonable approach. The evidence presented throughout these chapters appears to suggest that the more we move to hire the right people, eliminate disparity and prejudices, establish noble goals and high expectations, ease unquestioned submission to absolute rules, and move from conditioning workers to subscribe to a paycheck as reward, the closer we are to creating an engaged pipeline.

Profiles International emphasizes that engagement is cultivated through job match, a deliberate effort to ascertain what motivates each individual,[13] and through communicated expectations (six of eight engagement goals recommended by the ClearCompany's 2014 CEO, Andre Lavoie, emphasize improved communication, ranging from better communicated recognition, to improved feedback loops and transparency related to goal alignment, to more clearly articulated goals and values to defeat gossip.[14] Foremost, as suggested earlier, recognition should be a public exercise and performance-based, hallmarked by simple, systematic, daily, creative, and simple acts demonstrating appreciation and celebrating exemplary, "above and beyond," product.[15] Immediate, personal acknowledgments are more effective than extrinsic means, such as monetary rewards.

Recognition and communication can manifest themselves with much more than a literal pat on the back. At a community college at which I worked, to demonstrate our impact and reach, our chancellor chartered a bus to bring the founding faculty and administrators on a tour of our extensive service area. We stopped at schools, churches, restaurants, prominent landmarks, and state park, locations that many had never visited even though we lived within the 60 mile service area. The act served to communicate our mission but also served to thank all of us for our extensive start up efforts, and remind us of the groundbreaking work on which we had embarked.

Nonetheless, I have heard from plenty of dissenting voices who argue that recognition alone does not quench the nagging, conditioned economic thirst for money. No amount seems to be a fair and just monetized value. Of course, living in a capitalist society is accompanied by the pull of conspicuous consumption embedded in marketing. To demonstrate this tendency, Suzanne McGee poses two questions:

- **"Imagine for a minute, that your employer tells you that he's going to pay you 25 percent more and give you an extra week of vacation… [if you can] cut your division's annual budget by 5 percent. Do you take the offer?"**

- **"When your family member asked what you wanted for the holidays, did you say, 'nothing really' – and mean it?"[16]**

Of course, materialism ironically competes with the less conspicuous and more intrinsic motivators. Accordingly, another reasonable argument to affirm that money is a better motivator is that intrinsic rewards only work for so long, embodied, for instance, in sales people who walk away from jobs because of meager bonuses. Employees will eventually tire of or want more than praise, suggesting that recognition has less appeal.

In reality, however, rewards (promotion/raises) should follow opportunity. Opportunity should follow from equity and membership. Aside from the social celebrations that one hopes are part of the work culture, praise and appreciation appropriately linked to performance surely equals recognition and the prospect of more money.

To be sure, if there is a glimmer of truth that money has a longer lasting effect on performance or happiness, it remains effective only as a motivational variable when equity, relationship building, and growth, are accommodated, and work is meaningful (discussed more fully in Chapter 7, "Taxonomy of Engagement"). The combined interaction, extrinsic rewards coupled with intrinsic catalysts, can be significant. Work becomes more meaningful and passions flourish if one is able to generate impact (giving) and move away from the need for validation through rewards in the form of external stimuli (what's in it for me, paycheck, corner office).

The greatest focal change required is tapping the "intrinsic," which requires a change in some management styles, a greater emotional and cognitive shift of a belief system: help others achieve their highest callings. Of course, fair and meritorious compensation are provisions of valid intrinsic motivators. If the basic extrinsic variable are sound, engagement is then better seen as a conscious building of culture, where self-interest is supplanted by a pervasive want to care for, love, grow, value and serve others.

Real Engagement Efforts Cost Very Little

Engagement at all levels requires a personal investment and commitment, not necessarily a pay bonus. Again, the bonus should follow from personal initiative and commitment. Personal initiative and commitment do not follow from a raise; they follow from engaging opportunities and tasks. Leaders must cultivate, not circumvent the intrinsic. After all, some organizational development dollars, aside from compensation or bonus dollars, should be dedicated to incubate engagement. If we really want greater engagement, and we have discretionary resources at our disposal, deploying a few dollars to address the intrinsic variables of an engagement initiative will yield win-win results.

We know the key stimuli that affect engagement and motivation (see "Driver x Thought Leader" table[17], below). After a number of more intrinsic variables, "pay fairness" occurs, not pay excess.

Strategies and actions should focus on these factors. Some of the "how" is generic; others aspects are more institutionally variable, depending on what is currently in place. Most ask us to think more deeply about how to build trust, foster relationships, assure fearless communication, form and fuel effective teams, balance well-being, provide appropriate resources and tools, and connect personal purpose and legacy to institutional vision and values. All are seated in acknowledging others:

- **Do we recognize the value of others?**

- **Do we recognize how each person is interconnected to trust?**

- **Do we recognize the well-being of others?**

- **Do we recognize when a team is functioning well...? How do we know?**

- **How well do we recognize and allow talents of others to fit into the flow?**

Driver x Thought Leader ⇩　　　⇨	A	B	C	D	E	F	G	H	I
Growth Opportunity, Nature of the Job, Fit, Purpose (including Learning and Development) (9)	✓	✓	✓	✓	✓	✓	✓	✓	✓
Feedback Expectations, Clarity Information, Communication (7)	✓	✓		✓	✓		✓	✓	✓
Performance, Accomplishment Contribution, Quality (7)	✓	✓	✓	✓	✓	✓	✓		
Team, Coworkers, Culture (including e.g., Relationship w/ Managers, Manager Quality, and Respect/Caring) (7)	✓	✓		✓	✓	✓	✓	✓	
Recognition (6)	✓	✓			✓		✓	✓	✓
Trust, Integrity (5)	✓	✓	✓		✓				✓
Voice, Influence (4)	✓	✓			✓		✓		
Well-Being, Work-Life Balance (4)				✓	✓	✓	✓		
Connection to Values, Vision, Mission (4)	✓			✓	✓			✓	
Tools (3)		✓			✓			✓	
Job Security, Perceived Future (3)					✓	✓			
Pay Fairness (2)				✓	✓				
Pride in Company (2)			✓		✓				

Foremost, recognition is a higher psychological need (requisite to belonging), so annual evaluations and merit raises are not engagement drivers. Recognizing work that aids the bottom line (either interpreted as an employee's wage or profit margin) is important, but even more important are on-going efforts that result in knowing and recognizing the person.

Therefore, a complementary principle contained in acknowledging others, in addition to supporting and recognizing others, "every day in every way," is that concrete aspects of engagement, particularly recognition, once mastered, costs us very little.

Whatever time and treasure may be dedicated to achieve engagement, the result promises to be an increase in more productive use of time and literal profit. Longer term, the goal is that the practices and core goals tied to effective engagement become woven into the fabric of the institution (i.e., transparent communication and empowerment, coupled with honest and accountable recognition, all which leads to creating a trustworthy culture).

Final Notes

Losses to profitability and productivity are an effect of disengagement, yet we tend to be comfortable with absorbing such losses and shunting the costs of disengagement to the subconscious. More disastrous is that we have lost track of what value and values really mean. The core to engagement investment is contributing to valuing others' well-being. Career coach Jeffery Kudisch adds, "The costs of devaluing others are so great that we need to spend far more time thinking than we do now about how to hold people's value, even in situations where they've fallen short and our goal is to get them to change their behavior for the better."[18]

Engagement is inversely related to fear and punishment. Engagement leads to meaningful work, fun, flow, and passion. Further, the joy, excitement, and reinforcement is creative and generative. Engagement requires:

1) Organizationally, **unwavering leadership** belief and commitment, and some administrative expertise and guidance, will propel progress. Start something you are willing to perpetually be a part of, be cognizant of, champion, fund, and defend. When working with departments and pivotal individuals on engagement initiatives, this summary statement is always suggested to the highest level executives: manager's or engagement team members' annual performance plans should explicitly include a percentage of time dedicated to engagement tasks.

2) Hire within or bring in an engagement expert? In terms of knowledge and converting knowledge into practice, because prioritizing engagement remains in its infancy, and hard work remains, most of the needs that are uncovered will be emotionally charged and change management oriented. Engagement (thus management) requires **people-oriented behaviors**, not the least of which are empathy, objectivity, and emotional discernment. Whether mining from within or contracting from the outside, those selected require ample room to probe, grow, succeed or fail, as well as confront and challenge evidence of disintegration within the status quo.

3) Manager training should be a pervasive, long-term value and priority. If this mindset is not dominant, deeply embedded positions will tend to recoil, reject, and debunk science. If an outside consultant is considered, Deloitte and Gallup appear to offer the best understanding of how to move managers toward **building relationships** (not sales relationships, but long-term understanding of coworkers, and how to be better persons at work). A pragmatic "to-do": do everything possible to create a culture that embodies able, <u>people</u>-oriented, formative coaches. Relationship building and coaching others should dominate the cultural landscape and be a literal expectation of every manager's annual performance plan, including means of assuring accountability (this may include discussion groups on coaching methods, modeling, or other developmental needs of the manager). If an internal consultant is to be employed, significant development time, 6-12 months should be dedicated to research (in addition to data collection and subsequent training/intervention, and long-range post intervention plan).

4) If real progress has been made, over time core drivers of engagement should become pervasive and permanently blended into the organizational culture. An effective starting point is **forming an "engagement" or "recognition" committee** to help lead the way, including orchestrating a formal recognition program if one does not exist (this should not be relegated to HR branches; engagement movers and shakers should be internally harvested within departments, but HR can be serve a valuable consulting function). Managers have the greatest influence on success, so they should be active partners in engagement activities (either collaborative or separate but equal).

Engagement actions must eventually become **an ingrained culture of service**. The best measure of this transformation is being mindful of founding CEO of Amazon, Jeff Bezos, who reiterated, "Your brand is what people say about you when you're not in the room."[19] Ideally, if the work is culturally transformational, some of the nuts and bolts (pragmatics, ideologies, and actions) become integrated into each person. At least some of an engagement team's work should eventually become unnecessary if everyone contributes. This is why managers should be involved in changing from work-centric to people-centric behaviors. Your engagement brand should be ubiquitous, seen in each person, each team, each leader, and in the leader in you.

In closing, with respect to shareholding, equity, fairness, and the influence of salary and performance: we should be mindful that the average retirement amount of highly paid CEOs as of 2015 was $49.3 million dollars each while the average savings of the all other Americans was $50,000; 100 CEOS held more wealth than 40% of other Americans combined.[20]

Why is this an important closing note? The principle is universal, in "First Who, Then What: It's Who You Pay, Not How You Pay Them," Jim Collins states, "We found no systematic pattern linking executive compensation to the process of going from good to great. The evidence simply does not support the idea that the specific structure of executive compensation acts as a key lever in taking a company from good to great."[21] On this final note, of course, each reader can form his or her own conclusions about motivation and money relative to self and within the context of the taxonomy of engagement.

Chapter 7

A Taxonomy Of Engagement

"The normal curve is a distribution most appropriate to chance and random activity. Education is a purposeful activity, and we seek to have students [workers] learn what we would teach. Therefore, if we are effective, the distribution of grades [valuations, evaluations, product and profit] will be anything but a normal curve. In fact, a normal curve is evidence of our failure to teach." –Benjamin Bloom, et. al.

~

Assessing engagement and agreeing upon specific strategies to correct organizational breakdowns or stimulate improvement is easy enough. As suggested throughout this book, typical focus areas float to the top: communication, growth, involvement, recognition. Some strategies are universal; some specific to particular cultural needs.

Most drivers and strategies intersect; for example, meaningful coaching should result in forward movement and relationship building. Relationships and trust depend on unambiguous dialogue with clear agendas and absence of ulterior motives. Does distrust exist? Quality is an effect of fostering and evolving trust within interactions that value and include others. When formative design thinking is regularly solicited from those who toil most at implementation, we gain respect and trust. If we are attempting to instill the highest level recognition principle, growth through involvement is the foremost stimulant and recognition anyone really desires!

However, when we begin to grapple with complex human physiological and psychological variables— such as survival, self, relationships, and their related contextual perceptions, misperceptions, or behaviors— tricky dichotomies materialize.

Simply removing barriers or stimulating key drivers of engagement do not resolve the fundamental hierarchical order of these complex relationships. The engagement hierarchy proposed here— Equity, Membership, Opportunity, Meaning, and Service— adapting Barrett's model[1] (from Maslow) brings more clarity to understanding a high and seemingly unyielding nationwide disengagement rate. While Maslow's hierarchy of needs theory is concerned with the movement from physiological and psychological basic needs to self-actualization, Barrett's is concerned with how these levels translate into levels of consciousness.

The taxonomy presented here interprets Maslow and Barrett to better practice engagement modeling. Accordingly, the path to stimulating engagement begins with equity and ends with service.

Maslow's theory deals with innate human desires, hungers, and realizing capabilities and suggests that the basic needs must be satisfied before higher levels can be obtained. The Engagement Taxonomy presented here suggests interrelated interactions: especially the uppermost level, "service," requires a responsibility to enable and fulfill the lower levels:

Hierarchy of Needs.............. Taxonomy of Engagement

Physiological .... Equity or Self/Well-being
Safety .... Security/Fair, Just Surroundings
Love/Belonging..................... Membership
Esteem.................................. through Meaning & Purpose
Self-Actualization .... through Service

The degree to which behaviors move from basic needs and selfishness (and entitlements) to growth and selflessness, this hierarchy suggests, is the only chance leadership (anyone) has of significantly improving engagement.

A simplified example of these principles in action would include a flexible benefits program, discounted life insurance, work from home options to assure healthy work-life balance, weekly group huddles to strengthen collective aims, and opportunities to take ownership, including operational/process checklists, mentoring, and peer evaluation.[2] Even more simply, if I fall ill at the end of my shift, my concerned supervisor might compassionately offer, "Don't worry. I'll clock you out, take the rest of the day off." Internal audit might cry foul, but the employee's well-being has been served as has the company's. A significant difference, a categorical imperative, resides between breaking the law and acting consciously against a rule. "Do no harm" = situational no fouls.

A more complicated example are owners of start-up companies. They often live through inherent complications, risking the safety of a secure job to start up a company, sacrifice family as they eat, drink, and sleep the job, waging self-esteem and self-actualization on the business's success.[3] While obviously passionate and engaged, they may dabble in some of the other taxonomy's levels but probably have not ascended above the first level, self.

The hierarchical, elemental structure of the taxonomy is not an absolute, linear progression. In fact, the levels are reciprocal or recursive. Realizing basic needs of the engagement hierarchy, (equity) at the lowest level, requires unconditional intent (service) at the highest level. For instance, on the lowest level, I should know, feel, and believe my compensation equals that of others according to the value and performance I bring to the organization. While safety and security are prerequisite to reaching full potential and capitalizing on passion, a full-fledged and conscientious service ethic assures basic needs being equitably met. We trust that contributions and value(s) employees add are proportionately recognized and equitably compensated. The basic psychological needs are nested in trust. Trust, within an authentic, other-centric ethic, must be intact to build the relationships and meaningful experiences upon which engagement pivots.

Drivers and Change Factors:	Taxonomy of Engagement
Customer/Other-centric, Influence, Selflessness, Shared Leadership	Service
Vision/Values, Trust, Integrity, Autonomy, Purpose	Meaning
Mastery, Growth, Task Variety, Involvement	Opportunity
Belonging, Recognition, Team, Connectedness, Communication	Membership
Self, Security, Well-Being, Fair and Just Policies	Equity

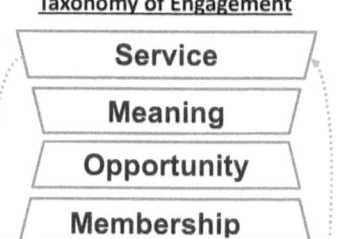

Miholic 2015

Level 1, Equity

The first level is perhaps the most rationalized yet, if realized, dramatically enables all other levels.

This fundamental prerequisite of engagement cannot be overemphasized. If dimensions of equity are not systematically and uniformly addressed, all other levels are diminished and unlikely to be actualized. Basic needs are met here: safety, security, survival. Moreover, meeting basic survival needs cannot be separated from ethics. Again, trust is deeply embedded in equity, which can be interpreted to include pay and workload parity, fairness, and equality, or may extend to ownership stakes; for detailed examples, see the "Equity Theory and Motivation (Case Study)" footnote.[4]

Trust fundamentally ensures that the employer cares for the employee's and the organization's well-being. This translates into assurance that the best methods are used to hire the best person for the job. For instance, in hiring new employees, at this level, if the "best" applicant does not meet standards of excellence, or does not meet the threshold to achieve excellence, re-advertising is necessary rather than hiring an immediately available but less desirable candidate. The criterion for filling a vacant position should not be desperation or driven by personal motivations. Moreover, without commensurate learning accommodations in place for all new hires, as well as expectations of continuous development, lowered standards will result, compromising effectiveness and diluting results.

We also trust that starting salaries and performance adjustments, as the Blanchard group states, are comparably fair and just.[5] Inequity remains pervasive. Facebook's COO, Sheryl Sandberg, reminds us that gender[6] disparities are still woven into our social and business fabric. Despite efforts to overcome forms of discrimination, workplaces continue to struggle with basic human and civil rights. On the national level, minimum wage remains leveraged as a political, rather than moral, issue; on the local level, political favoritism, cronyism, and nepotism cripple efficacy.

Thus, while one may argue the way of business is through networking, and to a degree, such social connections are grounded in confidence and trust, substantial equity needs remain unattended in most organizational cultures. To be sure, no level of this taxonomy speaks to prestige, self-preservation, excess or obtaining favors, position or trappings. These are not basic needs but overt indulgences. Clearly articulated by the Pew Research Center, if all were well, "Is the deck stacked?" would not be a fixture in sociological research.[7]

Trust is realized when all employees are equitably chosen, served, and valued. Accompanying the substantial disengagement percentage, reminded that 70 percent of the variance in moving the engagement needle depends on how leaders translate mission, values, and vision into action,[8] without deliberate, overt attention to and assessment of equity, the interior scaffolding of the hierarchy of the taxonomy collapses as does the effectiveness organizational hierarchy.

Engagement pivots on well-being and trust. Upon this foundation, relationships and meaningful work are built. Without equity, suspicion, skepticism, and cynicism spoil actualization of the interior hierarchal constructs— membership, opportunity, and meaning. Thus, unresolved conflict in lower levels, substantially at the equity level, will subvert individual, cultural, and organizational effectiveness by short-circuiting electricity transmission to the taxonomy's higher purposes.

Level 2, Membership

Moving higher on the hierarchy insists that all shareholders' best interests are in the minds and hearts of leaders. Gallup suggests that this progression is best achieved through a purposeful symmetry of accountability and inclusion.[9] Authentic membership is a catalyst for autonomy, experimentation, initiative, innovation, learning, and creativity— that is, best performance.

Since a great many hours of our days are conducted at work, we recognize that the quality of the work culture reflects the quality of relationships. Growth, communication, inclusion, and connections cultivate optimal performance. If any doubt exists, one need merely turn to *Fortune*'s "100 Best Companies to Work For" whose selection criteria, based on a "Trust Index," includes camaraderie. Additionally, membership repeatedly surfaces as a high impact variable in Bersin's[10] insights. This value is projected through relationships, ownership, and contribution, reinforcement that results in productive and stimulated employees, coaching, and community building.

Obviously, for membership to flourish, collaboration must be accentuated by each individual's contributions. Of course, balancing autonomy, and passion or lack of it, within collaborative teams, can be problematic. As we typically see in conventional classrooms, and likely as you have experienced, group personalities can pivot off balance, and without individual accountability, collaboration within teams is much more difficult to realize. A sole person can be unexpectedly saddled with or feel responsible to shoulder a disproportionate work load. Of course, before too long, the lopsided disparity is accompanied by an undercurrent of gossip. This disruption in flow, often unknown to formal leaders, tacks toward overarching malaise, indifference, and discontent.

Moreover, communication and membership are symbiotic. Communication, if highly valued, functions as the foremost hallmark of trust-building and includes authentic input processes for decision-making. Having worked with groups on engagement strategy, I heard universally, "We wish leaders would share more often" and "I learned something from an outside branch or client that I should have already known from within my work groups." Miscommunication or lack of timely updating devalues membership. Bottom line: proper and complete communication leaves very little room for distrust, suspicion or disenfranchisement. Incomplete, neglected or improper communication breeds distrust.

If leaders proclaim withholding information is in the best interests of stakeholders, we have a natural and practical obligation to question the tactics and integrity.

Membership is easily translated into everyday practice. Intimacy matters. Those in formal supervisory or leadership roles should regularly ask these questions: When I talk to others, am I guided by their well-being, positive regard, and am I showing it in actions? At the employee's office space, how regularly and how much time do I take to personally talk to, share with, or feel the pulse of

_____each subordinate?
_____fellow leaders (at every level)?
_____colleagues?
_____significant others?

Often? If yes, do employees have any reason to question that I have their best interests in heart and mind? No? Then, I truly subscribe to an open door policy, and therein I am a steward of true membership and am building trust and membership.

Level 3, Opportunity

Built from membership, opportunity allows confidence and self-esteem to soar. Successive responsibility follows workers who are respected, guided, and grown. But this responsibility does not follow if the person is disenfranchised. While membership is, in part, a product of the right hire, the right fit and the "right seat on the bus," fair opportunities assure mastery.

Opportunity is the invitation to initiate something more, something new. Autonomy and room for error increase opportunity and drive. For example, as founder and CEO of MediConnect Global, Inc., Amy Rees Anderson asserts, "Good employees make mistakes, and great leaders allow them."[11] Mistakes approached as means to excellence, and not as imperfections, result in growth and mastery. Micromanagement, conversely, cripples mastery and impairs opportunity. Confidence and self-esteem interconnect with effective processes, training, and non-threatening feedback to drive optimal performance and foster a desire to seek new challenges.

How is opportunity generally seen in everyday practice?

- **When your immediate supervisor casually visits your office.**

- **When your immediate supervisor pulls you aside and offers, "Take a minute, I'd like you to come with me to this meeting...."**

- **When coaching conversations explores, "Take a look at this contract, white paper, research, or report and tell me what you think?"**

- **When a supervisor asks, "What would you like to know more about our operations?"**

- **When a supervisor follows up, "You're asking to learn more about X to do Y better? I'd like you to cross-train or shadow with Z?"**

Every employee, not merely a select few, awaits opportunity. And leaders' effectiveness and legacy should be accurately evaluated by their ability to guide and provide opportunity for everyone.

Level 4, Meaning

Two of three engagement drivers identified by both Daniel Pink and Malcom Galdwell,[12] autonomy and mastery, are derived from shared values, opportunity, and in organizational citizenship behaviors derived from participation. The third driver, purpose, requires membership, from which opportunity follows and meaningful contribution resides.

Membership and opportunity are prerequisite to meaningful work. Meaning, then, can be measured by degrees of participation, growth, accomplishment, exertion, vibrancy, optimism, and entrepreneurial spirit experienced at work.[13] Hating going to work, encountering ostracism and isolation, and feeling bored, unchallenged or stagnant, all of these dispositions sit on the debilitating side of a meaningful spectrum.

The values to which we associate meaning also remarkably coincide with the taxonomy. Again, the highest level of meaningfulness, making a difference, is associated with service.

- **Making a Difference (Purpose/Service)**

- **Following Your Passion (Purpose)**

- **Using Your Talents/Earing Shares of Responsibility (Opportunity)**

- **Achieving Status/Sharing Authority (Membership/ Opportunity)**

- **Earning Shares/Money (Equity)**

The relationship between meaning and happiness[14] may at first appear to be akin to answering the riddle, "What comes first, the chicken or the egg?" But it is not difficult to tease out. Of course, each of us searches for meaning, yet management can create an incubator to find meaningful work and greater purpose. Happiness is more transactional when we directly derive pleasure from what we get; for instance, we earn enough money to buy things that make us happy. Meaningfulness, on the other hand, is more intrinsic and optimal when the sense of fulfillment and gratification is both personally satisfying and when we feel we make a difference; for instance, when we contribute to the food drive or otherwise help others. Meaning is a product of building the chicken coop, incubating, feeding, watering, protecting, and shining light. Happiness follows meaning.

When we move beyond transactional exchange (e.g., paycheck as a motivator) to more transformational motivators, happiness and meaning, are derived from, as leadership coach Cathy Greenberg asserts, "*exertion* that challenges but does not break us (creative 'flow states'), in the *service* of a goal that excites us (creating positive emotion and meaning)."[15]

Ultimately, "Each one of us creates our own definition of a meaningful career... that's what creates meaning."[16] Teresa Amabile and Steven Kramer's rigorous, naturalistic research demonstrates that meaning is derived from "incremental steps forward, small wins [to] boost 'inner work life.'" The strong caution is how easily a worker's quest for meaning can be disrupted;[17] among the ways managers short-circuit progress:

- **dismiss the importance of subordinates works or ideas and losing sight of an employee's perspective.**

- **prematurely switch people off project teams, start and abandon initiatives, or never discover if initiatives are working.**

- **neglect to communicate updates of changes to staff (lack of clarity).**

- **avoid risk, or conversely, create chaos or paranoia.**

- **cultivate the ordinary and mediocre.**

- **formulate unrealistic, unobtainable, and disconnected top-down goals.**

Meaning is found in participation and in the mutual support we find in our business communities. Social scientist Paul Loeb asserts, "My experience leads me to believe that the main distinction between those who participate fully in their communities and those who withdraw...[is that] they savor the journey of engagement and draw strength from its challenges."[18]

Meaning requires being. Being and nothingness are mutually exclusive, so we must be committed to creating meaning for others, to affirming their significance, assuring that all employees are, and thus *feel* they are, an indispensable part of the whole. Our meaningfulness is confirmed when contributions to outcomes are meaningfully acknowledged. Meaning requires giving and service.

Engagement turns an old adage on end. The whole is not greater than the sum of its parts. The whole is made great when talents of its individuals' parts are unleashed.

Level 5, Service

This hierarchy suggests that the only chance leadership has of significantly altering workplace engagement is in its capacity not to expect to get but to give. Consequent engagement depends on the degree to which leadership behaviors move from selfishness (perceptions of entitlements) to growth and selflessness. The path to stimulating engagement begins with leaders equitably attending to others' basic needs and ends with service; in fact, very basic needs (equity) recursively require membership and management practiced at the highest level— service to others.

If equity, membership, and opportunity are attended, each employee's engagement and leadership moves from survival, namely self and ambition, toward aspiration and inspiring others. Actualization of the highest level is significantly transformational, but only can be attained if we transcend ego, rise above self, and eliminate mistrust.

As equity foremost reflects organizational values in everyday operations, decision-making, or communication, not surprisingly, this engagement taxonomy shares two aforementioned derailers that contribute to team dysfunction articulated by Lencioni:[19] at engagement's core hierarchal level, the first dysfunction is absence of trust, and the second, at the top level, the preponderance of ego.

Let's look at illustrations of the extremes: Kim Kardashian's book, *Selfish,* literally a book of selfies, or *Mother Teresa CEO, Unexpected Principles and Practical Leadership.* Leadership and followership are synonymous. The exothermic energy of humble, giving leaders is inherited and continues to fuel unabated productivity accompanied by quiet, yet appreciative, fanfare. Self-serving leaders are endothermic (consuming the energy around them) and their followers, superficial, toxic, and self-limiting, at worst. Discovering self requires enriching others.

Workers who are entrenched in a "what's in it for me" entitlement or mentality, who rely on strict adherence to compliant behavior, or who are inordinately affected by other external drivers probably have not moved far beyond basic transactions bound to baser, excessive wants, and will find the journey to service difficult indeed.

No matter what occupation, collective purpose and real service are typically lost in competition and self-indulgence. Because of this, we witness the complication of many advancing, but not growing into consciousness. Service is as much learned as an innate disposition, so 100 percent engagement is a noble but unrealistic goal. However, if you are on a progressively formative path, you have likely compared your progress with theory and practice suggested by Robert Greenleaf, Kathleen Patterson, Don Page and Paul T. P. Wong.[20]

I offer a series of quotes to gauge progress on the taxonomy:

- **EQUITY**: "I've learned that people will forget what you said, people will forget what you did, but people will never forget how you made them feel." Maya Angelou

- **MEMBERSHIP**: "The utmost form of respect is to give sincerely of your presence." Mollie Marti

- **OPPORTUNITY**: "A good leader takes a little more than [her]/his share of the blame, and a little less than [her]/his share of the credit." Arnold H. Glasgow

- **MEANING**: "What difference will you make? What will be your legacy?" James Kouszes and Barry Posner

- **SERVICE**: "True leadership must be for the benefit of the followers, not to enrich the leader." John Maxwell

Basic laws of physics do not apply to the workplace: energy can be created *and destroyed*. In fact, building towering engagement can quickly crumble if the energy expended to erect its pillars sit in shallow, soft ground or a glimmering facade is fastened to questionable underlayment. Fuller engagement is more likely to occur when organizations:

- **choose to loosen bureaucratic constraints that subvert shared leadership.**

- **discard blame by allowing guided regulation and growth from mistakes or failures.**

- realize that "empire building" is inversely related to effective succession.

- cultivate initiative versus exercising control, and more equitably share the fruits of success.

Engagement becomes a mutual responsibility when the workplace conditions and processes share governance, allow risk-taking, promote opportunities, and encourage initiative. As work flow dynamics are inextricably linked to engagement, from hiring to stake-holding to succession, this taxonomy may help comprehension of how we can truly make a difference and assess progress.

Chapter 8

"The first problem with all of the stuff that's out there on leadership is that we haven't got a clue what we're talking about. We typically think of the leader as being the person at the top. But if you define a leader as an executive, then you absolutely deny everyone else in an organization to be a leader." –Peter Senge

~

This chapter asks the reader to ponder a number of first person, "I," questions. These questions, interspersed throughout this chapter, are complemented by a reflective leadership inventory that can be found in the Appendix as well a compact inventory that closes the chapter.

The first and most important question:

I most value _____.

Joking around the office, most of us would rightfully reply, "I most value Me!" And others should, too. Indeed, constant improvement (self, department, and business) is an effect of perpetuating noble values. However, the answers that follow "Me" are true indicators of engagement. The answer checks-in on our most cherished values at work or in life. Generally, our highest values eclipse work related functions. For instance, family members may be pronounced as being foremost valued; accordingly, more time is actually invested in reinforcing love, respect, helping, or commitment to family members. This may include holding a job to pay the bills.

If words are not fulfilled by actions, our values require redress, as well as the realities of our associated efforts and priorities. At work, we should ask,

- **Do my actions make a difference in improving my engagement or the engagement of others? If not, why not?**

- **Am I granted the autonomy to act in accordance with what I value?"**

- **Are these shared organizational values?**

- **Do I have a voice in bringing clarity to these values?**

If the answers are "Every day in every way," characteristics of shared leadership and engagement are supported. If not, I might be asking,

- **"Do I feel trapped in a compromise of integrity and well-being in order to survive? Is it worth it?**

- **Where am I leading myself?"**

"Leadership" itself is not usually listed as a key driver of engagement. The actions that ensure well-being and trust are drivers, so engagement initiatives are more likely to succeed over time only when engagement is championed, and its architects have gained the insurance of trust from the top. To gain the most out of engagement efforts, an authentic practice of shared leadership should, without question, be a core value.

Harvard Business School professor and former Medtronic CEO, Bill George, asserts in *True North,*[1] "You don't have to be born with the characteristics or traits of a leader; you don't have to wait for a tap on the shoulder; you don't have to be at the top of your organization; you can step up and lead at any point in your life." This point of view is complemented by John Maxwell, teaching pastor and author of *The 21 Irrefutable Laws of Leadership,* "Every person is a leader, many of us don't realize it. The question is do you act with intentionality."[2]

Perhaps more importantly is the whether we feel safe to act with intentionality. Secondly, who or what purpose does the intentionality serve? Do the formal leaders see my voice as vital, and do I actually see myself as a vital voice? If not, co-leadership has not been embraced as a cultural value. Productive and inclusive shareholding has likely been co-opted by secrecy, hidden agendas, or defensive tactics.

Even within disconnected, strictly hierarchal organizations, each individual can constructively influence effectiveness if given enough autonomy and appreciation within a team. Yet at work, the politics of the place may be at odds with a philosophy of joint leadership or personal triumph. The difficulty of the autonomy/ authority dichotomy is that not all workers are believed to add value nor are they proportionally acknowledged as informal leaders. We are reminded by Paul Loeb in *Soul of a Citizen: Living with Conviction in a Cynical Time* that the voices and vision of each employee can be defeated by pigeon-holing: "If the theories of developmental psychology are right, there are no natural leaders or followers…, only individuals who through happenstance or habit have had their voices and vision sufficiently encouraged."[3]

Of course, a consciously directed tactical disenfranchisement is a recipe for distrust. Consequently, as explored in the prior chapter, if the organizational structure employs a heavily top-down chain of command, the effect is that little room may exist for ground-breaking entrepreneurial acts. Furthermore, information sharing may be highly scripted and controlled. Then, unfortunately, little room is created for all to lead, and opportunity for improvement or innovation is sacrificed. As autonomy and information sharing is sacrificed, the oxygen of shared leadership is exhausted. And as autonomy diminishes, defects in authoritarian decision-making surface, particularly a tendency to gravitate toward debilitating like-mindedness.

On the other hand, when everyone has a true, participatory opportunity to lead, we meet people where they are. Engagement, and the questions and productive risk-taking it cultivates, flourishes when we embrace the leader in everyone and profit from each other's style, grace, and giftedness. Every other person's unique leadership qualities and abilities, if embraced and properly acknowledged and valued, augments our own strengths and serves as a quality control check to compensate for our failings.

Informal walkabouts[4] and open invitations to meetings (which, in an interdependent organization, implies an invitation to freely participate) provide access to all employees, be they fledgling, emergent or continuing leaders. All must be encouraged, perhaps even required, to enter into the leadership conversations. More importantly, as previously stated, leadership development opportunities should be programmed in and available as soon as new employees join an organization to improve their respective journeys, whether they move into formal leadership roles or are leaders in their specializations.

Traditional leadership development tends to be designed for those who have already ascended into managerial positions. Most commentary on the subject suggests, however, that this strategy results in development lags: proper leadership reflection falls behind the role in which formal leaders are placed.

Thus, elite leadership development programs populated through selective admissions should be complemented with other open-admissions leadership options and on-going educational opportunities to assure more inclusive and timely saturation. Current team leaders should be participating in continuing peer-based leadership discussions in order to assess their habits.

Sometimes the simplest acts, or absence of them, provide insights to cultural malignancies and exemplify the depth and breadth of personal leadership commitment. Our leadership inventory, therefore, requires that we ask a general question:

- **Does the organization capitalize on situations in a positive, active, pervasive, and universal way or succumb to control or the status quo?**

Again, if the organization's culture does not capitalize upon inclusion, critics are right to argue that advertising, "Everyone is a Leader," is hollow and disingenuous.

The Leader as Horologist

Have you ever entered a room and noticed an idle clock on the wall?

The first reaction is that no one has noticed. But if the clock continues to be unattended for weeks, we can conclude either that the importance of the location for the clock was either ill-assessed or had faded over time, or the clock simply does not work. If broken, surely someone would have removed it. Or the person who installed it moved on. It has outlived its usefulness, or surely someone who loved clocks would have adjusted the time, just to help maintain the order of things. Obviously, even if initiative was lacking, i.e., the troubling refrain, "It's not my job," or we were fearful to break some sort of protocol, someone would have taken a minute to call building maintenance. At the very least, one would expect someone to move the clock to a place where it could serve its proper purpose.

At the very least, the clock's importance to anyone else being a moot point, we might be amused enough to test the "clock doesn't work" hypotheses. Not because the clock is important. Watches and cell phones are readily available, and other clocks are hanging around. Nevertheless, testing the hypothesis by inserting an AA battery, we find that the second hand begins to tick.

In reality, leadership is an inclusive synergy of both individual choice and action as well as a reflection of collective well-being. Our engagement is about aligning ourselves as agents of progress and being mutual partners as catalysts of change or improvement. Order the battery, change the battery, exchange the clock, move the clock, alter the purpose....

We must order the battery, change the battery, or recharge the battery to maximize the energy in our purpose.

Engagement requires taking time to demonstrate that every person matters and quickly finding new purposes or challenges for people who no longer *appear* to matter. Administrative negligence, walking by and not attending to the clockworks, which sets the tone and models others' behaviors, is a core driver of disengagement. Yes, every person has a personal choice to make, but disengaged leaders are taproots for disengagement we see in others. A formal leader may not need be involved in the minutiae of the clock, but that no other person took the lead, and acted or bothered to ask the question, "What about that clock?" hints at either a lack of a sense of humor or a symptom of cultural malaise and, most certainly, is indicative of an engagement breakdown.

A 2014 Korn Ferry survey[6] revealed that 72 percent of global business leaders found culture to be extremely important to performance, but only 32 percent said their culture aligns with their business strategy, and more importantly, 75 percent said they have not identified nor sufficiently communicated cultural expectations. Of course, we are obligated to not only point at or laugh about the clock, but investigate what attitudes and neglect resulted in the breakdown causing idle clock (or the idle worker). To blame the worker or the clock ignores the core issues. Culture aligns with strategy only through awareness, care, and action about people clockworks.[7]

Importantly, central to changing the engagement outlook is altering our conditioning about who we see as the visionaries. We are conditioned to believe that vision is the exclusive purview of the CEO (in the same breath that we're all asked to be leaders), and the worker's role is to translate that vision. But we must also see how complex, current workplace conditions, interactions, and situations hinder or accelerate realizing the vision. Leadership and meaning at work is equally about simple actions that either propel or impede change. Of course, this change also requires a change in attitude, something as simple as picking up a piece of debris on the floor because we should all care about the appearance of the space in which we work (and know that the janitorial staff cannot be expected to police all areas at all times).

How all leaders incorporate engagement in everyday discussions and actions matters. Of course, no matter how we and others define ourselves as leaders, when we are invited to be autonomous, innovative and take initiative in our work, we emerge and grow as leaders. Our actual participation is a mixture of not only the little things, but how our leadership capabilities are utilized within the context of the bigger things. Parallel to the important, everyday little things, Jim Collins elaborates on the "One Big Thing,"[8] to propel business decisions or its application to graphing personal leadership trajectories.

Collins suggests reducing our focus to essential, gut level questions (below and revisited in Chapter 8, "Transform Thyself"). The central tendency in the answer to these questions is not only attributable to highly successful companies but also serves as a hedge against disengagement:

- **What makes your clock tick? In what activity does your passion reside?**

- **What is your best work? Does your job allow you to do your best?**

Not only do successful businesses reduce their core production to mastery and passion, but all workers at every level should triangulate and assess their own passion, best work, and safety needs to help refuel individual engagement.

Whether standing on a high ladder rung or on the first rung, in "Awaken the Leader in You," Sharif Khan suggests that if your job is not fulfilling, your hedge against disengagement rests inward, and resides outside of work:

> Whatever it is that you enjoy doing, be it writing, acting, painting, drawing, photography, sports, reading, dancing, networking, or working on entrepreneurial ventures, set aside time every week, ideally two or three hours a day, to pursue these activities. [Your] doubts, anxieties, fears, and worries are demons and dragons guarding the door.... Being an alive and vital person vitalizes others. When you are pursuing your passions, people around you cannot help but feel impassioned by your presence.[9]

Vincent Miholic, Ph.D.

Beware Clouded Vision

Leadership development and clarity of vision requires that we constantly challenge ourselves to see beyond the familiar. Latching onto others who affirm our position requires little effort. Finding a kindred spirit certainly feels better, especially one who supports justifications to complain or assume a siege mentality. We associate with others who agree with our perceptions because we are hard-wired to seek out supportive and shared interpersonal relationships.[10] New patterns emerge only when they prove to be more satisfying or more fulfilling than the old pattern, and this change occurs only after repeated, positive experiences. We fail to learn new behaviors from not having the opportunity to try them out, accompanied by lack of support.

With respect to that clock battery, as educational thought leader Fred Lunenburg reminds us, unused or misused power adversely affects worker behavior, performance, task completion, job satisfaction, absenteeism, and turnover.[11]

Consider if you have ever spoken or heard variations of these laments, "It's really bad around here!" "We improved the process, but I still suffer from other people's procrastination." "The micromanagement is stifling." "Nothing's ever good enough." "If I even muster the courage to offer the most useful advice, I'm accused of not rowing in the same direction...."[12]

In many instances, fear cripples being honest with others and with ourselves. Authenticity, on the other hand, including the strength to be transparent, paves the way to engagement. Thus, being authentic, being true to ourselves and others, how we lead ourselves, can help us leverage engagement and ourselves as leaders.

Unfortunately, we have all seen unscrupulous individuals leverage themselves by attempting to destroy others. For instance, you may have encountered an individual who demonstrates a most joyful and generous spirit, a genuinely giving countenance. Enter the superior, scolding, "Stop doing that [fill in the blank]." Essentially, a good soul is punished and admonished with malicious coaching, "Stop being yourself."

We have no other legitimate and conscious choices but to build up ourselves and others. Neglect destroys engagement. Any opportunity not used to uplift others is squandered growth. We either work at passion (matching our job to our desires), build passion (cultivate joy). Ownership requires periodic upgrades, repairs, and improvements to maintain the value of our home and neighborhood. Lacking that support, we become like the homeowner who did not realize she/he actually has a vested interest to maintain the home in which he/she invested. Without on-going maintenance, the house falls into disrepair and decay.

The peril lies in any unrecognized tendencies or motivations that paint a false image, glad-hand, placate, patronize or polarize, or deliberate actions that ostracize, ignore, or deter. Another danger is that everyone tends to reinforce old patterns, including those patterns possessed by leaders who are responsible for providing new opportunities and evaluating new attempts. In the end, we cling to a few positive experiences that reaffirm what we think we already know is true (even though the conclusion may be false).

Within constrained, dysfunctional, or hostile situations, each person has a conscious decision to make: be on the leading edge of improving others, oneself, and our workplaces or succumb to complaint.

Turning Leadership Posture into Discovery and Possibility

The counter-weight to bias and old patterns, according to Shawn Achor's workplace happiness research,[13] is in expressing thankfulness, giving, and gratitude in order to generate the greatest energy, happiness, and satisfaction. This appreciation is most pragmatically conveyed through regular encouragement, feedback, reinforcing, and coaching. We should always strive to advance the well-being of others, which mutually benefits the collective.

A crucial sounding board for self-discovery is clearly found in empowering and developing others as well as ourselves, demonstrating vulnerability and humility, doing the right thing at the right time for the right reasons, and knowing why these choices make the most sense, thereby practicing open, participatory, servant leadership.[14] Effective coaching, for instance, cannot be accomplished if hidden agendas or authoritarian tendencies corrupt communication.

All employees have reciprocal responsibilities. We must honestly assess all the variables that affect our choices, our level of personal involvement, empowerment, commitment, and the effort and risks to overcome self-limitations. We must also assess our viability and seek well-being. At every stage of our careers, we should attempt to understand the degrees to which we have followed our passion.

- **Does my job reflect activities and time that I enjoy?**

The answer is fundamental to evaluating our own gravitational pull to engagement. If our investment feels like and is a substantial personal commitment of time and effort, accompanied by tangible affirmation, we can improve ourselves and others, and our workplace.

In addition to fulfilling our passions, either at work or away from work, based on substantial research from the Gallup organization, Marcus Buckingham and Curt Coffman's *First, Break All the Rules*[15] relays tangent touchstones (see summary below) for exploring our purpose at work. These touchstones and others are explored in greater depth in the next chapter, "A Taxonomy of Engagement."

Transactional: (New Role, Basic Needs) What is expected of me? What do I get in return? What conditions apply?

Formative Membership: What am I able to give? Am I any good at the job? Do I fill a role in which I can excel? What conclusions have others drawn about my present and future performance (requires no ambiguity)? Will they help?

Belonging: Do I push the envelope? Do my opinions count? Is my job important? Do I have a reliable colleague/friend?

Opportunity: Is growth mutual and collaborative? Is reliable, unbiased coaching provided? Is feedback a motivational device to advance progress? Can I avail myself to other opportunities to learn, grow, and excel?

Meaningfulness: Are answers affirming? If so, I have reached the summit with clear focus and a recurring sense of achievement.

Adapted from Marcus Buckingham & Curt Coffman, *First, Break All the Rules: What the World's Greatest Managers Do Differently* (New York: Simon and Schuster, 1999), 43-46.

Chapter 9

"People subtly and carefully 'massage' the evidence to make it consistent with their expectations... and are also prone to self-serving assessments when it comes to apportioning responsibility for their success and failures. In numerous studies across a wide range of situations, people have been found to attribute their successes to themselves, and their failures to external circumstances." –Thomas Gilovich, *How We Know What Isn't So: The Fallibility of Human Reason in Everyday Life.*

~

As mentioned earlier, the characteristics of disengagement in any enterprise are easily identified. Our choices, to approach what we sense, matter most. We can reliably agree that the disengaged *appear* complacent, compliant, disinterested, close-minded, manipulative, cynical, dishonest, or as complaining, disingenuous, bored, dysfunctional, average, or selfish. Interactively, all are inversely related to improvisation, innovation, change, and both critical and creative thinking.

If, in fact, workers do exhibit these undesirable traits, leaders should be asking themselves, "How did these workers get there? Have I, as a leader, contributed to the malaise? How do we collectively move from dysfunction to innovation? What has to change in me, or others?" Engagement, as explored, is accompanied by some of the following attributes:

- **EQUITY**: truthfulness, transparency, egalitarianism, influential, fairness.

- **MEMBERSHIP**: inclusiveness; functional collaboration.

- **OPPORTUNITY**: receptiveness (evidenced by seeking feedback from those who offer valid perspectives contrary to a fixed disposition or sequestered councils).

- **MEANING**: vibrancy, optimism; entrepreneurial spirit (as seen in avenues that enable discretionary effort).

- **SERVICE**: absence of personal agendas; graciousness, reinforced personal valuing; appreciation, recognition, and giving.

Engagement increases when exclusive and secretive top-down hierarchies are replaced by matrices of dynamic organizational interactions. Rather than collide over functions and posts, engaged communities share interest and assimilate information from multiple sources embedded in the contexts of values and valuing, where multiple points of view are invited and accommodated without prejudice.

Some sort of pulse– capacity, will, and disposition– must be present to move from lethargic to athletic teams and organizational momentum.

The previous chapters have attended to dissecting organizational and people needs. Foremost, sometimes the lack of influence or direction presents insurmountable obstacles. First, the upper echelon of leadership, wherever the key movers and shakers reside on the organizational chart, must admit a need to break out of self-protective behaviors, personal status, and the status quo. People managers must lengthen their reach out to employees.

"Leaning in"[1] requires the courage to reach out. Leaders must have the courage to listen and break away from the comfort of voices that only confirm their truths. Distorting truth to best fit a personal agenda is destructive. Leaders can easily fall prey to allowing their image (emperor's clothes) to become more important than listening, understanding, and helping everyone. Their self-portrait is usually reinforced by a reliance on feedback from too few. Image is self-satisfying at the expense of others.

How I am perceived, my image (or personal brand), gets in the way of how I can shift my attention away from self and toward growing the continued success of others. A legacy is not measured by what I have done but the enduring impact of my actions have had on everyone, positive or negative, long after I have retired.

Closed-mindedness, thus, confuses loyalty with cronyism. Cronyism is conditional and often dishonest. Loyalty, on the other hand, relies on unconditional openness and honesty. When information is controlled and personal image or brand is more important than relationships, leaders are likely to sacrifice authenticity. Moreover, in dysfunctional cultures, when workers speak up they earn the coincidental label of being unproductive. The dismissal or suppression of individuals, rather than gaining their investment, causes disengagement. Leaders who are not concerned with their image, create energy by listening rather than expending energy by scapegoating or negatively labeling others. Singing off key is not entirely a bad thing. Because we get by "with a little help from our friends,"[2] a choir master is able to listen, gain greater clarity, and build trust by welcoming the cognitive dissonance that occurs when all voices are heard.

A fearless leader will fully evaluate the culture by careful and deliberative accounting of all perceptions, with a suspect eye cast toward selfishness. Because everyone gravitates toward consonant tones, tones that reinforces our own prejudices, we also tend to dismiss voices that offer greater depth to deriving fact and truth. The danger is misjudging others' intents, condemning the innocent, victimizing an opposing voice.

Alex Turnbull, CEO & founder of software company Groove provides the reason why leaders need to listen more, "If an employee is having a bad day or week, or is unhappy in his role, or if just about anything else is wrong in their eyes, it's easy to hide it. And that's very scary. Cultures where important things remain unsaid are unproductive, unpleasant, and frankly toxic to business." He relates a story of a friend who concluded the one thing he would have done differently is to have blocked off time to check in, one-on-one, with everyone on the team. Of course, in larger organizations intimacy is more difficult to do, but generating random samples of employees is not. Turnbull, having adopted that advice relays the positive effects: connection, honest substantive talks that promoted a sense of safety, even when discussing negative issues. It helped customer service and employee needs better intersect. Explaining the "why" behind decisions minimizes mistrust. Employees came forward more willingly, which nipped issues in the bud and resulted in happier employees. And finally, clarity allowed the leader to self-assess and correct failings.[3]

Vanity and ego function only to distort truth and clarity. Like the leader in Hans Christian Andersen's tale, "The Emperor's New Clothes,"[4] too vain to notice he has been stripped bare, the more leaders block themselves off from the reality of multiple truths and all feasible good intents, and the more leaders surround themselves with comforting, agreeable voices, the more likely they are to declare, "The pretense must go on!" Unfortunately, susceptible chamberlains, who are subtly, culturally coached to unquestionably follow in vanity's footsteps, continue to walk behind and carry the leader's illusionary train. Essentially, this "my bus" parade mentality preserves the status quo. Some of these workers who support the emperor do so to curry favor. Others are manipulated to believe that if they do not agree, they are responsible for breeding negativity. For leaders, hearing all voices, leads to insight, and with this modern allusion to Andersen's story, resolution pivots on seeing the plain spoken truth, not opportunistic nor manipulative renditions of truth.

More and different individuals and groups should be provided access to communicate their perceptions, ideas, and questions without fear of retribution. Perhaps the most interesting empirical proof of turning toward truth was captured in the rehiring of a respected Market Basket grocery CEO, Arthur Demoulas.[5] A long and sometimes tumultuous immigrant family rags to riches story dating back to 1917, culminated in Arthur being dismissed by the corporate board in 2014, essentially for being a kind leader. His employees boycotted work until the board reconsidered and reinstated him. The months-long crisis included company officials firing supervisors who helped organize support for the ousted leader. Not only did the employees boycott the store, but they were joined by thousands of customers and scores of ascending political voices. In this instance, the reversal of fortunes coupled doing the right thing with recovering profits.

One of the most heinous cases of distorting truth was captured in the Jimmy Savile British broadcast scandal.[6] Silence, and turning away from the truth, accompanied years of sexual abuse. Sycophants and cronyism led to the silence. Savile allegedly committed years of sexual assaults upon scores of victims, an investigation found a "culture of separation, competition and even hostility between different parts of the BBC, so that concerns arising in one part would not be discussed with others." The truths of Savile's acts were only beginning to be addressed after his death in 2011, but allegations dated 40 years earlier. We can very likely attribute the greatest weakness in leaders to whenever advantages are enjoyed by a select few. Such behavior is often accompanied by further prosecuting of the victim. Thus, we should all be careful to check for the pitfalls of our self-certainty or confidence in our expertise which increases closed-mindedness or "Earned Dogmatism."[7]

Optimally, organizational leadership provides sufficient doubt, room for mistakes, and a supportive ear to support reflection and course correction, inclusion, and recognition, that is, adaptive room for transformation. Effective cultures do not accept nor promote silence nor exclusion. Those who come forward with a concern, speak out because they have been excluded, and usually by extension, aggrieved, which, business writer John Kador suggests, requires a leader to understand that "it's always the victim who responds with justified anger."[8]

Despite debilitating workplace circumstances, some overcome incredible odds. Others succumb to debilitating oppression and roadblocks. Some of us rebound from failure or rebuke. Others plummet into despair or learn to exercise extreme caution, often accompanied by warranted paranoia and internalized trauma, after recoiling from being blind-sided. The real misgiving, particularly when an employee stumbles, is unwillingness to effectively and honestly see and listen beyond self. The real failure is a leader's prejudicial response and conscious choice, or perhaps deeply rooted unconscious choice, not to honestly coach.

Finding the Way

Often workers find themselves wanting more but not knowing how to get there. Where we currently find ourselves, however, is only a single page of much larger narrative. Some engagement tune-ups, particularly within the context of leadership evolution, remain a personal, private journey. Our immediate supervisors may choose to find a fitting and noble story arc or idly ignobly stand apart.

Each person makes a conscious decision to be engaged or disengaged, but each individual choice to be disengaged radiates beyond self and can slow collective flow and growth. To learn how to respond to ever-changing game rules and adversity, we must understand and capitalize on our own strengths, talents, and gifts. In many cases, we, as workers, default to Maslow's fundamental need; we consciously sacrifice integrity, or abandon the pursuit of work that we love in order to gain job security. Nevertheless, each person must be willing to think beyond merely fulfilling a function in order to purse the ideal match between what one loves and where one is.

In many cases, this response involves an honest assessment by those who are charged with driving engagement and by those who feel the pangs of disengagement. Employees, however, must honestly reconcile conditions and situations in which we find ourselves. Employers must ask, "What more can I do to help all workers, not just a select few, realize their highest aspirations?" Despite the obstacles, what is my strategy to realize my personal best?

When we sacrifice vitality, we also are willing to sacrifice effectiveness, ours, at our workplace, and at home. The choice we make is both ethical and moral. Are we the very best person at work? If not, for whatever reason, we have an obligation to strive to be our best rather than one of the rest. How willing are we to sacrifice or abandon our best contributions, gifts, and abilities, knowing that we are not demonstrating our best?

Given an imperfect world, are we willing to grow within constraints and beyond our position to become the best of who we are within the place we find ourselves? Unfortunately, the odds are greatly weighed against authenticity. Industry leader Deloitte Consulting has found virtually everyone is susceptible to "covering" who we really are to protect ourselves against workplace biases.[9] Nevertheless, when we look at work as an opportunity and every day a new possibility, we are more likely to break down engagement barriers.

Within this context, rather than providing a survey, this book has offered key questions to personally guide your approach to work and engagement.

The Central Engagement Needs & Listening Inventory

A grand engagement survey is not required, but introspection is, particularly by leaders. Questions that help us listen do not require extensive statistical validation although many of the questions that follow are research based. They simply ask each person to examine aspirations in the context of where we currently are, what we need, and where we would like to be.

Managers, especially in one-on-one meetings with direct reports, should not be afraid to ask:

- **"How am I (me as your manager) doing?"**

- **"What can I do differently?"**

- **"What more would you like to know about _____?"**

- **"What concerns do you have?"**

These questions are quite simple and reliable barometers, and if asked in an untrusting environment, might take patience and perseverance for employees to feel safe enough to honestly and candidly reply. More central questions that should be part of this dialogue follow at the end of this chapter.

Part of the *Good to Great* maxim borrows Isaiah Berlin's adage (from the Greek poet Archilochus). Each should compare her or his personal leadership reflections and doubts to the sly fox and the simple hedgehog.[10] The fox supposedly is the smarter predator, but the hedgehog, rolling itself in a protective ball, reduces all challenges and dilemmas into a simple act (or idea). Our simple acts of kindness, for instance, determine how we nourish others' engagement and our own. Again, we return to an honest capitalization of strengths.

Thus, in the context of Hedgehog framework originally explored in Chapter 1, tangent answers to engagement questions can fill in a few more of the Venn intersections to help ascertain our personal big pictures. Revisiting, below, Collin's three questions, we can ask ourselves not only what is in the business's best interest but in our best interests. What drives our economic engines, passion, and excellence? The intersection of passion, purpose, mastery, and autonomy addresses the feasible risk we are willing to accept to break beyond the usual.

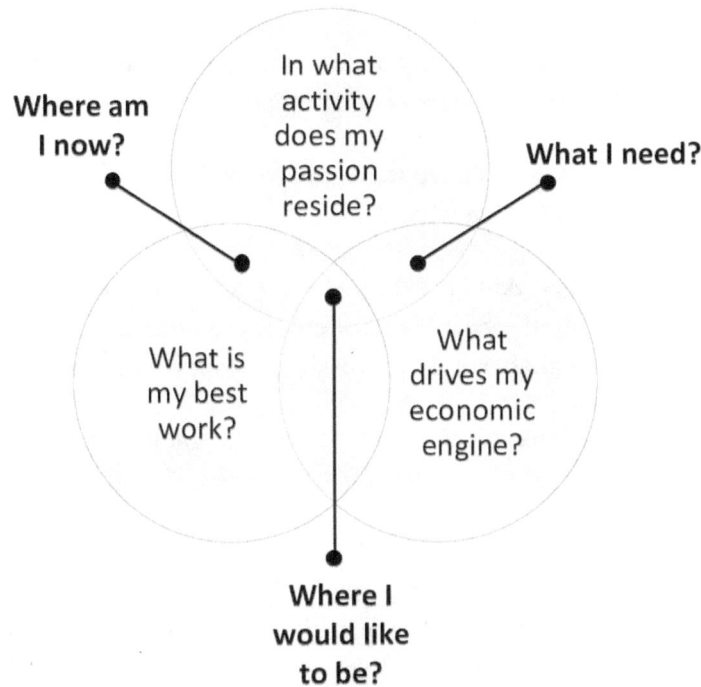

The additional self-inventory questions below are included to aid personal, mutual contributions in negotiating fulfillment at work.

Each person, organization, and leader could do much worse than carving out time to privately explore these questions (or pursue them as a means for collective planning). The following inventory is intended to provide a foundational context for how engagement should influence attitudes, participation, and work product. Hopefully, they also provide a catalyst for examining workplace dynamics and lend greater perspective to understanding your place and participation in deriving the greatest pleasure in and a fuller contribution at work in which all should find personal and professional fulfillment as well as improved measures of success.

1) **Employee**: Am I working at what I love?

   Manager: Do I fully understand each employee's desires to leverage the best fit and potential future contributions?

2) **Employee**: If I have sacrificed following my passion, have I grown to love what I do?

   Manager: Am I providing unrestricted encouragement for reaching the best blend of employee interest and passion with available and progressive job opportunities?

3) **Employee**: Aside from salary and monetary bonuses, have I told my supervisor what types of motivation work for me?

   Manager: Does my supervisor enable, affirm, and provide for frequent expression of a variety of rewards or recognition for the employees I serve? If there are costs, are they justified and built into the budget?

I highly recommend accessing Gallup's core Q12 engagement areas.[11] Two related questions tap into a link between business success and personal fulfillment:

4) **Employee**: Am I cared for as a person?

   Manager: Am I frequently checking in with each of my direct reports? Have I established networks of mentors, coaches, and encourage interactions so that no one employee feels isolated? Have I helped create an atmosphere and culture that cultivates positive relationships?

5) **Employee**: What is my purpose; how do I fit?

Manager: Do I purposefully review activities in the context of mission, vision, and purpose, and do supervisors regularly connect the dots between departmental or organizational needs and each person's impact (time is scheduled in to attend to this need)?

Aside from leadership responsibility to create a culture where engagement is a goal, executive coach Marshall Goldsmith explores the leader's responsibility to create a culture where engagement is the goal, and he focuses on engagement as an individual enterprise that requires personal and administrative commitment. He adds these tangent questions:[12]

6) **Employee**: Do I bring my best to increase my happiness?

   Manager: Do I take a personal interest in my employees? Am I a task-manager (subject matter dominant) or a person manager (emotionally intelligent)? – Note: The latter is infinitely more important. Am I driven by image and what my shareholders might think about me (selfish), or am I driven by other people's and customers' best interests (selfless)? Managers tend to forget, while the buck appropriately stops at the leader's desk, praise for anyone reflects a collective win.

7) **Employee**: To the best of my ability, do I set clear personal goals and progress to achieving the goals?

   Manager: Do I meet with employees on a regular basis to take the temperature of their investment at work and guide their growth and developmental needs, or do I rely predominantly on compliance and solely on annual reviews?

Lenny DeFrano, author of "The (New) Definition of Employee Engagement," reduces the engagement equation to two fundamental questions:[13]

8) **Employee**: How invested do I feel in the quality of my work output?

   Manager: Regarding quality, are my formative evaluations, efforts, and expectations consistent? Are our standards high enough; should we examine the height of the bar for entry and to ensure return on investment?

9) **Employee**: How empowered am I to achieve good quality work? Questions a-d, below, are sample subordinate questions to gauge applications of "empowerment": Every day, I contribute my best self and my best work:

   (a) through arising opportunities?*
   (b) in the access to tools and resources?*
   (c) through growth and learning coaching and options?*
   (d) through input and contributions to decision-making?*

   Manager: *If employees are not able to affirmatively answer these questions, these awareness aspects are problems for managers to resolve. Thus, as a manger, do I take time from other tasks to step back and fully support workers' best interests and enable interactions that promote a-d above?

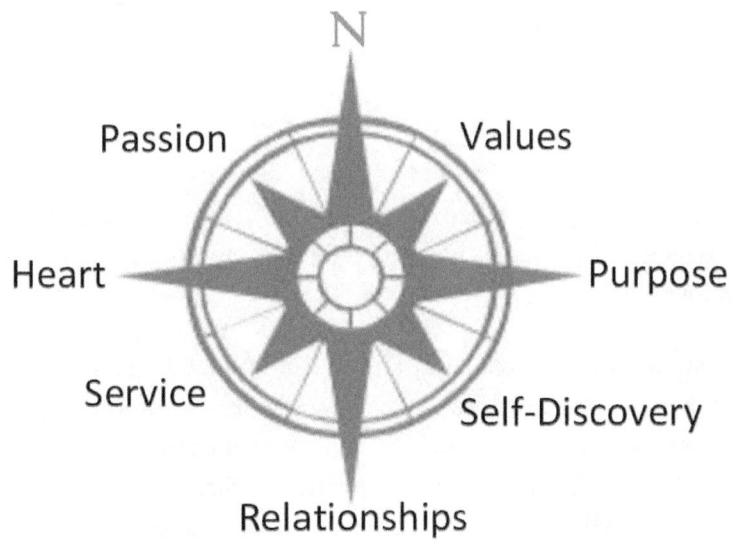

Chapter 10

WHY EMPLOYEES LEAVE: FOR "BOSSES" ONLY

"The role of the CEO is to enable people to excel, help them discover their own wisdom, engage themselves entirely in their work, and accept responsibility for making change." –Vineet Nayar

~

Mustering the humility and will to play more outside of our comfort zones is the backdrop for this chapter. We return to the reason why productive and effective employees leave their employers.

One stream of management thought is convinced that only select high performers are the "go to" people for accomplishing the majority of key work tasks. Such managers may well claim a sly, entitled grin and claim innocence, "Pareto's 80/20 rule is irrefutable! My best 20 percent compete 80 percent of the work. We cannot move the immovable 80 percent." However, this de facto surrender is premature. [1]

Surrendering to mediocrity avoids the pivotal administrative responsibility necessary to stimulate above average performance in everyone. While each worker is independently accountable for at least part of personal connectedness, commitment, and finding joy in one's work, Gallup has also found 70 percent of the variance in creating positive stimuli to reduce disengagement and increase worker happiness rests in management's hands.[2]

What occurs at work to instill mediocrity and abandon excellence? Engagement is a product of a healthy, interactive workplace. The more people connect to and understand each other's roles, each other's strengths, goals, and contributions, the more they can appreciate each other. The more each employee surrenders to favoritism, survival of the meanest, threat, competition at all costs, then the goal of engagement gains by all is impossible.

Most would agree that no one arrives at work wanting to perform poorly. First-year employees and interns are typically the most highly engaged with a precipitous drop off in engagement during the following years. The fit is wrong. Ill-will may creep in, or the employee senses dysfunctions: employees are usually quite knowledgeable about the factors and breakdowns leading to disengagement. In dysfunctional and disengaged surroundings, leaders tend to be consciously oblivious, especially when they admonish and silence workers by tacitly propagating silos and a "stay in your own lane" philosophy.

Another sobering statistic from Gallup, one that probably tells us much about disengaged employees, is that "companies fail to choose the candidate with the right talent for the job 82 percent of the time."[3] Given the relatively high number of disengaged, we forget the managerial domino effect, the effect on the disposition and attitude of workers as a consequence of reporting to disengaged managers and the chain reaction set off by a woefully underprepared manager. At the very least, we can conduct a causal analysis that reflects, hiring, training, or many of the previously listed unattended variables.

We cannot discount the need for individual initiative across the entire organization regardless of periodic setbacks or changing priorities (engaged behavior and strategy is part of change and shifts). However, breakdowns in trust, errant hires, misaligned, ill-equipped, side-lined personnel, or employees who feel stagnant or complacent in their occupations, these factors reflect the heart of leadership. And the best place to pick up the pieces, to reinvigorate morale and productivity, these needs reside primarily at leadership thresholds. Unfortunately, Grossman,[4] citing a Dale Carnegie study, indicates that 80 percent of disengaged employees are dissatisfied failings of their direct managers. For all personnel caught in the middle, the interactions may seem akin to slightly askew dominoes resulting in a disappointing chain reaction, or an absurd Rube Goldberg contraption.

Obviously, the key question is what to do with those managers who fail in their shares of leadership and either claim subject matter superiority, or admit some culpability but choose not to change or simply reject the significance and existence of disengagement (theirs and others'). Having and sharing ownership requires facing hard questions from all fronts, from introspection complemented by objectively listening to all and crucially resisting prejudgment in the face of brutal, sometime painful truths.

First, leaders must acknowledge they are not executing enough people-oriented objectives. In fact, we need to constantly remind ourselves that workers are not wired to criticize, but to support each other, nor to act out but to contribute. No one wants to fail; no one wants to be excluded.

Everyone wants to contribute her or his best work, but if a leader is convinced that an employee who offers high value and high potential is not good for the company, again, take stock in what's driving the decision: the employee's best interests or the leader's?

There are, also, a few ineffective balms or catch phrases leaders may preach to placate work groups. "We need to *fake* it until we make it," for example. Vulnerability, however, is an attribute of authenticity. "Fake" implies giving up who you are and releases leaders from accountability. If a leader's expectation is for anyone to pretend to be engaged, happy, or challenged until leadership fulfills promises, they have certainly mastered fake. Of course, sometimes our authentic selves require some regulation or moderation, but this does not imply fake; rather, it requires always fueling our better selves. Leaders fuel fates.

The next, "*Faithing* it," resting exclusively on hope, too, requires first and foremost the good faith of leaders. If leaders want employees to "faith it," leaders must model the way, not some of the way but complete commitment to all employees. Faith requires, unwavering commitment to each employee demonstrated by appreciable action rather than obfuscation, penalty, or hidden agendas. For employees to have faith, leaders must practice believable values.

Therefore, if a leader coaches others to faith it, the leader's actions must, then, advantage every employee, and must explicitly direct and focus others in relation to mission by repeatedly connecting decisions, actions, and assignments to each employee. Far too often, leaders who have grown to understand equity, membership, opportunity, and meaning, fail at the last level of the engagement taxonomy, being in service to all, which includes stimulating, meaningful discourse and dialogue.

A sampling of resources[5] (see the following comparative chart) reveal remarkable convergence of general reasons for employee dissatisfaction. Like engagement, predictors of turnover, especially influence of the boss and job fit, appear relatively stable and consistent over time. While we know connections grow stronger when leaders stimulate employees, numerous studies identify we have not gained much traction in responding to the outstanding needs.

Branham	Robinson (2008)	Heathfield (2015)	Schappel (2015)
(2005) Based on Saratoga Institute (Third Party Exit Interviews Study)	Based on Gallup Meta-analysis; (*Top 5 predictors)	Naturalistic Observations	Bamboo HR Survey
Lack of Trust in Senior Leadership; Too Little Coaching or Feedback	Connect to Senior Management* Relationship with Manager* (sum 75%; 2013: 50% Escape Manager)	Relationship with Boss	Boss
Job Fit; Misleading Work Expectations	Job Fit* (20%)	Opportunities to Use Skills; Relevance of Job to Business Goals	Did Not Like the Path Chosen; Work Expectations
	Coworkers Relationships, re: Commitment to Quality*	Coworker Relationships	
Growth Opportunities	Advancement, Promotion (32%)		Training
Overwork; Work Life Balance	Flexible Scheduling (8%)		
Worker Value and Recognition		Recognition for Performance	
	Job Security (1.7%)	Organization's Financial Stability	
	Work Environment (17%)	Overall Culture	Job Was Not Fun
	Pay and Benefits* (22%)		
		Meaningful Work	
		Autonomy and Independence	

One of the very basic responses leaders and managers should ponder can be taken out of the Intel playbook. The late Andrew Grove, founder of Intel, was purported to balance seriousness with humor. Complementing being at ease during daily operations, part of Intel's success can be attributed to company members who were interactive, collaborative, good natured, but most importantly, argumentative.[6] Particularly, with respect to cultivating trust, communication, relationships, and training, all are centered in willingness of leaders to be open to honest debate.

Because we can be accomplishing so much more, nested together, the aforementioned findings should arrest the confidence of our accomplishments (even if we factor in +/- 5-10% reasonable doubt):

82% Candidate Selection Error

70% Disengaged

74% Cannot Define Engagement

70% of Probable Change Attributable to Management, yet 80% Dissatisfaction with Management

Year after year, we continue to read similar findings, yet the findings do not move us toward more concerted action. For instance, risk management firm Aon Hewitt found that after collecting engagement feedback from European team managers, 38 percent viewed an engagement survey but did nothing with the results or merely ignored the results.[7]

Initial but aggressive personal steps to combat indifference must rule out the disconnected and depersonalized effects inherent in surveys and the antiquated suggestion box (we are legitimately talking to employees and building trust, or we are not). Rather than feeling free to talk directly, exactly, and clearly to each other about needs, some managers might adopt the use of an anonymous suggestion box, which, ironically, actually works to perpetuate distrust. Our immediate and open appreciation should answer these questions:

- **How can I listen better?**

- **How can I avert succumbing to an "earned dogma effect"?** (Explored in Chapters 5 and 9)

- **How do I reduce prejudicial thinking?**

- **How can I better respond to the positive effects of dissonance?**

The following scenarios approach how to apply what we know about engagement to avert the workers' absence from the collective enterprise. Each describes some of the intervening complications hindering engagement and points to possible pathways to constructive solutions.

1) The "Peter Principle" Compounded by the Plight of the Task-Oriented Manager

"The Peter Principal" adage[8] still appears to ring true: people get really good at something (for instance, as subject matter or process experts), then are rewarded by promotion from analytical or specialized business functions and work tasks into people appreciation tasks.

The habits/steps that advanced them to higher rungs are not necessarily the habits that work best once they have reached that higher rung. Think, for instance, Jacob Marley in Charles Dickens' *A Christmas Carol.* You are an accountant seeking to publish error free books. Turning a microscopic eye at your own work is a prudent behavior. In the manager's role, however, using that micromanaging skill to berate others who toil tirelessly and struggle with reconciling their own balance sheets does not work. Years of conditioning to be unforgiving in my own work, then being expected to shift to a different, more hospitable person, rather than hostile, is nearly impossible (unless, of course, you are visited by enough ghosts to scare up a proportionally corrective consciousness responsive to the fear and resentment previously instilled in others).

In workplaces where salary caps exists, workers are motivated to abandon what they do best and rise up into managerial positions to gain additional compensation. As a partial solution, in his chapter "The Blind, Breathless Climb," Buckingham argues for structural 'broadbanding,"[9] or allowing a wide variety of salaries independent of position, which enables greater salary parity across job descriptions; i.e., if you're really good at something, you should not have to ascend to management as your only means to earn more money. You do not risk a rise into incompetence in order to make ends meet or more fairly compete.

An incredibly gifted and effective elementary mathematics teacher, for example, may have no other means of substantial pay advancement but through hierarchical advancement into administration. The teacher may have thoroughly mastered the art of teaching, garnered awards, present at conferences, loves the subject area and working with students, understands grade level learner scaffolding, in other words has reached his or her calling with an admirable mastery and service level yet is reduced to abandon a calling to gain equity. Especially in government public service, a few years into a career, workers begin to calculate the retirement formula, and realize that moving into management or administration could increase post-career income by 30 percent or more.

Have you ever encountered a similar type of situation?: "Jos," an admirable employee, is an incredible widget counter. Given the task of counting 10,000 widgets, Jos will count 20,000! This incredible ability and drive is noticed, and Jos is moved into management to instill this work ethic in others. The C-suite calculates the possibilities of "transforming everyone on the floor into prolific widget counters!"

A promotion is offered with tenure accompanying the move, and a substantial pay increase, to which Jos thinks, "Why not?" The "not" part is that management has only noticed Jos's disposition while counting widgets. Prior to noticing this remarkable performance benchmark, management has provided no leadership development (or it has been very restricted to a select few already at the top). With just the slight hint of power and authority, and an uncanny ability to interact with widgets but possessing zero people skills, Jos starts ordering people around. Mistakes and abilities are criticized; gains are expected and unheralded. Jos disguises disgust behind fleeting smiles. Lacking leadership ability, Jos reveals a particularly mean and angry demeanor. There may have been infrequent but inconsequential coaching interventions. Mostly, the employees are faulted. Within a year, Jos is disliked by everyone. Morale is declining as is productivity. By this time, the horse is out of the barn, and no amount of training can fix this problem. Regardless, with little if any prior leadership mentoring, and some floor personnel possessing at least as much leadership experience, some more, it's far too late to consider Jos's road to improvement.

Jos's position is found no longer necessary. Management decides this situation is untenable and attempts to pawn Jos to a different department. However, word has spread. No one wants to work with Jos, nor can Jos move back to widget counting. Jos's former position has been filled, and now commanding a much higher salary, the move cannot be reconciled in the budget or with other co-workers. Moreover, tenure was a standard contract agreement attached only to managerial positions, not to front-line positions.

Attracted by the higher salary, but without proper organizational succession steps to assure best fit and employee success, Jos, the consummate widget counter, turns into a human resource nightmare, is blamed for the turmoil and ultimately laid off. The company loses an expert widget counter and mops up the mess but does not take the time to exchange the water in the bucket. The cycle is likely to reoccur.

In other workplaces, the worker ascends into management, but often the job does not appreciably change. The manager conducts annual performance reviews, checks time statements, mitigates conflicts, facilitates processes, etc., but in many cases, remains a functional player performing the same tasks as direct reports in addition to newly managing people. With a scarcity of human resources and time, managing people, however, is almost always sacrificed to reverting to task management. The tendency is to be confined in an office toiling away at the same tasks as all the others in the office, rather than truly engaging in people-oriented needs.

In the worst-case scenario, not only have these upwardly mobile employees departed from passion, but now, relatively ineffective and unhappy, they lack an admission (particularly when more money is involved) that they perhaps were promoted to and languish in the wrong position. No one wants to admit a mistake in cultures that do not acknowledge improvement, or the promotional regulations permit the most expedient, if least effective route, so no one is really willing or has time to work on change.

As discussed earlier, this denial is often compounded by the inefficiencies that accompany lagging, non-existent, or incorrectly designed leadership enrichment.

Not surprisingly, reciprocal failure results, and often self-protection takes the form of controlling knowledge to secure and protect a position, and which is kept secure through micromanagement. A new manager, for instance, caught in this precarious position, is gratified by the monetary security and position but almost invariably blind within an insular bubble.

What novice managers fail to see is that they must now give up the subordinate tasks to navigate big picture issues. They are no longer needed as the functional expert. Leaders direct their attention to support, direct, and help to propagate others' successes. New managers, however, are easily caught up in demonstrating their importance than being concerned about coworkers' issues and aspirations.

Solution: Awareness, humility, and...view Vineet Nayar's "Employees First, Customers Second *Ted Talk*."[10]

Of course, those who do choose to pursue management should be required to participate in growth experiences much earlier in their careers (once they've reached a higher post, they rarely find the time or recognize the need). Leadership development should be seamlessly realized, from employee entry to exit, through coaching, modeling, and learning opportunities, accompanied by fair and credible accountability measures.

Clearly, in effective and engaged cultures, micromanagement is made unnecessary through constructive coaching behaviors, shared or distributed power, and supportive guidance. The employee's fear of failure and mistakes are often negatively compounded by a manger's image, ego, status, or air of indispensability. In order for engagement to gain traction, management must replace the cultural imprints of status with an ethic of helping others become ready, equally essential, which stimulates each worker's aspirations by advocating everyone's hand in leadership.

Human Resources expert Susan Hearthfield suggests thinking about employee retention every day, and asking yourself, "What are you purposefully doing or ignoring to make employees leave or stay?"[11] This is supported by organizational behaviorist Eean Crawford's extensive research findings that "hindrances" were negatively associated with engagement while "challenges" were positively associated.[12] Allowing an employee to be complacent, average, or to let talents and gifts escape, conveys more about the leader's flaws than the employee's.

Honestly evaluate yourself using the "How to Run an Unproductive Company" checklist (Appendix A[13]). Concern yourself with serving others, rather than worrying, "How will this look? How will this reflect on me?" Properly served, employees look engaged and are reciprocally supportive.

2) My Growth Versus "Your/Our Bus" Paradox

If I am a manager who understands that 1) no one is perfect, 2) every new job presents learning opportunities, 3) much is gained from making mistakes, and 4) if my fundamental priority is growing people to maximize potential, I must be compelled to abandon the dubious formula, "Past behavior predicts future behavior."

Growth, coaching, and repeated opportunity to gain mastery are catalysts for progress. The past is not a foregone conclusion but springboard to the future. The leader's resolve should not be nested in the past, especially if failures are *mutual* learning opportunities. The resolve should be nested in tenaciousness and perseverance to moving beyond past and striving toward a complementary world view.

Recognition (which requires a leader's full range of skills: objectively seeing, comprehending leadership blind spots that inhibit true knowing, taking time to notice and take notes, morally acting, advocating, actively listening...) is a true interpretation/realization

157

of "the right seat on the bus," [3] not the seat I want to put others in. Understanding the person means understanding the person's talents, accompanied by rigorous, unceasing actions that create the seat. This, of course, requires a strategic plan and avoiding the perils of "tracking" based on faulty and subjective evaluations, imprecise or misleading testing, and confirmation bias.

Perhaps the greatest challenge for leaders is understanding plasticity, interposed against fixed attitudes and work strictures. Personality may well be fixed– research tells us that personality is infused by seven years of age. Behavior is not. LifeScience.com reports that 30 years of age appears to be the balancing point of genetic disposition and formative experience; fortunately, as we grow older, we still possess the capability to grow more agreeable and more altruistic.[14]

This is good news because, all factors considered, engagement appears to be a product of altruism, and most importantly, intrinsic motivation devoid of ego. Again, chief architects of engagement are wise to attend to forensic psychologist Karen Franklin who insists that we should retire the past behavior predicts future behavior myth.[15] The American Psychological Association reports that as scaffolding connects past and future habits, new habits are formed within "stable, supporting environment."[16]

If leaders want more of the same half-hearted work habits, the answer is to discount and punish workers. In fact, growth and change are products of positive reinforcement and recognition more than products of punishment or being ostracized. Leaders who want to fully realize the talents and gifts of others need to continue to test each employee's mettle, as well as their own, by endorsing an exercise of acceptable risk, creativity, capacity, and abilities. Managers need to continue to provide opportunities for employees to flourish rather than banish employees to the mundane, stagnant tasks, or to insignificance. Disrespect and disregard of talent and gifts, rather than active pursuit and cultivation, are surely signs of an insecure and uncertain manager.

Talent expert Lou Adler concurs by arguing that the inability to discard the "past behavior" formula instills mediocrity and, at worst, results in tendencies to rationalize scapegoat, wrap targeted individuals into pigeon holes, or reinforce self-fulfilling prophecies of the manager's making.[17] As seen above, we may be not so adroit at getting those seats right on the bus; therefore, carefully listening to, and not judging or discounting the employee, helps mitigate replacements.

Thus, contrary to the general notion that leaders should be paranoid about competition, etc., in the case of the profitable and productive growth of others, a leader's worst enemy is self-paranoia: "Who's out to get me (throw me under the bus)?" Often, managers create their own counterproductive subcultures by misjudging and labeling others. As psychologist Barry Schwartz emphasizes, "False ideas about human beings will not go away if people believe that they're true. Because if people believe that they're true, they create ways of living and institutions that are consistent with these very false ideas."[18] The best leaders, again, are not concerned about how they look. On the other hand, some leaders lose their way because the trappings of prestige are so alluring, and as leadership co-author Bill George, states in *True North*, "their distortions convince them they are doing nothing wrong."[19]

Therefore, the best corollary is not "the best predictor of future behavior is past behavior," but the adage attributed to Peter Drucker and Abraham Lincoln (perhaps reminded of his "failures" before ascending the American presidency), "The best way to predict the future is to create it."

Can people and places change? The answer is a resounding "Yes!" All the time. Leadership requires the risk to jump out of insular comfort zones.

Solution: Awareness and..., Paul Brown, author of *Entrepreneurship for the Rest of Us*, offers an elegant solution to defeatist management styles (particularly those who tout on my bus, off my bus extremes, or cannot quite get the seats right), "Act, Learn, Build, Repeat":[20]

- **"Figure out what [a worker and you want].**

- **Take a small step toward making it reality, and keep the principle employee(s) in the information loop.**

- **Pause to think about what they learned from taking that step.**

- **Build that learning into their next step, and if that means adjusting from the initial path, so be it."**

Notice the solution above emphasizes encouragement. It implies, as Vineet Nayar argues, "Employees First!"

The true objective is to help each other, and among the inherent challenges, trust others. This choice to help others is not leading lemmings into the sea (a myth, too, just like the past/future behavior fortune telling myth). In fact, the choice is just the opposite. Providing the spring board to elevate others assures that employees feel safe. Knowing that the sky's the limit includes the understanding that we are allowed to fail without risk of being branded malcontents, disloyal, not fitting, or "not on the bus." Supportive leaders assure the right fit, including their own.

The best leaders, therefore, entrust people to bring higher level thinking to their work, to question, and challenge authority. Again, on-going, genuine coaching and/or training must be in place to allow the best to lead others to be even better. David Sturt, author of *Great Work: How to Make a Difference People Love,* argues that interacting with employees daily strengthens relationships between peers and with managers, which improves morale and bolsters engagement.[21] Managers are responsible to provide the paint, canvas, and the room (with a view) from which to create.

3. After All the Reflection, Introspections, Inventories, the 360, and Escaping the Sensory Deprivation Tank, then What?

Is this your first rodeo? Seen leaders come and go? Are one? Aspire to be one? We can inventory ourselves to death, figure out if we are introverted, extroverted, compliant, commanding, top-brained, bottom brained…. Psychological testing is not going away, nor are its proponents. Some of it is actually useful, but none of that knowledge guarantees a change in our behaviors. If anything, it provides, with perhaps greater awareness, an excuse to do nothing else, and further imprint "That's just the way I am," confirmation bias.

Leaders are teachers, not tyrants nor despots, and should not be striving to be idols. With respect to coaching, teaching, mentoring, and promoting learning, we need to always return to the notion that everyone wants to do his or her best; everyone wants to succeed; and everyone wants to learn more. This last factor, growth and development (and constant diligence to reward these), is at the core of engagement. Particularly in interviewing, a candidate should be able to identify what more he or she can learn or has a desire to learn. Barring this priority, an employee has not failed as a learner; supervisors have failed as teachers and employers.

As growth remains engagement's common denominator, teaching is the variable that bridges work dynamics and engagement. Therefore, a discussion about engagement requires attention to what effective teaching looks like. Blending received theory with the latest neuroscience[22] yields a widely applicable formula to apply to a variety of business situations but particularly to avoid succumbing to faulty biases. Effective learning opportunities connects instructional content to the learners' prior experiences and readiness (emotional and cognitive) to accommodate new material and behaviors. No matter what design "model" used, instruction/coaching/training/relationship building must carefully and creatively deliberate facets of this specific learning pattern:

Access Existing Personal Cognitive Structure
⬇
Activate Current Frameworks to Stimulate Connections
⬇
Receive New Information
⬇
Rehearse New Information
⬇
**Discard Inaccurate Understanding by
Accommodating Correct Information**
⬇
Adjust Schemata, Build New Structure
⬇
Apply, Practice Accordingly to Gain Mastery
⬇
Refresh to Imprint Over Time
⬇
Access Existing Structure...

One of the crucial interior components is that what happens during rehearsal and discoveries during application influences the discarding of spurious conclusions and beliefs. Leaders must be willing to let workers experiment with the "how" and make mistakes without punishment and with positive guidance, provide substantive context about the "why": "This is the best way we have found to do it; this is why we constructed and agreed on this process; but keep asking why, and if you have found a better way, don't be afraid to come forward and share your impressions and ideas."

Secondly, knowledge is subsumed and engrained within the dynamic of the Bloom's taxonomy: application, analysis, synthesis, evaluation, and creation.[23] The goal is to move the learner from surface knowledge acquisition to create meaning through deep integration. Where we often fail is on the front end of inquiry by not probing at the starting points:

- **"Where do you want to go; how do you want to get there?**

- **What do you need?**

- **How can I help you get there?"**

Secondly, we are prone to fail by focusing on the "how" without providing authentic "why"s. Employees should be stimulated through clarity and progress, not derailed by frustration or disenfranchisement. They should be provided multiple avenues to advance personal priorities in consort with business outcomes. Objectives or goals are, ideally, measured through a variety of different means and match the employees' current strengths and abilities to move toward acquiring and employing new skills.

Solution: The general framework necessary to create the learning opportunities that result in an engaged workers includes:

163

- **Ownership of content by integrating new information to personal experience. Start where the employee is, and find deep, emotional connections to heighten impact.**

- **Distributive, spaced learning to aid retention and impact (one-shot learning sessions without meaningful follow-up will likely have the _least_ long-term effectiveness; for instance, again, a core need is to bridge the differences between single annual reviews and on-going formative coaching by including continued, follow-up discussions and exploration).**[24]

Think about a time when you were a frustrated learner, confronted with a difficult problem or ill-equipped to address a confusing task. What would you have liked to have told the instructor or manager? Sometimes out of sheer embarrassment, shyness, reluctance, or fear, we choose not to share our frustration or difficulties. While managers, coaches, or teachers can attempt to diagnose needs, they aren't mind readers. The corollary is that when workers/learners do speak up, leaders have an obligation to affirmatively respond to their insights. When workers feel safe to professionally engage, managers need to muster the courage to deviate from the routine and maximize the person in order to capitalize on meaning and purpose.

The most important of Steven Covey's habits cuts to the core of the relationship between content, learner's readiness, and teacher approach. Teachers/leaders need to "seek first to understand" (the learner's strengths and potential connectedness), "then to be understood."[25] None of the other core drivers can be useful if this prerequisite learner piece is missing. In addition to closely listening, other developmental parallels present in Covey's philosophy include candor, self-awareness, principled-centered actions, and mutual gains. Each of these (with Covey's accompanying quotations[25]) is expanded below:

First, most people want to be heard, but the listener tends to pursue self-centered interests without truly consuming equally valid perspectives (welcome new or contradictory information, discard old or faulty beliefs, adjust conclusions). We are all guilty of remaining blind to inconsistencies or contradictions in professed values. A failure to really stop, listen, and consider what the learner/employee at any level brings to the table prohibits us from understanding truths about relationships, within another person's point of view or errors in our own; thus, an honest exchange is the foremost important character trait. Understanding depends on compassion and empathy.

To the degree that the teacher/manger advantages any one person over another as a product of image, ego, or status, favoritism, cronyism, patronage, or hidden agendas indicates our own failings as authentic co-workers, co-learners, co-leaders and teachers.

Second, "self-awareness (teachers' and learner') enables us to stand apart and examine the way we see ourselves," but what we derive from such awareness is only profitable if our growth is used to help others grow.

Third, each person is a leader whose actions are a matter of principles: "Our lives need to be principle-centered with deep, fundamental truths, classic truths, and generic common denominators."

Fourth, implicit in the need to honesty evaluate all points of view is facing "the brutal facts."[26] The facts, often hidden in multiple subjective truths, can sting a little if honestly assessed. Any action that hurts or inhibits another is a direct contradiction to the instructional mission and values, but reframing and behavioral change takes, hard and sometimes painful work in the light of honest discovery and willingness to accommodate both our well-being and change.

If we are truly open to growth and self-improvement, what helps us through transcendence from false facts and faulty reasoning is also one of Covey's principles, "looking out for and looking for the good in others." Not just saying what we plan to do, but enabling palpable steps; doing it. Right-flowing work feels energizing and creative.

Recognizing the good in all should be foremost, complemented by the willingness to openly work through conflict or confront a defensive posture that may occur in the light of uncomfortable truths. All (teacher and student) "should be able to express ideas, feelings, and experiences in a way that will encourage others." Unfortunately, a great many people selfishly operate under a win at all costs mentality. Learners, teachers, and managers who approach performance outcomes with passion and collaboratively feel mutually and emotionally satisfied. Unfortunately, in playing the "insufficient time" or similar "overriding priority" (i.e., "get out of jail") cards, we are unable to unfold the winning hand echoed in Allen Toussaint's lyric, "You will not lose, not if you use your heart.[27]

4. Distrust: the Primary Engagement Killer

Mistrust and distrust take various forms, ranging from micromanagement's unfulfilled commitments or clipping a willing worker's wings. Performance consultant Gregory P. Smith asserts:

> Management doesn't allow the rank and file to make decisions or allow them pride of ownership. A visitor to my website emailed me a message that said, 'Forget about the professional decisions. How

about when you can't even select the company's holiday card without the President rejecting it for one of his own taste?'[28]

Gaining trust is a matter of integrity and honest, uncompromised interaction. If I continue to worry about how any action, positive or negative, reflects on me, my ego disrupts cultivating trust. One of the surest means of determining if ego is in the way is to determine the degree of control imposed on others.

Rather than allowing flexibility, unnecessary ambiguity in information sharing distorts clarity and compromises leadership integrity. Excluding the necessity of legal, proprietary or confidential requirements, obfuscation typically follows from control. Naturally, suspicion and discontent arise from perceptions of exclusion.

Warren Bennis emphasizes the great values of curiosity, daring, errors, questioning, integrity, originality, the new, authenticity, and eschews hierarchy and convention. He argues freedom to be original is complimentary to trust. In *On Becoming a Leader*, he shares AIDS scientist Mathide Krim's commentary:

> I have little tolerance for institutional restraints. Institutions should serve people, but unfortunately it's often the other way around. People give their allegiance to an institution, and they become prisoners of habits, practices, and rules that make them ultimately ineffectual.[29]

Dissent, on the other hand, is a fundamental good in an open culture. Dissent is essentially a means of questioning, fact finding, and finding the missing links in interactions. Everyone should invite feedback loops to lend different points of view or to aid corrective action. Leadership fuels distrust when it ignores, rather than accommodates questions, concerns, and feelings. And the adage "perception is truth," is more accurately stated as a sole perception is one of many skewed truths. Since truth is revealed through alternative perceptions, cutting through the noise and inaccuracies require dissent.

This approach to dissonance should not be confused with Daniel Goleman's analysis of malignant leaders who use dissonance as a means to mislead and manipulate. In fact, as the authors suggest of emotional intelligence in *Primal Leadership,* "Leaders give praise or withhold it, criticize well or destructively, offer support or turn a blind eye to people's needs." Authentically listening to dissonance, and not misusing it, creates resonance.[30]

Solution: Easy answers are out of reach when reciprocal mistrust is entrenched. A pervasive understanding of business issues should flow throughout the workplace. Leadership should not expect workers to solicit information, but they should anticipate questions and feedback and readily respond with detailed answers, constantly and clearly explain the "why" while reconnecting to values, mission, and vision.

The methods employed to stimulate conversation and communication are personal choices, which require time to share and explore. A leader either seeks value or seeks to devalue, and this conscious choice is inextricably connected to a commitment to be honest and transparent with each employee. If trust is an outstanding issue for employees, formal leaders/managers should first delve deeper into self-exploration, see Appendix B, "Leadership Inventory."[31]

As each person models culture, we should ask, "Are we on an honest trajectory to encourage and improve each other and avoid the spiral of confirming faults in others?" Employees regularly take the temperature of culture at the water cooler. Murmurs shared in hushed sidebar conversations test principles and reveal much about the actions that have increased or decreased levels of trust. If seeking information or judging are common in such sidebars, the leadership has likely not modeled an honest trajectory to foster trust nor to encourage, include, and improve.

The simplest action is taking time to connect with each employee. We gain trust from honesty with self and others and through concern and unconditional love. At a minimum, any supervisor who evaluates the performance of others should take time to meet, apart from annual reviews, and ask each person:

- **What more do you need to know to be better connected and increase the substance of your contributions?**

5. "All You Need is Love"[32]

Some would argue that truth does not equal love, but truth, beauty, God, all are synonymous with love. We engage others when we exercise love. When we welcome the eyes of many beholders, we grow in love. Conversely, when we block or minimize others, we succumb to a war footing. The Arbinger Institute clarifies that when we inhibit others, we see other people as "objects, vehicles, or irrelevancies." When truth prevails, we see others "whose hopes, needs, cares and fears are as real as any others."[33]

As explored earlier, an applied taxonomy of engagement parallels social and psychological theory. For instance, love and true leadership or wisdom is consistent with Lawrence Kohlberg's post-conventional and principled conscience levels of a "clear effort to define moral values and principles that have validity and application apart from authority of the groups or people holding these principles apart from the individual's own identification with these groups."[34] It also echoes Erik and Joan Erikson's stages of psychosocial development, specifically the basic state, "hope versus mistrust," through progressive states to "despair and disgust versus integrity."[35]

And finally, love, woven into transparent communication, harkens back to Carl Rogers's humanistic principles and classic listening challenge:

> **The next time you get into an argument with your wife, or your friend, or with a small group of friends, just stop the discussion for a moment, and institute this rule. 'Each person can speak up for himself/herself only after he/ she has first restated the ideas and feelings of the previous speaker accurately, and to that speaker's satisfaction....'**

You will discover it's the most difficult things you have ever tried to do,"[36] and, in fact, rarely a routine practice.

Would you agree that most people in the business world do <u>not</u> love each other or do not enjoy each other's company? If so, find a way to fix that. Start by using Rogers's exercise above. If the question is an oversimplification of negotiation, politics, posturing, etc., how should the complexities be viewed? Would you say that colleagues lack the capacity or the ability to embrace loving each other? Some leaders tell us they love us all the time, but no one believes them. If we are not emotionally honest and intelligent (head and heart), we need to work more on accepting others and sorting through the complexities of conflict. Taking time to identify and repair fissures matters. This begins with accepting our own limitations. No one is perfect.

We are all humans who make mistakes, yet we attempt to make best decisions possible given situations and circumstances surrounding the pursuit of goals. Politically, leaders can choose a manipulative position by criticizing the choices, actions, or positions others have taken. Love levels criticism.

Solution: The difficulty resides in making the effort to do the right thing for the right reasons (which eliminates selfishness) even in the face of recalcitrance, resistance, or rejection. Part of this complication is corrupting the meaning of "positive" workplace. Those who approach management with concerns should not be met with dismissing labels, "being negative," nor met with manipulation: dismissed as uninformed, rejected as not understanding complex issues, ignored for meddling outside their area of expertise, discounted because others on the team disagree with their perspective.

Whistle blowers are usually cast as destructive, but their appeal, often outside of the accepted chain of command, is almost always in response to leaders' refusal to listen or cultural constraints that interfere with listening.

Thus, the ultimate test of prevailing good, as always, is not seeking confirmation, or acknowledgement of self or own beliefs, but acting in a supportive way to receive, accept, value, and affirm the opinions of others even if they are different from our own. Bad things happen to good people when they are summarily rejected for no good reason or to protect selfish interests.

On the other hand, engagement and love is, foremost, other-centric. All truths, thus love, require fair hearing, not defensive blocking, to arrive at best, prudent, ethical, and moral answers.

Granted, complaints and gossip can be malicious, debilitating and rabid. But even if input is erroneous, suspect, or unfounded, our biases lead us to be tone deaf to the input that is not. While an ethical leader will relentlessly maintain an equitable and fair foundation on which to build solid communication and engagement, Kellogg School of Management faculty remind us that people are messy, and toxic workers are selfish.[37]

A conscious choice to dismiss others is disrespectful. Disregard devalues others.

We have all known leaders who confuse loyalty with cronyism, who create insular, political "kitchen cabinets," or who deliberately create ambiguity to control or coerce (as if the naturally occurring variety of ambiguity alone is not sufficiently destructive). "Good Leaders engage. Bad leaders entrap," Warren Bennis admonishes in *On Becoming a Leader*. "Leaders know the importance of having someone in their lives who will unfailingly and fearlessly tell them the truth."[38]

The evening that I was drafting this closing section, I received David Dye's "Engage" email newsletter. In the article, "Is Service Leadership Bulls--t?" he suggests that the most important questions do not revolve around conditions (stress, tools, resources), rewards, insecurity, or those blind to their own behaviors. Dye reiterates that everyone's actions reveals each person's reciprocal leadership potential:

> "Ultimately, the most important question isn't about *those* managers. The most important question is, 'What [kind of person] *will you be*?' Will you enjoy your work, or will it suck the life out of you? Will you build lasting results and leave a legacy, or will people be glad to see you leave?"[39]

Therefore, we return to some of the business thought leaders and their conclusions. Pick up any of the top leadership books, and you will find a consistent, independently verified morale of the story: find ways to say and live "I love you." If the words are too difficult or appear inappropriate, others understand that your love is conveyed through your actions.

And of those who know the pain of unrelenting ill-will and questionable intent? To make engaging progress, we must work toward excellence rather than conceding to lower expectations. On one hand, for example, anonymous, random acts of kindness are simple expression of commitment to others. On the other, any obstacles we construct, such as negative assessments or judgmental opinions of others, or actions that block others from growing, are opposite of love. Sometimes we must be the spiked, round-balled hedgehog. The fox sniffs and pushes us around a bit; we roll around a bit, but once the Fox tires, we continue, unhindered and unbounded, to move forward.

Caring for our well-being and care for the others who symbiotically care for us, loosens the tangled knot tied by those who choose to interrupt productive flow. Caring always puts others' advancement and well-being first. Even when we may disagree, our hearts insist that we always share an explicit formula for another's successes. If we choose to do nothing, we teach others not to love and not to care. Engagement and effective business practices begin and end with a core ingredient, love:[40]

- The best managers... employ tough love,... a mind-set, one that reconciles an uncompromising focus on excellence with a genuine need to **care**.... It frees the manager from blaming the employee. - Marcus Buckingham, *First Break All the Rules.*

- Love your passengers… that is, make time, listen, and recognize, **serve**, and bring out the best in them. - Jon Gordon, *The Energy Bus*

- Of all the things that **sustain** a leader over time, love is the most lasting…. Leadership is not an affair of the head. Leadership is an affair of the heart. - James Kouzes and Barry Posner, *The Leadership Challenge.*

- [Love at its core] is the movement of evolution, to higher and higher levels of mutuality, recognition, union, and **embrace.**' People see the marketplace as a jungle of competition; they fear that businesses that emphasize love and care cannot possibly be competitive and win. In fact, the opposite is true. Love and care are not weak virtues; they are the strongest of all human traits. Companies that operate on fear are the ones headed for extinction. - John Mackey and Raj Sisodia, *Conscious Capitalism*

- You must have love in your heart for the **people** under your leadership. - John Wooden, *Wooden on Leadership.*

Where we need to most develop management acumen is honestly and unconditionally connecting with others by actually exercising and resurrecting compassion, play, and bringing more love and enjoyment to our work.

Whether culture is revealed in what people say behind our backs or how we are treated, Steven Covey coaches us:

> People are a function of the social mirror, scripted by the opinions, the perceptions, and the paradigms of the people around them. As interdependent people, you and I come from a paradigm which includes the realization that we

are a part of that social mirror. We can choose to
reflect back to others a clear, undistorted vision
of themselves.[41]

If we choose to let others make work miserable, dull, combative,
and dreary, we might be reminded of the lesson in Jean Paul
Sartre's play, *No Exit*. Three characters cannot escape a mirrorless
room in which they find themselves. Their eternal existential
hell is created from the reflections they cast and the indignities
they suffer upon each other. At work that miserable eternity lasts
between 6 months to 35 years for the disengaged unless "the better
angels of our nature"[42] prevail.

Chapter 11

"The greatest thoughts come from the heart." –Marquis de Vauvenargues

~

For as long as engagement statistics have been reported, the "engaged" of us has nested at around one-third. At the lunch table, then, the person on whom we should first cast a glance is not the person sitting to the right or left but ourselves and our capabilities.

Engagement must rise above anxiety, apathy, and boredom. And to traverse these symptoms, the high-water marks of engagement are clarity of purpose and intense, unhindered involvement.

To incorporate comprehensive engagement strategies and planning, we first need to learn what motivates ourselves and our colleagues to work to full potential, to explore and capitalize on what propels all of us and makes everyone better. To that end, this book included aspects on how to better engage employees and mitigate discontent by responding to the most common reasons for disengagement. Pertinent take-aways are found in each chapter's closing paragraphs and accompanying appendixes and footnotes.

Engagement includes the initiative, and the choice, to tackle tough questions and telling observations. The questions posed throughout the book were provided to help objectively weigh personal well-being and your ability to affect engagement, both yours and others. Bridging the engagement gap means finding ways to assess and improve a psychological state (in you and your colleagues) embodied in positive, meaningful involvement, where potential is maximized and where pride of membership is demonstrated through initiative, purpose, energy, discretionary effort, and persistence. Realizing this state should be a continuing personal quest and institutional goal, woven into the cultural fabric of daily work.

While the mathematical steps can be a bit tricky, the engagement formula is not extraordinarily difficult to solve, nor expensive. These "x"-factor formulas are found in Chapter 2:

- **Maximizing Worker Realities and Potential = Unrealized Profits.**

- **Personal Productivity =**

  Meaningful, Progressively Appropriate Growth Tasks

  – Hidden Agendas

  ÷

  Manager's Relationship Building Responsibility
  (i.e., Employee Input

  + Valuing Talent

  + Right Expectations

  + Fair and Culturally Acceptable Recognition)

- **"Intimacy + Access = Trust"** (see Burke, Ch. 3).

At each workplace, anywhere in the process, beginning, middle or end, at any pivotal year within a career and in life, we can collectively brainstorm these formulas, perhaps synthesize and refine a more elegant formula to better meet our needs and purposes. Regardless, we know how to solve for x. We know the variables that positively affect engagement.

Sometimes, however, the person working the equation misses a step, forgets a sequence, or misassigns a value. How, for instance, do students typically fall out of mathematics? They chose not to do the homework, and when beset by a logical or formulaic quandary, they forsake logic, succumb to frustration, and choose not to review the formula nor rethink their work. Out of embarrassment (I cannot admit that I did not do my homework) or frustration (I have asked before and the teacher/manager just was not there for me), they do not ask for help. Some surrender.

To bridge engagement gaps each individual is required to rethink her or his place at work and how each of us models, inspires, challenges, enables, and encourages[7] or, conversely, adds to discontent, rejection, and disenfranchisement. Yes, work complications can be frustrating and defeating. We may feel undervalued and ignored while pivotal decision-making is taking place, especially when the processes being discussed involve us. We may feel stuck or betrayed. We may find ourselves agreeing to disagree more than we'd like. And, in fact, those red flags tell us much about dysfunctional or disengaged teams,... or about ourselves if we choose to remain in the company of worst practices.

Finding new pathways, arduously defending and seeking a culture of discovery, with the enduring support of others, may be the ultimate lifelong challenge and test of engagement, so we should continuously strive for the new inside and outside of our jobs, a deeper future, yet exercise gratitude of life in the present.

Economic and social conditions can impede our journey, and out of immediate necessity, our patience and perseverance may be our most useful assets.

But we must remember despite the obstacles encountered in the present, wherever we reside on the organizational chart or in the economic picture, we remain our own self-managers, our own contemporaneous co-leaders, regulating clear choices about the roles we perform and the others we serve among the company we keep. Too often, selfishness gets in the way of community. Personal agendas, power trips, and position can foul a mission and subvert values, vision, and culture, and hurt others. When our ultimate purpose is self-service, we defeat collective purpose. Sometimes we hold a double-standard by not offering each person the same standard nor courtesy to prove themselves.

Even in worst case scenarios, when we feel and know our talents are being squandered, taken advantage of, or we work for a terrible manager, if we are misplaced or do not feel appreciated, we must hone an awareness that the way we shape our actions and feelings either impede our spirits and also disrupt our engagement, or our awareness can carve a path to lift and stimulate others' sprits.

If our current assignments do not capitalize on a particular strength or gift, vocational expertise, or avocational joy,[3] if these aspects of our lives, work, or play are important to us, then, at whatever age and stage we reside within our work lives, we must in some way choose to spend discretionary effort in an attempt to defeat decay and overload as well as pursue improvement, foster collaboration, and accelerate growth. We can move toward excelling at our current work functions or move toward more personally satisfying ones. The key is to always seek to cultivate greater participation, learning, questioning, affirmation, and continuously seek answers.

"It's a Family Affair"[4]

What more do we need to consider to attend to engagement basics? Practically:

- **Where do we begin?**

- **Where do we pick up where we left off?**

- **What did we miss, and why did we miss it?**

The more complex question: despite all of the research, consultants, and information at our disposal, why have we not gained greater ground? Even if we have attended to necessary variables and experiences positive gains, are we in denial about or subconsciously or consciously avoiding other factors that inhibit growth? Do we deliberately blind ourselves to co-workers who work only two feet or an elevator ride away?

There is no perfect world. If world religions, governments, and educators have conflict within their own houses, we can breathe a sigh of relief that we serve within much smaller populations within our work groups. Neither are workplaces perfect. Some folks just cannot seem to get out of their own ways. And perhaps for this reason alone, a central value merely should be to cultivate others' and our own enjoyment at work.

Nonetheless, fostering engagement is hard work, so our responses to disengagement should be as much fun as possible. Moreover, at the end of the day, it's a family affair. Start and end with the pleasure that is derived from unconditional service to and love for others. Preserve appreciation, compassion, and lending hand in house, as a product of coming together, for instance, to host a fun, collaborative "Toys for Tots" campaign or canned food drive.

Each other of us is handed an opportunity to shape the community, the family, in which we reside. We should be asking, "How can I help?" We should be driving 30 miles at 3 a.m. to help Pat fix a flat tire.

Our membership is similar to how responsible parents assure their children, "You might not like what I have to say, you might not agree with my decision, but never, ever doubt that I have your best interests in my mind and heart."

And in some families, this is followed by a frantic search, "You know Uncle Sal is divorced from reality, right!? You know he gets confused and forgets where he is! Please tell me, you didn't leave him alone, outside?!"

Did you? The answer to this frantic search and plea, our capacity to corral wide-ranging engagement challenges, requires a methodology grounded in a moral and ethical practice: "Do all the good you can. By all the means you can. In all the ways you can. In all the places you can. At all the times you can. To all the people you can as long as ever you can."[5]

Chapter References and Tangents

Introduction

1   For a great illustration of the difference between authoritarian and transactional to self-less leaders conducting empowered workers, see Talgram, Itay. "Lead like the Great Conductors," *TED Conferences/LLC/TEDGlobal*, June 2009, http://www.ted.com/talks/itay_talgam_lead_like_the_great_conductors.

2   Michelle Burns, "How to Determine Employee Engagement ROI," *C. A. Short, Inc.* June 11, 2015, http://www.cashort.com/blog/determining-employee-engagement-roi.

3   To argue a case, access these lists of engagement statistics and indicators:

"Social Knowns: Employee Engagement Statistics (August 2011 Edition)," *The Social Worlkplace.com*, August 8, 2011, http://www.thesocialworkplace.com/2011/08/social-knows-employee-engagement-statistics-august-2011-edition;

Brandon Carter, "Employee Engagement and Loyalty Statistics: The Ultimate Collection," *Access Development.com* (blog), December 21, 2015, http://blog.accessdevelopment.com/index.php/2014/08/employee-engagement-loyalty-statistics-the-ultimate-collection;

Max Niesen, "These Charts Reveal the Secrets to Motivation," *Business Insider.com/Strategy*, March 29, 2013, http://www.businessinsider.com/charts-about-performance-and-motivation-2013-3?op=1.

4   Phil Wahba, "How Starbucks CEO Howard Schultz Says He Can Win in China," *Fortune.com,* January 12, 2016, http://fortune.com/2016/01/12/starbucks-china/.

5   Mortimer Adler, "How to Write a Book," originally in *The Saturday Review of Literature,* July 6, 1940, reproduced, *UNZ.org,* https://www.unz.org/Pub/SaturdayRev-1940jul06-00011.

Chapter 1 Work

Mary Field Belenky, et. al., Women's Ways of Knowing: The Development of Self, Voice, and Mind (New York: Basic Books/Perseus, 1997), 149.

1   Studs Terkel, *Working: People Talk about What They Do All Day and How They Feel about What They Do* (New York: MJF Books, 1974), "Introduction" xi; xxiv.

2   Daniel Pink, *Drive: The Surprising Truth about What Motivates Us (*New York: Penguin/Riverdale), 2009.

3   Sources of conclusions:

Michelle L. Buck, "Management Lessons from *Undercover Boss,*" *Business Week.com/Bloomberg Business/Kellogg School of Management,* March 23, 2010, http://www.businessweek.com/managing/content/mar2010/ca20100322_429067.htm#p1;

Coretta Jackson, "10 Reputation Lessons from the TV Show *Undercover Boss,*" *Trackur.com,* September 27, 20102, http://www.trackur.com/10-reputation-lessons-from-the-tv-show-undercover-boss;

David Kiger, "Top 4 Leadership Lessons from *Undercover Boss,*" *Buisness2community.com/Business and Finance Leadership,* February 23 2015, http://www.business2community.com/leadership/top-4-leadership-lessons-undercover-boss-01165684;

Meridith Levinson, "Leadership and Management Lessons from *Undercover Boss,*" *Cio.com/Careers/Staffing,* March 4, 2010, http://www.cio.com/article/2420026/careers-staffing/leadership-and-management-lessons-from--undercover-boss-.html;

Julie Rains, "7 Business Lessons from *Undercover Boss*," *Americanexpress.com / Open Forum*, July 2015, https://www.americanexpress.com/us/small-business/openforum/articles/7-business-lessons-from-undercover-boss/.

4   Quotes, respectively: Meridith Levinson. "Leadership and Management Lessons from *Undercover Boss*," *Cio.com/Careers/Staffing*, March 4, 2010, http://www.cio.com/article/2420026/careers-staffing/leadership-and-management-lessons-from--undercover-boss-.html;

Michelle L. Buck, "Management Lessons from *Undercover Boss*," *Business Week.com/Bloomberg Business/Kellogg School of Management*, March 23, 2010, http://www.businessweek.com/managing/content/mar2010/ca20100322_429067.htm#p1.

5   James Allen, *As You Think*, 1ˢᵗ Edited Version (Novelo, CA: New World Library, 1998), 23.

6   "9 Ways Senior Leaders Subconsciously Sabotage Innovation," *Center for Creative Leadership/Insights and Research*, 2016, http://media.ccl.org/wp-content/uploads/2016/02/Sabotage-Innovation-for-web.png#_ga=1.8490737.59416281.1424277971.

7   Steven King, *The Green Mile. Internet Archive. archive.org*, 2014, https://archive.org/stream/pdfy-Xznac6YLQRd-NyUo/Stephen%20King%20-%20Green%20Mile_djvu.txt, Chapter 10, 75.

8   Scott M. Peck, "Entropy and Original Sin," in *The Road Less Traveled (*New York: Touchstone/Simon & Schuster, 1978), 275.

9   Robert Snow, "Reviews of Classic Movies: 'Brazil,'" *Wordpress.com*, January 29, 2015, https://robertsnow.wordpress.com/2015/01/29/reviews-of-classic-movies-brazil/.

10 Jim Collins, "The Hedgehog Concept: Simplicity within the Three Circles," Ch. 9, and "From Good to Great to Built to Last," Ch. 5, *Good to Great* (New York: Harper Collins. 2001), 109/209.

See also: Heidi Grant Halvorson, "The Key to Choosing the Right Career," *Harvard Business Review*, April 8, 2013, https://hbr.org/2013/04/the-key-to-choosing-the-right.

Chapter 2 Engagement Redefined

Dottie Gandy, "The High Cost of Low Trust," Ch. 3, in *30 Days to a Happy Employee: How a Simple Program of Acknowledgement Can Build Trust and Loyalty at Work* (New York: Fireside/Simon & Schuster, 2001), 51.

1   Modern Survey, "The State of Employee Engagement – Spring 2015," *Modern Survey*, June 5, 2015, http://www.modernsurvey.com/resources/whitepapers.

2   William A. Kahn, "Psychological conditions of personal engagement and disengagement at work," *Academy of Management Journal* 33, no. 4 (1990): 692. See also: Andie Burjek, "Re-engaging with William Kahn 25 Years after He Coined Term Employee Engagement," December 14, 2015, *Workforce Magazine*, http://www.workforce.com/articles/21779-william-kahn-engagement.

3   Wilmar Schaufeli and Arnold Bakker, "UWES Utrecht Work Engagement Scale, Preliminary Manual, Version 1," *Occupational Health Psychology Unit/Utrecht University,* November 2003, http://www.beanmanaged.com/doc/pdf/arnoldbakker/articles/articles_arnold_bakker_87.pdf 4-5.

4   David Sirota, et. al., *The Enthusiastic Employee: How Companies Profit by Giving Workers What They Want* (Upper Saddle River, NJ: Pearson Educational, Inc., Prentice Hall, 2005), 25.

5   The definition is synthesized from these sources:

Joseph Dawsey and Edward Taylor, "Empirical Evidence of Engagement and Active Disengagement in an Organizational Setting," *Advances in Business Research*, 3, no. 1, (2012): http://journals.sfu.ca/abr/index.php/abr/article/viewFile/86/6067-71;

Hogan Associates, "Why Engagement Matters," *Hogan White Papers*, Hogan Assessment Systems, 2014, http://info. hoganassessments.com/whyengagement-matters;

Kevin Kruse, "What is Employee Engagement," *Kevin Kruse Newsletter*, November 22, 2012, http://www.kevinkruse.com/what-is-employee-engagement/;

Michael Schrage, "Engagement Is a Means, Not an End," *Harvard Business Review/Managing People*, February 22, 2016, https://hbr.org/2016/02/engagement-is-a-means-not-an-end.

5   Christina C. Maslach and Michael P. Leiter, *The Truth about Burnout: How Organizations Cause Personal Stress and What to Do about It* (San Francisco, CA: Jossey Bass, 1997), 23-38.

6   Towers Watson, "Engagement at Risk: Driving Strong Performance in a Volatile Global Environment, Global Workforce Study," *Towerswatson.com*, July 2012, http://employeeengagement.com/wp-content/uploads/2012/11/2012-TowersWatson-Global-Workforce-Study.pdf.

7   Lenny DeFranco, "The (New) Definition of Employee Engagement," *blog.grovo.com/Grovo*, November 17, 2015, http://blog.grovo.com/definition-employeeengagement/?utm_source=linkedIn&utm_medium=social&utm_campaign=SocialWarfare.

8   Daniel Pink, *Drive: The Surprising Truth about What Motivates Us* (Penguin/Riverdale, New York, NY, 2009).

9   David Larcher and Scott Saslow, "2014 Report on Senior Executive Succession Planning and Talent Development," *Stanford GSB Corporate Governance Research/Slideshare*, 2014, http://www.slideshare.net/StsanfordCorpGov/2014-report-on-seniorexecutive-succession-planning-and-talent-development.

10 "Median Employee Tenure Unchanged at 4.6 Years in January 2014," *The Economics Daily/Bureau of Labor Statistics*, September

25, 2014, http://www.bls.gov/opub/ted/2014/ted_20140925.htm; and
see the following: http://www.bls.gov/news.release/pdf/tenure.pdf;
and "Turnover," *Talx.com/Equifax,* 2016, http://www.talx.com/
benchmarks/turnover/index.asp.

11 See Richard Barrett, "What Motivates Employees? A New Look
at Employee Engagement and Culture Risk," *www.valuescerte.
com/Barrett Values Centre,* 2013, https://www.valuescentre.com/
sites/default/files/uploads/2013-08-05/What%20Motivates%20
Employees.pdf;

Hogan Associates, "Why Engagement Matters," *Hogan
White Papers/Hogan Assessment Systems,* 2014, http://info.
hoganassessments.com/whyengagement-matters;

Kevin Kruse offers this summary: "People give loyalty and
discretionary effort to those who foster growth, show appreciation,
share a compelling vision and are trustworthy," in "The One
Sentence Employee Engagement Course: 20 Words to Gain
Emotional Commitment." *Forbes.com/Leadership,* February
8, 2016, http://www.forbes.com/sites/kevinkruse/2016/02/08/
employee-engagement-course/?inf_contact_key=4349e3a
5b0c3807dedf5faaece65db8471e229274fcdd1a2a4b9716435f5f4f9
#4d410e3c1810. See also: Kevin Kruse, "Employee Engagement: The
Wonder Drug for Customer Satisfaction," *Forbes.com / Leadership*,
January 7, 2014, http://www.forbes.com/sites/kevinkruse/2014/01/07/
employee-engagement-the-wonder-drug-for-customer-satisfaction/.

12 For more research, see these historic figures: "…pro-growth/
pro-engagement behaviors are social (John Dewey and Maria
Montessori), involve mastery (Benjamin Bloom), construct meaning
(Jerome Bruner), require modeling (Robert Gagne), empathy (Carl
Rogers), purpose (Eric Erickson) and reflection (Socrates), the sum
of which affects culture, levels of satisfaction, or the fun we derive
from our toil (Lev Vygotsky)."

13   The Arbinger Institute, "People or Objects," in *Leadership and Self Deception*, (San Francisco, CA: Berrett-Koelhler Publishers, Inc., 2010), 42-50.

14   Josh Bersin, "New Research Unlocks the Secret of Employee Recognition," *Forbes.com/Leadership*, June 13, 2012, http://www.forbes.com/sites/joshbersin/2012/06/13/new-research-unlocks-the-secret-of-employee-recognition/.

Chapter 3 Active Values

Bertrand Russel, from *Unpopular Essays* (London/NewYork: Routledge Classic/Taylor & Francis Group, 1950/2009), 106. https://books.google.com/books?id=n-Zamjv7TkUC&pg=PA106&dq=Bertrand+Russell,+Unpopular+Essays,+Collective+Fear+stimulates&hl=en&sa=X&ved=0ahUKEwisybfuiuXPAhWCZCYKHfDXAqkQ6AEIITAA#v=onepage&q=Bertrand%20Russell%2C%20Unpopular%20Essays%2C%20Collective%20Fear%20stimulates&f=false

1   Marcus Aurelius, "Book III, 7," in *Meditations* (Mineola, New York: Dover Publications, 1997), 16.

2   David A. Garvin and Michael A. Roberto, "Change Through Persuasion in *On Change Management* (Boston, Massachusets: Harvard Business Review Press, 2011), 17/30.

2   Shunryu Suzuki *Zen Mind, Beginner's Mind: Informal Talks on Zen Meditation and Practice* (Weatherhill *New York, NY*, 34th Printing, 1995), http://terebess.hu/zen/mesterek/Suzuki-Zen-Mind.pdf.

3   Mihaly Csikszentmihalyi, "Flow, The Secret to Happiness," *www.ted.com/TED2004*, February 2004, http://www.ted.com/talks/mihaly_csikszentmihalyi_on_flow.

4   John Mackey and Raj Sisodia. "Capitalism: Marvelous, Misunderstood, Maligned" in *Conscious Capitalism* (Boston, MA: Harvard Business Review Press, 2014), 11.

5   Elizabeth W. Morrison, "Employee Voice and Silence," *Annual Review of Organizational Psychology and Organizational Behavior* 1, no. 2 (January, 2014): http://www.annualreviews.org/doi/full/10.1146/annurev-orgpsych-031413-091328.

6   Lewis Garrad, "Correcting the Grammar of Employee Engagement," *Human Capital Exchange, The Conference Board*, November 11 2015, https://hcexchange.conference-board.org/blog/post.cfm?post=5075.

7   Sydney Savion, "Culture: The Enemy at the Gate of Innovation" *Training Industry Magazine* 9, no. 2 (Spring 2015): http://www.nxtbook.com/nxtbooks/trainingindustry/tiq_2015spring/index.php?startid=45#/44.

8   Susan Fowler, "The Motivation Dilemma" in *Why Motivating People Doesn't Work...and What Does: The New Science of Leading, Energizing, and Engaging* (San Francisco: Berrett-Koehler, 1st ed., 2014), 16-17.

9   Ken Blanchard, "Not Making Progress on Your Employee Engagement Initiative? 3 Keys for "Moving the Needle," *www.kenblanchard.com,* (Blanchard Blogs), *The Ken Blanchard Companies*, 2014, http://www.kenblanchard.com/Leading-Research/IgniteNewsletter/September-2014?elq=e3a10a91605a4dc7b23b4a33c6b974ac&elqCampaignId.

10   Dan Harrison, "Engagement is a Shared Responsibility!" *Harrison Assessments/Lakewood Media Group*, 2016, http://whitepapers.lakewoodmediagroup.net/sites/default/files/EngagementisSharedResponsibility-Article%202016.pdf.

11   Brue Cameron, See Garson O'Toole, "Not Everything That Counts Can be Counted," *Quote Investigator.com*, September 5, 2011, http://quoteinvestigator.com/2010/05/26/everything-counts-einstein/.

Regarding metrics, collecting qualitative engagement data, and alternatives to "SMART" goals: Amit S. Mukherjee, "It's Time to

Do Away with SMART Goals, *Chief Executive Magazine*, March 4, 2016, http://chiefexecutive.net/its-time-to-do-away-with-smart-goals/; among others: Scott Christ, "When SMART Goals Don't Work, Here's What to Do Instead, Entrepreneur, April 17, 2014, http://www.entrepreneur.com/article/232909; Peter Economy, "Forget SMART Goals – Try CLEAR Goals Instead," *Inc.*, January 3, 2015, http://www.inc.com/peter-economy/forget-smart-goals-try-clear-goals-instead.html.; Mark Murphy, "Are SMART Goals Dumb?" *Leadership IQ.* June 22, 2015, http://www.leadershipiq.com/blogs/leadershipiq/35353793-are-smart-goals-dumb.

12 Benoit Hardy-Vallee, "A Successful Engagement Program: 10 Lessons from World-Class Organizations," *IBM/Kenexa Canada*, 2014, https://www-950.ibm.com/events/wwe/grp/grp101.nsf/vLookupPDFs/A%20successful%20engagement%20program%20TO%20SHARE/$file/A%20successful%20engagement%20program%20TO%20SHARE.pdf.

13 David Lee, "Why Your Employee Engagement Efforts Are Not Producing Results," *Human Capital Institute Management & Leadership Community* (Blog), September 14, 2015, http://www.hci.org/blog/why-your-employee-engagement-efforts-are-not-producing-results?utm_campaign=TOFU1%3A%20Employee%20Engagement&utm_content=20950685&utm_medium=social&utm_source=twitter#.Vfc5nZjGr_A.twitter.

14 "A Ten-Step Guide to Working More Human: Lessons Learned from WorkHuman 2015," *Globoforce*, http://go.globoforce.com/rs/862-JIQ-698/images/WorkHumanWhitepaper.pdf.

15 "Trends in Employee Recognition," *WorldatWork/ITA Group*, May 2015, https://www.worldatwork.org/adimLink?id=78679.

16 Dawn Burke, contributor at Fistful of Talent," The HR Gateway Drug = Candidate Experience," *Fistful of Talent*, November 10, 2015, http://fistfuloftalent.com/2015/11/the-hr-gateway-drug-candidate-exerience.html?utm_source=

feedburner&utm_medium=email&utm_campaign=Feed%
3A+FistfulOfTalent+%28Fistful+of+Talent%29.

17   Marcus Buckingham and Curt Coffman, "The Fourth Key Find the
     Right Fit: Three Stories and a New Career," Ch. 6, in *First, Break
     All the Rules* (New York: Simon & Schuster, 1999), 201.

18   See Nick Scheidies, "11 Life-Changing Business Lessons from
     Zig Ziglar," *incomediary.com,* (undated), http://www.incomediary.
     com/zig-ziglar-life-changingbusiness-lessons.

19   James M. Kouzes and Barry Z. Posner. "The Five Practices of
     Exemplary Leadership" in *The Leadership Challenge* (San
     Francisco: John Wiley & Sons, 4th ed. 2007. 14-6. Print.

20   Ted Bauer, "Employee Engagement Ideas: Cut the BS,"
     ThecontextofThings.com, (May 2, 2016), http://thecontextofthings.
     com/2016/05/02/employee-engagement-ideas/.

Chapter 4 Disengagement and The Walking Dead

George A. Romero, "George A. Romero: 'Who Says Zombies Eat
Brains?" VF Hollywood, May 27, 2011, http://www.vanityfair.com/
hollywood/2010/05/george-romero.

1   See "Engagement Defined," Chapter 2, footnote 22.

2   Gallup, *State of the American Workplace.* (Annual), http://www.
     gallup.com/services/178514/state-american-workplace.aspx. Of
     course, this number fluctuates, depending on the study, but based on
     the inclusiveness and randomness of the research, Gallup's number
     is probably the most representative. In 2014, "Igniting Workplace
     Enthusiasm, How to Create Engaged Employees," Dale Carnegie
     Training, http://www.icajapan.jp/wp-content/uploads/2013/07/ICA-
     2013-7-24-How-To-Create-Engaged-Employees.pdf, comparative
     2009 numbers, cumulative "not engaged" and "actively disengaged,"
     includes Blessing White reporting 69%, Towers Watson at 79%,
     and Dale Carnegie at 71%. Furthermore, The *Insurance Journal*

cites a study conducted by Proudfoot Consulting asserted that 29% of all employees are unproductive: http://smallbusiness.chron.com/effects-unproductive-workplace-10881.htm.

3   Josh Bersin, "Culture: Why It's The Hottest Topic in Business Today," *Forbes.com/Leadership*, March 13, 2015, http://www.forbes.com/sites/joshbersin/2015/03/13/culture-why-its-the-hottest-topic-in-business-today/. See also the introductory material offered by this vendor: "Winning Culture," *New West Institute,* 2008, http://www.newwestinstitute.com/winning_culture.html#cm.

4   Edward Hall, "The Paradox of Culture" in *Beyond Culture* (New York: Anchor Random House, 1ˢᵗ ed. Vol. 1, 1976), 9.

5   Enrique (Henry) Trueba, "The Social and Cultural Contest of Life in the Valley" in *Latinos Unido: From Cultural Diversity to the Politics of Solidarity* (Oxford, England: Rowan & Littlefield Group, 1ˢᵗ ed., 1999), 154.

6   Mark J. Cotteleer and Timothy Murphy, "Ignoring Bad News: How Behavioral Factors Influence or Avoid Negative Messages," *Deloitte Development LLC/Deloitte University Press*. 2015, http://d27n205l7rookf.cloudfront.net/wp-content/uploads/2015/08/DUP_1214_IgnoringBadNews.pdf.

7   Maria-Paz Barrientos, et al., "Amplifying Employee Voice: How Organizations Can Better Connect to the Pulse of the Workforce," *IBM Institute for Business Value and IBM Smarter Workforce Institute*, October 2015, http://public.dhe.ibm.com/common/ssi/ecm/gb/en/gbe03697usen/GBE03697USEN.PDF

James Detert and Ethan R. Burris, "Can Your Employees Really Speak Freely?" *Harvard Business Review.com/Communication*, January 2016, https://hbr.org/2016/01/can-your-employees-really-speak-freely?utm_source=newsletter&utm_medium=email&utm_content=Can%20Your%20Employees%20Really%20Speak%20Freely%3F&utm_campaign=HR_NB_100715

8   See footnote 2, *Gallup*, 13. Percentages for pie chart graphic: Amy Adkins, "U.S; Employee Engagement Reaches New High in March," *www.gallup.com*, April 13, 2016, http://www.gallup.com/poll/190622/ employee-engagement-reaches-new-high-march.aspx?g_source= EMPLOYEE_ENGAGEMENT&g_medium=topic&g_ campaign=tiles.

9   Lauren   Parkhill,   "A   Controversial   Look   at   Employee Engagement   [Infographic],"   *Sonomaleadership.com*, February   11,   2016,   https://www.sonomaleadership.com/ blog/a-controversial-look-at-employee-engagement-infograph ic?utm_campaign=Blog+Subscriptions+Campain&utm_source= hs_email&utm_medium=email&utm_content=26162579&_ hsenc=p2ANqtz-8pkss-XyfVeMcCKnaI4_4HzNC9YjVcVNGVH ngWBpUwm7ltVWRRTrgQVcSEC7GokuPjgoM7oWbI0n3F8gUj RwmXy8FJJg&_hsmi=26162579

Infographic: Jeff Fermin, "Personality Trains of a Disengaged Employee," *Officevibe* (Blog), May 26, 2014, https://www. officevibe.com/blog/infographic-disengaged-employees.

10 Yuri Noguchi, "Behold the Entrenched – and Reviled – Annual Review." *NPR/Morning Edition*, October 28, 2014, http://www. npr.org/2014/10/28/358636126/behold-the-entrenched-and-reviled-annual-review.

11 Janice Min, "The Hollywood Reporter to End Rankings for Women in Entertainment Power 100," *The Hollywood Reporter*, November 11, 2015, http://www.hollywoodreporter.com/features/ hollywood-reporter-end-rankings-women-839046.

12 See Michael Zigarelli, "Ten Leadership Theories in Five Minutes," *YouTube,* August 17, 2013, https://www.youtube.com/ watch?v=XKUPDUDOBVo.

13 Jim Collins, "First Who… Then What," Ch. 3, in *Good to Great: Why Some Companies Make the Leap... and Other's Don't (*New York: Harper Collins, 1st ed., 2001), 44.

14　Doris Kearns Goodwin, "Introduction" and "I Am Now Public Property" in *Team of Rivals: The Political Genius of Abraham Lincoln* (New York: Simon & Schuster Paperbacks, 2005), xvii/319, respectively.

15　Claudio Feser, Fernanda Maol, and Ramesh Srinivasan, et. al, "Decoding Leadership: What Really Matters," *McKinsey Quarterly*, January 2015, http://www.mckinsey.com/global-themes/leadership/decoding-leadership-what-really-matters?cid=other-eml-ttn-mip-mck-oth-1604.

16　Profiles International, "The Ultimate Guide to Employee Engagement," *Profiles International*, 2015, http://info.profilesinternational.com/eBook-The-Ultimate-Guide-to-Employee-Engagement.

17　The holistic aspect of self-improvement is discussed in Habit 7 of Steven Covey's *The Seven Habits of Highly Effective People.*

18　Everett M. Rogers, "The Four Main Elements in the Diffusion of Innovation" in *Diffusions of Innovation* (New York: Free/Simon & Schuster, 5th ed., 2003), 11.

19　Viktor E. Frankl, "Experiences in a Concentration Camp," Part 1, in *Man's Search for Meaning* (Boston: Beacon Press, 2006), 65;

　　Hellen Keller, *The Story of My Life* (Boston: Houghton Mifflin Company/The Riverside Press Cambridge, 1905), 99.

20　Alvin Toffler, *Future Shock* (Random House: New York, 1st ed., 1970).

21　Chris Argyris, "Introduction" in *Organizational Traps: Leadership, Culture, and Organizational Design* (New York: Oxford University, 2012), 2. See also the summary of Aryris's findings regarding leadership failures "to avoid discrepancies between principles espoused and courses of action advised," as summarized in "Chris Argyris (1923-2013): An Appreciation," *Thinkers 50,* http://thinkers50.com/blog/chris-argyris-1923-2013-appreciation/.

22 Malcom Gladwell, "The 10,000-Hour Rule" Ch. 2, in *Outliers: The Story of Success* (New York: Back Bay Books/Little Brown, 2008), 40.

23 Recounted by numerous HR authors, for instance: John Nemo, "What a NASA Janitor Can Teach Us about Living a Bigger Life," *The Business Journals*, December 23, 2014, http://www.bizjournals. com/bizjournals/how-to/growth-strategies/2014/12/what-a-nasa-janitor-can-teach-us.html?page=all;

   Jackque Vilet, "Company Goals: Do Your Employees Have a 'Line of Sight' to Them?" *Eremedia.com/TLNT*, June 7, 2012, http://www.eremedia.com/tlnt/company-goals-do-your-employees-have-a-line-of-sight-to-them/;

   Benjamin Dyer, "Are You Aiming for the Moon?" *businesszone.co.uk*, October 29, 2009, http://www.businesszone.co.uk/community-voice/blogs/benjamindyer/are-you-aiming-for-the-moon.

24 Explore the allegory more, the inflexibility of monarchs, and the usefulness of models, in the Henry James short story "The Real Thing."

25 Peter W. Hart and David Zinger, *People Artistry at Work: The Ennoblement Imperative* and *People Artists: Drawing Out the Best in Others at Work* (Canada: Rideau Recognition, Inc.), 2015.

26 Employment New Zealand, *employment.gov.nz/Ministry of Business, Innovation & Employment, http://employment.govt.nz/er/bestpractice/worklife/casestudies/index.asp.*

27 Josh Bersin, "New Research Unlocks the Secret of Employee Recognition," *Forbes Leadership*, June 13, 2012, http://www.forbes.com/sites/joshbersin/2012/06/13/new-research-unlocks-the-secret-of-employee-recognition/.

28 See this animated translation of Pink's findings in *Drive*: "The Surprising Science of Motivation: An Illustrated Guide to How

Motivation Really Works," *BKVideos, RSAnimate*, August 2014, http://bkvids.blogspot.com/2014/08/the-surprising-science-of-motivation.html; see also Daniel Pink, *Drive: The Surprising Truth about What Motivates Us* (New York: Penguin/Riverdale), 2009.

29 Roy Saunderson, "Top 10 Differences between Rewards and Recognition," *www.incentivemag.com*, November 3, 2013, http://www.incentivemag.com/Strategy/Ask-the-Experts/Roy-Saunderson/Top-10-Differences-Between-Rewards-and-Recognition/.

30 Meghan M. Biro, "5 Ways Leaders Rock Employee Recognition," *Forbes Leadership*, January 13, 2013, http://www.forbes.com/sites/meghanbiro/2013/01/13/5-ways-leaders-rock-employee-recognition/.

31 Christine M. Riordan, "We All Need Friends at Work," *Harvard Business Review*, July 3, 2013, https://hbr.org/2013/07/we-all-need-friends-at-work/.

32 Charlotte Fritz, et al., "It's the Little Things That Matter: An Examination of Knowledge Workers' Energy Management," *Ross Center for Positive Organizations/School of Business/University of Michigan*, 2011, http://positiveorgs.bus.umich.edu/wp-content/uploads/ItsTheLittleThingsThatMatter.pdf.

33 Thad Peterson, "You Either Lead by Example or You Don't Lead at All," *Globoforce*, October 8, 2013, http://www.globoforce.com/gfblog/2013/you-either-lead-by-example-or-you-dont-lead-at-all/.

34 Darcy Jacobsen, "The Power of Workplace Gratitude: A Brief Bibliography," *Globoforce*, November 21, 2013, http://www.globoforce.com/gfblog/2013/the-power-of-workplace-gratitude-a-brief-bibliography/.

35 See Cary Cherniss, "The Business Case for Emotional Intelligence," *Consortium for Research on Emotional Intelligence Organizations*, 1999, http://www.eiconsortium.org/reports/

business_case_for_ei.html. See also: "About Emotional Intelligence: What Everyone Needs to Know," *wwwtalentsamrt. com*, (undated), http://www.talentsmart.com/about/emotional-intelligence.php; and Meridith Levinson, "Are You the Strong, Sensitive Type, *CIO Magazine* 16, no. 10 (March 1, 2003): https://books.google.com/books?id=hw0AAAAAMBAJ&pg=RA2-PA81&lpg=RA2-PA81&dq=EI+is+notably+a+strong+indicat or+of+overall+success&source=bl&ots=W7rSIFRk9U&sig= MaDWe3FS4B4Ttnko7nkeLke8va8&hl=en&sa=X&ved=0ah UKEwjct_-GwebLAhXD7SYKHYCfCFsQ6AEIHDAA#v= onepage&q=EI%20is%20notably%20a%20strong%20 indicator%20of%20overall%20success&f=false, 78.

Also, apart from emotional intelligence, current research suggests that appealing to unrelated learning styles does not improve learning outcomes, see Harold Pashler, et al., "Learning Styles: Concepts and Evidence, *Journal of the Association of Psychosocial Science/Sage Journals* 9, no. 3 (December 2008): http://psi. sagepub.com/content/9/3/105.abstract. While Garner is often erroneously cited as a supporter of learning styles, he weighs in: Valerie Struass, *The Washington Post*, "Howard Gardner: 'Multiple Intelligences' Are Not 'Learning Styles.'" October 16, 2013, https://www.washingtonpost.com/news/answer-sheet/wp/2013/10/16/howard-gardner-multiple-intelligences-are-not-learning-styles/.

Take one of the free tests (see also *Psychology Today* website for a variety of tests): or TalentSmart, "Take the Test." Emotional Intelligence 2.0" *TalentSmart Inc.* 2015. Web. <http://www.talentsmart.com/test/>, or take the test in Levinson's article, above, but be careful, while we have learning preferences, there is not causal effect attributed to appealing to learning styles.

36 Warren Bennis, "Understanding the Basics," Ch. 2, *On Becoming a Leader* (Philadelphia, PA: Basic Books, 20th Anniversary Edition, 2009), 41.

Chapter 5 Derailed

Paulo Coelho, The Alchemist (New York: Harper One/Harper Collins, 1998), 16/22.

1   Jim Collins, "Level 5 Leadership," Ch. 2, in *Good to Great: Why Some Companies Make the Leap... and Other's Don't* (New York: Harper Collins, 1st ed., 2001), 39.

2   Jeffrey Sugerman, et. al., "The 8 Dimensions of Leadership, Ch. 1, in *The 8 Dimensions of Leadership: DiSC Strategies for Becoming a Better Leader* (San Francisco: Berrett-Koehler, Pub. Inc./Inscape, 2001), 7.

3   Nancy L. Maldonado and Candace H. Lacey, "Defining Moral Leadership: Perspectives of 12 Leaders," *Florida Journal of Educational Research* 41, no. 1 (2001): http://www.coedu.usf.edu/fjer/2001/FJERV41P7900. pdf, 79-101; see also, Center for Creative Leadership, "What's Your Leadership Culture?" *Leading Effectively E-Newsletter*, November 2014, http://www.ccl.org/leadership/enewsletter/2014/NOVwhat.aspx? utm_source=SilverpopMailing&utm_medium=email&utm_ campaign=Leading%20Effectively%20-%20November%202014%20 (1).

4   Alfred Lansing, *Endurance: Shackleton's Incredible Voyage,* Part VI, Ch. 4, (New York: Basic Books/Perseus, 2007), 236.

As identified by Modern Survey, "Dealing with Prisoners in the Workplace," *www.modernsurvey.com*, 2015, http://www. modernsurvey.com/wp-content/uploads/2015/03/Dealing-with-Prisoners-in-the-Workplace.pdf. Or turn to slightly later in in the century and what might seem to us utterly barbaric. We can compare 20th and 21st century "prisoner" workers, Upton Sinclair's *The Jungle* (excerpt below) to today's "comfortable, preoccupied, and overpaid prisoners":

"There were the men in the pickle rooms, for instance, where old Antanas had gotten his death; scarce a one of these that had not some spot of horror on his person. Let a man so much as scrape his finger pushing a truck in the pickle rooms, and he might have a sore that would put him out of the world; all of the joints in his fingers might be eaten by the acid, one by one…. The hands of these men would be crisscrossed with cuts, until you could no longer pretend to count them or trace them…. There were men who worked in the cooking rooms, in the midst of steam and sickening odors, by artificial light; in these rooms the germs of tuberculosis might live for two years (p. 101). And yet there were things even worse. You would begin talking to some poor devil who had worked in one shop for the last thirty years, and had never been able to save a penny; who left home every morning at six o'clock, to go that tend a machine, and come back at night too tired to take his clothes off; who had never had a week's vacation in his life, had never travelled, never had an adventure, never learned anything, never hoped anything…." (Upton Sinclair, *The Jungle*, Ch. 9 & 30, New York: New American Library of World Literature, Signet. 1960, 101/320).

5   Angeles Arrien, "Lessons from Geese." Speech at the Organizations Development Network, http://suewidemark.com/lessonsgeese.htm, 191. (Note: Based on the work of Milton Olson, original authorship has been attributed to Robert McNeish).

6   Ariana Eunjung Cha, "Beware the Rule-Following Co-Worker, Harvard Study Warns, *The Washington Post*, December 15, 2015, https://www.washingtonpost.com/news/to-your-health/wp/2015/12/15/beware-the-rule-following-co-worker-harvard-study-warns/?tid=sm_fb&utm_source=newsletter&utm_medium=email&utm_content=Watch%20Out%20for%20the%20Rule-Follower&utm_campaign=HR_NB_121815.

7   Victor Ottati, "When Self-Perceptions of Expertise Increase Closed-Minded Cognition: The Earned Dogmatism Effect," *www.sciencedirect.com/Journal of Experimental Social Psychology*, June 30, 2015, http://www.sciencedirect.com/science/article/pii/S0022103115001006.

8   Justin Barrett, "The Science of Intellectual Humility" (Abstract), *www.thethrivecenter.org*, June 20, 2015, http://thethrivecenter.org/ research/research-projects/the-science-of-intellectual-humility/.

9   Jim Collins. "First Who... Then What," Ch. 3, in *Good to Great: Why Some Companies Make the Leap... and Other's Don't (*New York: Harper Collins, 1st ed., 2001), 60.

10 Educator bell hooks speaks about "the will to share the desire to encourage excitement, was to transgress ("Introduction," 7). "It is the absence of a feeling of safety that often promotes prolonged silence or lack of engagement." bell hooks, "Embracing Change," in *Teaching to Transgress: Education as the Practice of Freedom* (New York: Routledge, 1994), 39.

11 The Arbinger Institute, "Part 1: The Heart of Peace" in *The Anatomy of Peace: Resolving the Heart of Conflict* (Oakland: Berrett-Koehler, Expanded 2nd. ed., 2015), 34-54.

12 Melany Gallant, "Employee Engagement Is Not a Racket," *TalentSpace*, www.halogensoftware.com (Blog), October 10, 2012, http://www.halogensoftware.com/blog/ employee-engagement-is-not-a-racket.

13 Center for Creative Leadership, "What's Your Leadership Culture?" *Insights.cc.org*, 2015, http://insights.ccl.org/articles/ leading-effectively-article/whats-your-leadership-culture/? utm_source=SilverpopMailing&utm_medium=email& utm_campaign=Leading%20Effectively%20-%20November%20 2014%20(1).

14 Informal Networks, Ltd., "Making Employee Engagement Natural," *YouTube*, September 21, 2015, https://www.youtube.com/watch?v=- GuIyTeZvG8>. See also, Cameron Anderson and Courtney E. Brown's research, "The Functions and Dysfunctions of Hierarchy," *Research in Organizational Behavior* 30 (December 2010). For the research abstract, go to Science Direct, http://www.sciencedirect. com/science/article/pii/S0191308510000031.

15   Bourree Lam, "Why Are So Many Zappos Employees Leaving?" *TheAtlantic.com*, January 15, 2016, http://www.theatlantic.com/ business/archive/2016/01/zappos-holacracy-hierarchy/424173 /?utm_source=newsletter&utm_medium=email&utm_content= Read%20More&utm_campaign=HR_NB_100715.

16   Wikipedia offers a useful description of Skinner's *Walden Two*, or see Deborah E. Althus and Edward K Morris, *www.ncbi.nlm. nih.gov,* "B.F. Skinner's Utopian Vision: Behind and Beyond Walden Two," *National Center for Biotechnology Information/U.S. National Library of Medicine/Association for Behavioral Analysis International* 32, no. 2 (Fall 2009): http://www.ncbi.nlm.nih.gov/ pmc/articles/PMC2778813/.

17   James M. Kouzes and Barry Z. Posner. "Leadership is Everyone's Business," Part 6, "Encourage the Heart," "Recognize Contributions" Ch. 11, and "Celebrate the Values and Victories" Ch.12, in *The Leadership Challenge* (San Francisco: John Wiley & Sons, 4th ed., 2007), 279-333.

18   John Wooden, Comp. Steve Jamison, "Introduction, The Secret of Success" in *Wooden on Leadership* (New York: McGraw-Hill, 1st ed., 2005), 6-8.

19   Steven R. Covey, "Express Your Voice – Vision, Discipline, Passion, and Conscience," Ch. 5, in *The 8th Habit: From Effectiveness to Greatness,*" (New York: Free Press, 2004), 62.

Chapter 6 At What Price Engagement?

Jessie J., "Price Tag," by Claude Kelly, Bobby Ray Simmons, Lukasz Gottwald, and Jessica Cornish, on *Who Are You*, Sony/ATV Music Publishing LLC., Warner/Chappell Music, Inc., Universal Music Publishing Group, produced by Jessie J. Dr. Luke, 2015, compact disc.

1   From various sources: Barb Sanford, "The High Cost of Disengaged Employees: A Q&A with Curt Coffman," *Gallup Business Journal,*

April 15, 2002, http://www.gallup.com/businessjournal/247/high-cost-disengaged-employees.aspx;

James O'Brien, "How Much Disengaged Employees Really Cost You," *American express.com* (Open Forum), October 22, 2013, https://www.americanexpress.com/us/small-business/openforum/articles/how-much-disengaged-employees-really-cost-you/;

Ariana Ayu, "The Enormous Cost of Unhappy Employees," *Inc. com/People*, August 27, 2014, http://www.inc.com/ariana-ayu/the-enormous-cost-of-unhappy-employees.html;

Resse Haydon, "Show Me the Money: The ROI of Employee Engagement," *Decision-wise.com*, (undated), https://www.decision-wise.com/show-me-the-money-the-roi-of-employee-engagement/;

Jennifer Giholl, "The Real Cost of Employee Disengagement," *Linkedin.com/Pulse*, 2015, https://www.linkedin.com/pulse/real-cost-employee-disengagement-jennifer-gilhool;

Alyss Retallick, "The Cost of a Disengaged Employee," *Glassdoor. com/for Employers*, May 25, 2015, https://www.glassdoor.com/employers/blog/the-cost-of-a-disengaged-employee/.

2   Jordan Weissmann, "This Study of Happiness Convinced a CEO to Pay All of His Employees at Least $70,000 a year," *Slate.com*, April 14, 2015, http://www.slate.com/blogs/moneybox/2015/04/14/money_and_happiness_when_does_an_extra_dollar_stop_making_us_more_content.html>. See also, Paul Keegan, "Here's What Really Happened at That Company That Set a $70,000 Minimum Wage," *Inc.com*, 2015, http://www.inc.com/magazine/201511/paul-keegan/does-more-pay-mean-more-growth.html.

3   Also a key premise in Arianna Huffington's book, *Thrive*: money is not nearly as important as well-being. Shankar Vendantam, "There's More to Wage Cuts than Just Lost Pay," *Hidden Brain/www.NPR.*

org, November 20, 2015, http://www.npr.org/2015/11/18/456459455/there-s-more-meaning-behind-wage-cuts-than-lost-pay.

4   (Unidentified author), "Randstad US Survey Reveals More Employees Leave Jobs for Career Growth Than Money," *www.prnewswire.com/randstadusa*, June 24, 2015, http://www.prnewswire.com/news-releases/randstad-us-survey-reveals-more-employees-leave-jobs-for-career-growth-than-money-300103779.html.

5   (Unidentified author), "Dealing with Prisoners in the Workplace," *Modernsurvey.com/resources/whitepapers. Modern Survey*, 2015, http://www.modernsurvey.com/wp-content/uploads/2015/03/Dealing-with-Prisoners-in-the-Workplace.pdf. Modern Survey: Workers who "feel they have been at their jobs long enough and deserve the pay they have without earning it." Problems outside of work influence their work behaviors and productivity: "Employees may be interested in leaving, but they've done the research and have found that you are paying in the open market," 8.

6   Jeffrey Jolton, et al., "2015 Employee Engagement Landscape Study: Championing Greatness or Capturing Mediocrity," *www.pwc.com,* November 2015, http://www.pwc.com/us/en/hr-management/publications/assets/pwc-hrs-employee-engagement-landscape-2015.pdf.

7   "Escape to Comptopia: 2016 Compensation Best Practices Report," *payscale.com*, http://www.payscale.com/cbpr, 17-18.

8   Josh Bersin, "New Research Unlocks the Secret of Employee Recognition," *www.Forbes.com,   Forbes/Leadership/Forbes LLC*, June 13, 2012, http://www.forbes.com/sites/joshbersin/2012/06/13/new-research-unlocks-the-secret-ofemployee-recognition/.

Tomas Charmorro-Premuzic, "If Money Can Buy Engagement, Should Happy Employees Earn Less?" *Forbes.com/Leadership*, August 8, 2014, http://www.forbes.com/sites/

tomaspremuzic/2014/08/08/if-money-can-buy-engagement-should-happy-employees-earn-less/;

Juliana Schroeder and Ayelet Fishbach, "How to Motivate Yourself and Others: Intended and Unintended Consequences," *Research in Organizational Behavior*, 2015, http://faculty.haas.berkeley.edu/jschroeder/Publications/ROB%20paper.pdf;

And very good commentary from Nicolai Andersen, et. al., "Nothing for Money: A Behavioral Perspective on Innovation and Motivation," *Deloitte University Press/Deloitte Review* 18 (January 25, 2016): http://dupress.com/articles/cultivating-innovation-at-work/?id=us%3a2em%3a3na%3adup2886%3aawa%3adup%3a021616&elqTrackId=cdeb50908bd74b01bd494b11a608eb87&elq=a03a34db981c4c388be638133e502076&elqaid=15465&elqat=1&elqCampaignId=4730.

9   Dina Gerdeman, "How to Demotivate Your Best Employees," *Harvard Business School Working Knowledge Baker Library/Bloomberg Center*, April 8, 2013, http://hbswk.hbs.edu/item/6946.html.

10   Tony Schwartz, "The Human Era @ Work: Findings from the Energy Project and Harvard Business Review," 2014, *The Energy Project*, http://documents.kenyon.edu/humanresources/Whitepaper_Human_Era_at_Work.pdf.

11   Malcom Gladwell, "The Three Lessons from Joe Flom," Ch. 5, in *Outliers: The Story of Success* (New York: Back Bay Books/Little Brown, 2008), 149-150.

12   Kathleen D. Vohs, "Money Priming Can Change People's Thoughts, Feelings, Motivations, and Behaviors: An Update on 10 Years of Experiments," *Journal of Experimental Psychology* 1 (2015): find in "General" at https://carlsonschool.umn.edu/faculty/kathleen-vohs.

13   Profiles International, "The Ultimate Guide to Employee Engagement," *Research Library. Profiles International*, 2015,

http://info.profilesinternational.com/Portals/63683/docs/Ultimate Guide to Employee Engagement eBook.pdf.

14 Andre Lavoie, "8 Goal-Oriented Steps to a More Engaged Workforce," *HRMorning.com*, September 17, 2014, http://www.hrmorning. com/8-goal-oriented-steps-to-a-more-engaged-workforce/.

15 See Achievers, "Engaging Gen X and Gen Y Employees: Three Significant Trends in Recognition," *www.achievers.com/Achievers/ Inc*, 2011, http://www.achievers.com/sites/default/files/Achievers - Whitepaper - Engaging Gen X and Gen Y Employees.pdf.

16 Suzanne McGee, "Bernie Sanders Has a Problem: Sometimes Greed is Good," *The Gaurdain.com/us-nes/us-money,* January 7, 2016, http://www.theguardian.com/us-news/us-money-blog/2016/ jan/07/bernie-sanders-greed.

17 A) ˉKenexa engagement metrics study across 40 countries, reported in Jeffrey A. Jolton, "A Candid Look at Employee Engagement: Five Global Truths," *IBM Software Group*, 2014, http://www-01.ibm.com/common/ssi/cgi-bin/ssialias? infotype=SA&subtype=WH&htmlfid=LOW14061USEN, 8.

B) Gallup 263 meta-research of 192 organizations (across 49 industries, 34 countries), reported in James K. Harter, et. al., "The Relationship between Engagement at Work and Organizational Outcomes, 2012 Q12® Meta-Analysis." *Gallup*, 2013, http://www. gallup.com/services/177047/q12-meta-analysis.aspx, 8-9.

C) Conference Board summary of twelve studies by various entities, reported in Patricia Soldati, "Employee Engagement: What Exactly Is It?" March 8, 2007, *Management-Issues. com*, http://www.management-issues.com/opinion/4008/ employee-engagement--what-exactly-is-it/.

D) Ken Blanchard Companies conclusions, reported in David Witt, "The Big Problem with Employee Engagement," *Blanchard International*, November 17, 2014, http://www.

blanchardinternational.co.in/wordpress/problem-with-employee-engagement/. See also: http://www.blanchardinternational.co.in/blog/problem-with-employee-engagement/.

E) Organizational Intelligence Institute survey of perceptions by 159 leaders, representing 29 industries reported in Salvatore Falletta, "The Hidden Drivers of Leader Engagement, Part1," *www. oi-institute.com/Skyline Group*, 2015, http://employeeengagement. com/wp-content/uploads/2015/03/Leader-Engagement-Drivers-Final.pdf.

F) Modern Survey's survey of 2,004 respondents, reported in Don MacPherson, "Creating a Culture of Employee Engagement" webinar. *Modern Survey*, January 2016. See also: "The State of Employee Engagement," Fall 2015, http://www.modernsurvey.com/blog.

G) Keith Branham reported in Stephen Bruce, "Engagement Suddenly a Priority? 6 Universal Drivers," *HR Daily Advisor*, July 8, 2013, http://hrdailyadvisor.blr.com/2013/06/30/engagement-suddenly-a-priority-6-universal-drivers/.

H) Kevin Sheridan from "Building a Magnetic Culture® Presentation for Human Resource Executive®, November 13, 2014, http://www.hreonline.com/pdfs/Kevin%20Sheridan%20Webinar%20%20on%20Magnetic%20Culture.pdf, 18.

I) Kevin Kruse reported in Jennifer Miller, Book Review: "Employee Engagement Is for Everyone," *People-equaliton.com*, July 2013, http://people-equation.com/employee-engagement-is-for-everyone/.

18 See Jeffery Kudisch, "Career Coach: Building Your Personal Brand," *Washington Post.com/Capital Business*, November 9, 2014, https://www.washingtonpost.com/business/capitalbusiness/career-coach-building-your-personal-brand/2014/11/07/de71810c-645f-11e4-9fdc-d43b053ecb4d_story.html.

19 Quoted in Tony Schwartz, "Why Appreciation Matters So Much," *Harvard Business Review/hrb.org,* January 23, 2012, https://hbr.org/2012/01/why-appreciation-matters-so-mu.html.

20 Catey Hill, "These 100 Execs have More Retirement Savings than 40% of America Combined," Market Watch, October 31, 2015, http://www.marketwatch.com/story/these-100-execs-have-more-retirement-savings-than-40-of-america-combined-2015-10-28.

21 Jim Collins, "First Who... Then What: It's Who You Pay, Not How You Pay Them," Ch. 3., in *Good to Great: Why Some Companies Make the Leap... and Other's Don't* (New York: Harper Collins, 1st ed., 2001), 49.

Chapter 7 A Taxonomy of Engagement

Benjamin Bloom, John Thomas Hastings, and George F. Madaus, *Handbook on Formative and Summarize Evaluation of Student Learning* (New York: McGraw Hill, 1971), 52-53.

1   Richard Barrett, "The Barrett Model," *Barrett Values Centre,* (undated), https://www.valuescentre.com/mapping-values/barrett-model. Josh Bersin plays with an engagement transposition of Maslow's hierarchy in his article, "New Research Unlocks the Secret of Employee Recognition," *Forbes.com/Leadership,* June 13, 2012, http://www.forbes.com/sites/joshbersin/2012/06/13/new-research-unlocks-the-secret-of-employee-recognition/. Abhishek Seth also toys with the notion in "Maslow's Hierarchy of Corporate Needs," www.huffingtonpost.com, October 15, 2013, http://www.huffingtonpost.com/abhishek-seth/maslows-hierarchy-of-corp_b_3756841.html.

2   Business Case Studies/Kellogg's/Building a Better Workplace through Motivation, *Business Case Studies.co.uk,* (undated), http://businesscasestudies.co.uk/kelloggs/building-a-better-workplace-through-motivation/maslow.html#axzz46ZNPHLri.

3   Doug and Polly White, "Entrepreneurs Turn the Classis Theory of Maslow's Hierarchy of Needs on Its Head," *www.entrepreneur.com*, November 3, 2015, https://www.entrepreneur.com/article/252362.

4   Abdulrazzak Zamzon, "Equity Theory and Motivation (Case Study)," www.linkedin.com/Pulse, February 4, 2015, https://www.linkedin.com/pulse/equity-theory-motivation-case-study-abdulrazzak-zamzom; or ownership share case studies from the National Center for Employee Ownership, http://www.nceo.org/assets/ESOP-employee-ownership-case-studies/, or Project Equity, http://www.project-equity.org/case-studies-business-conversions/.

5   Drea Zigarmi, et al., "Employee Work Passion: What's Important in Creating a Motivating Work Environment and Whose Job Is It." *The Ken Blanchard Companies, Perspectives, Employee Work Passion* 4 (2001): http://www.kenblanchard.com/getattachment/Leading-Research/Research/Employee-Work-Passion-Volume-4/Blanchard_Employee_Passion_Vol_4-(1).pdf;

    Ken Blanchard and Scott Blanchard, "The Role Money Plays in Engaging Employees," *Fast Company.com*, April 15, 2011, http://www.fastcompany.com/1747509/role-money-plays-engaging-employees.

6   See Sheryl Sandberg with Nell Scovell, "Sit at the Table," Ch. 2, in *Lean In: Women, Work, and the Will to Lead* (New York: Alfred A. Knopf/Random House, 43rd printing, 2013), 27-38. See also: http://leanin.org/.

7   Drew Desilver, "5 Facts about Economic Inequality," *Pew Research Center*, January 7, 2014, http://www.pewresearch.org/fact-tank/2014/01/07/5-facts-about-economic-inequality/.

    As a purely capitalist argument, economist Richard Thaler argues, "Firms that act responsibly [fair] are going to have loyal customers over the long run." See also: James Guszcza, "The Importance of Misbehaving: A Conversation with Richard Thaler," *Deloitte University Press/Deloitte Review* 18 (January

25, 2016): http://dupress.com/articles/behavioral-economics-richard-thaler-interview/?id=us%3A2em%3A3na%3Adup2885%3Aawa%3Adup%3A021616&elqTrackId=1dd71319c9f542e49c3b7a61e5737c5d&elq=a03a34db981c4c388be638133e502076&elqaid=15465&elqat=1&elqCampaignId=4730.

8   See Chapter 3, "Disengagement and the *Walking Dead,*" footnote 2.

9   Annamarie Mann and Ryan Darby, "Should Managers Focus on Performance or Engagement?" *Gallup.com*, August 5, 2014, http://www.gallup.com/businessjournal/174197/managers-focus-performance-engagement.aspx.

10   Josh Bersin, "The Five Elements of a 'Simply Irresistible' Organization," *Deloitte.com*, April 1, 2014, http://hrtimesblog.com/2014/04/01/the-five-elements-of-a-simply-irresistible-organization/.

11   Amy Rees Anderson, "Good Employees Make Mistakes. Great Leaders Allow Them To," *Forbes.com/Forbes Entrepreneurs*, April 17, 2013, http://www.forbes.com/sites/amyanderson/2013/04/17/good-employees-make-mistakes-great-leaders-allow-them-to/.

12   Daniel Pink, *Drive: The Surprising Truth about What Motivates Us* (New York: Penguin/Riverdale 2009). See also Chapter 5, footnote 12 (Gladwell).

13   Katherine Brooks, "Finding the Meaning in Your Work," *Psychology Today.com*, February 25, 2014, https://www.psychologytoday.com/blog/career-transitions/201402/finding-the-meaning-in-your-work.

14   Jessica Amortegui, "Why Finding Meaning at Work is More Important than Feeling Happy," *Fast Company.com*, June 26, 2014, http://www.fastcompany.com/3032126/how-to-find-meaning-during-your-pursuit-of-happiness-at-work.

15   See Cathy Greenberg's *What Happy Companies Know* in "The Birth of Positive Psychology," *Fearless Leaders Group, LLC*, 2014, http://www.fearlessleadersgroup.com/the-science-of-happiness.

For more on "flow states," see Mihaly Csikszentmihalyi, *Finding Flow: The Psychology of Engagement with Everyday Life* (New York: Basic Books/Perseus, 1997). For more on chickens and protecting the eggs, go to Pilpel and Rechavi's "The Lamarckian Chicken and the Darwinian Egg https://biologydirect.biomedcentral.com/articles/10.1186/s13062-015-0062-9.

16 Margaret Steen, "Moving Toward a Meaningful Career: Six Ways to Find Meaning in Your Job – No Matter What It Is," *Monster. com*, 2016, http://career-advice.monster.com/job-search/career-assessment/moving-toward-a-meaningful-career-hot-jobs/article.aspx.

17 Teresa Amabile and Steven Kramer, "How Leaders Kill Meaning at Work," *Mckinsey.com/ McKinsey Quarterly*, January 2012, http://www.mckinsey.com/insights/leading_in_the_21st_century/how_leaders_kill_meaning_at_work.

18 Paul Rogat Loeb, "An Antidote to Powerlessness" in *Soul of a Citizen: Living with Conviction in a Cynical Time* (New York: St. Martin's Griffin, 1999), 8-9.

19 Patrick Lencioni, "Conquer Team Dysfunction," *The Table Group*, 2014, http://www.tablegroup.com/imo/media/doc/Conquer_Team_Dysfunction.pdf. See also, *The Five Dysfunctions of a Team: A Leadership Fable* (San Francisco, CA: Jossey-Bass/Wiley, 2002).

20 Paul T. P. Wong and Don Page, "Servant leadership: An Opponent-Process Model and the Revised Servant Leadership Profile," *Regent University School of Leadership Studies/Servant Leadership Roundtable*, October, 2003, Virginia Beach, VA, http://www.drpaulwong.com/wp-content/uploads/2013/09/Wong-Servant-Leadership-An-Opponent-Process-Model.pdf;

Robert K. Greenleaf, *Servant leadership: A Journey into the Nature of Legitimate Power and Greatness* (New York: Paulist Press, 1977);

Kathleen A. Patterson, "Servant Leadership: A Theoretical Model," *Regent University School of Leadership Studies/Servant Leadership Roundtable*, August 2003, Virginia Beach, VA, https://www.regent.edu/acad/global/publications/sl_proceedings/2003/patterson_servant_leadership.pdf.

Also, see synopsis: http://www.google.com/url?sa=t&rct=j&q=&esrc=s&source=web&cd=5&ved=0ahUKEwiQr-fjst3PAhWqr1QKHdZUDqYQFghBMAQ&url=http%3A%2F%2Fwww.servantleadersineducation.com%2Fimages%2FIntroduction_to_Servant_Leadership.doc&usg=AFQjCNF2D5hVnD4SmnJXqqgio8iCSEnP-w&sig2=eluoa6KrsUqH2usellDFWw&bvm=bv.135974163,d.cGw&cad=rjt.

Chapter 8 Everyone Is a Leader

Mark K. Smith, "Peter Senge and the Learning Organization," *infed. org/YMCA George Williams College*, 2001, http://infed.org/mobi/peter-senge-and-the-learning-organization/.

1   George Bill and Peter Sims, *True North: Discover Your Authentic Leadership* (San Francisco: Wiley/Josey Bass, 2007), xxviii. For reflective leadership exercises, see "True North Exercises" at http://www.billgeorge.org/page/true-north.

2   Maxwell, John. 8/31/2015. "A Minute with Maxwell." <http://johnmaxwellteam.com/2015-leadership?i=qfPT daliymwm@johnmaxwellteam.net>; on behalf of; John Maxwell john@johnmaxwellteam.com, via email from Martinelli and Associates.

3   Paul Rogat Loeb, *Soul of a Citizen: Living with Conviction in a Cynical Time* (New York: St. Martin's Press/Griffin, 1st. ed., 1999), 48.

4   See examples, such as community walkabouts: http://www.plymouthcommunityhomes.co.uk/our-community/how-to-get-involved/community-walkabouts/; or 1-800 Flowers founding CEO Jim McCann's practice: "Leadership Secrets of the Walkabout

CEO," *Inc*, March 26, 2104, http://www.inc.com/leigh-buchanan/jim-mccann-1800flowers-conversation.html.

5   John P. Kotter, "What Leaders Really Do," *Harvard Business Review*, December 4, 2001, https://hbr.org/2001/12/what-leaders-really-do/ar/5.

6   Stu Crandell, "Real World Leadership, Part 3: Create an Engaging Culture for Greater Impact," *Korn Ferry Institute*, September 13, 2015, http://infokf.kornferry.com/rs/243-WPI-042/images/RWL-R3.pdf.

7   Reminded that readers are left to their own devices to construct meaning from print, Tom Robbin's admonition may be a useful touchstone: "A book no more contains reality than a clock contains time. A book may measure so-called reality as a clock measures so-called time; a book may create an illusion of reality as a clock creates an illusion of time; a book may be real, just as a clock is real (both more real, perhaps, than those ideas to which they allude); but let's not kid ourselves– all a clock contains is wheels and springs and all a book contains is sentences." Tom Robbins, Ch. 34, in *Even Cowgirls Get the Blues* (New York: Houghton Mifflin/Bantam, 1976).

8   Jim Collins, "The Hedgehog Concept (Simplicity within the Three Circles)" Ch. 5., in *Good to Great: Why Some Companies Make the Leap... and Other's Don't* (New York: Harper Collins, 1st ed., 2001), 96.

Based on Isaiah Berlin's adage from the Greek poet Archilochus. See also Troy Patterson, "On the Origins of Foxes and Hedgehogs," *Slate*, March 19, 2014, http://www.slate.com/blogs/browbeat/2014/03/19/foxes_vs_hedgehogs_a_history_from_nate_silver_fivethirtyeight_and_isaiah.html

Compare your leadership assessment to the sly fox and the simple hedgehog. The fox is supposedly the smarter predator, but the hedgehog, rolling itself in a protective ball, reduces all challenges and dilemmas into a simple idea and act. But we should view engagement as an enabling act, not offensive nor defensive act. Our pro-other acts determine how we nourish others' engagement and our own.

9   Sharif Khan, "Awaken the Leader in You," *www.sharifkhan. bogspot.com* (Blog), February 16, 2005, http://www.sharifkhan. blogspot.com/2005/02/ten-easy-steps-to-developing-your. html>; further, a 2004 study by the Family and Work Institute concluded that "having a life outside of work does not detract from work success" but enhanced it, see: http://familiesandwork.org/ downloads/OverworkinAmerica.pdf.

10   Dennis E. Coates, *Enhance the Transfer of Training: Tips, Tools and Intelligence for Trainers, ASTD Press, InfoLine*, 2007, Issue 0710, http://www.2020insight.net/Docs4/IL0710-READ%20ONLY.PDF.

11   Fred C. Lunenburg, "Power and Leadership: An Influence Process," *International Journal of Management, Business, and Administration* 15, no. 1 (2012):15-1, http://www.nationalforum. com/Electronic%20Journal%20Volumes/Lunenburg,%20Fred%20 C%20Power%20and%20Leadership-An%20Influence%20 Process%20IJMBA%20V15%20N1%202012.pdf.

12   Compare to *Louder than Words* author and engagement expert, Bob Kelleher's illustration: "Employee Engagement – Who's Sinking Your Boat," *You Tube.com/The Employee Engagement Group*, August 20, 2013, https://www.youtube.com/watch?v=fUXdrl9ch_Q.

13   Shawn Achor, "The Happiness Advantage: Linking Positive Brains to Performance," *TEDxBloomington*, June 30, 2011, https://www. youtube.com/watch?v=GXy__kBVq1M.

14   See Paul T. P. Wong and Don Page, "Servant Leadership: An Opponent-Process Model and the Revised Servant Leadership Profile," *Regent University School of Leadership Studies/ Servant Leadership Roundtable*, October, 2003, Virginia Beach, VA., http://www.drpaulwong.com/wp-content/uploads/2013/09/ Wong-Servant-Leadership-An-Opponent-Process-Model.pdf.

Robert K. Greenleaf, *Servant leadership: A Journey into the Nature of Legitimate Power and Greatness* (New York: Paulist Press, 1977).

Kathleen A. Patterson, "Servant Leadership: A Theoretical Model," *Regent University School of Leadership Studies/Servant Leadership Roundtable*, August 2003, Virginia Beach, VA, https://www.regent.edu/acad/global/publications/sl_proceedings/2003/patterson_servant_leadership.pdf.

Larry C. Spears, "Reflections on Robert K. Greenleaf and Servant Leadership," *Leadership & Organization Development Journal* 17 (1966): 33-35.

15 Marcus Buckingham and Curt Coffman, "The Measuring Stick: Mountain Climbing," Ch. 1, in *First, Break All the Rules* (New York: Simon & Schuster, 1999), 43-46.

Chapter 9 Transform Thyself

Thomas Gilovich, "Seeing What We Expect to See: The Biased Evaluation of Ambiguous and Inconsistent Data," Ch. 4, *How We Know What Isn't So: The Fallibility of Human Reason in Everyday Life* (New York: Free Press/Macmillan, 1991), 53/78.

1 Sheryl Sandberg with Nell Scovell, *Lean In: Women, Work, and the Will to Lead* (New York: Alfred A. Knopf/Random House, 43rd printing, 2013).

2 The Beatles, "With a Little Help from My Friends," on *Sgt. Pepper's Lonely Hearts Club Band*, written by John Lennon and Paul McCartney, Northern Songs, EMI Studios/Parlophone Producer: George Martin, June 1, 1967, $33^{1/3}$.

3 Alex Turnbull, "How Regular One-on-One Meetings Saved Our Company Culture," *Grovehq.com* (Blog), https://www.groovehq.com/blog/one-on-one-meetings-for-company-culture.

4   D. L. Ashliman, "The Emperor's New Clothes and Other Tales of Aarne-Thompson-Uther Type 1620, 1999-2014," *University of Pittsburg* (landing page), revised April 16, 2014, http://www.pitt.edu/~dash/type1620.html.

5   Kyung Kim, Eun. "'He's One of Us': Workers Willing to Lose Jobs for Supporting Fired Supermarket CEO," *Today.com*, August 6, 2014, http://www.today.com/news/workers-customers-protest-firing-supermarket-ceo-hes-one-us-1D80024391.

6   (Unnamed staff), "Savile and Hall: BBC 'Missed Chances to Stop Attacks,'" *Bbc.com/BBC News*, February 25, 2016, http://www.bbc.com/news/uk-35658398.

     Or identically, the same culture of silence and complicit behavior in Robert Huber, "The Sins of Penn State: The Untold Story of Joe Paterno's Fall," *Philadelphia* Magazine, February 20, 2012, http://www.phillymag.com/articles/the-sins-of-penn-state-the-untold-story-of-joe-paterno-s-fall/#D2r1hJMR4l7oM0E1.99 http://www.phillymag.com/articles/the-sins-of-penn-state-the-untold-story-of-joe-paterno-s-fall/.

7   Earned Dogmatism: when self-perceptions of expertise, multiplied by business norms, increase close-mindedness. See Victor Ottait, et. al., "When Self-Perceptions of Expertise Increase Closed-Minded Cognition: The Darned Dogmatism Effect," *Elsevier.com, Journal of Experimental Social Psychology* (2015): http://nathanaelmu.com/academic/wp-content/uploads/2013/10/2015-Earned-Dogmatism.pdf.

8   John Kador, "The 7 Deadly Sins of Apology," *Chief Executive Magazine*, March 17, 2016, http://chiefexecutive.net/the-seven-deadly-sins-of-apology/.

9   Kenji Yoshino and Christie Smith, "Uncovering Talent: A New Model of Inclusion," *Deloitte University/The Leadership Center for Inclusion*, December 6, 2013, https://www2.deloitte.com/

content/dam/Deloitte/us/Documents/about-deloitte/us-inclusion-uncovering-talent-paper.pdf, 5-13.

10 Jim Collins, "The Hedgehog Concept (Simplicity within the Three Circles)," Ch. 5, in *Good to Great: Why Some Companies Make the Leap... and Other's Don't* (New York: Harper Collins, 1st ed., 2001), 96.

11 Gallup, "Feedback for Real," Q12/12 Engagement Questions, *Gallup Business Journal,* March 15, 2001, http://www.gallup.com/businessjournal/811/feedback-real.aspx.

12 Marshall Goldsmith, "6 Questions that Will Set You Up to Be Super Successful," *INC/5000 Conference*, 2015, http://www.marshallgoldsmithlibrary.com/cim/articles_print.php?aid=1526.

13 Lenny DeFranco, "The (New) Definition of Employee Engagement," *Grovo*, November 17, 2015, http://blog.grovo.com/definition-employee-engagement/?utm_source=linkedIn&utm_medium=social&utm_campaign=SocialWarfare.

Chapter 10 Why Employees Leave: For "Bosses" Only

Vineet Nayar, "Recasting the Role of the CEO: Transferring the Responsibility for Change," in *Employees First, Customers Second: Turning Conventional Management Upside Down* (Boston: Harvard Business School, 2010), 164.

1 Corey Rosen, "The Pernicious Myth of the 80-20 Rule," *Inc/ www.inc.com*, December 10, 2015, http://www.inc.com/corey-rosen/the-pernicious-myth-of-the-80-20-rule.html.

2 Randall Beck and Jim Harter, "Managers Account for 70% of Variance in Employee Engagement, *Gallup.com*, April 21, 2015, http://www.gallup.com/businessjournal/182792/managers-account-variance-employee-engagement.aspx.

3   See p. 10 of Gallup's "The State of the American Manager: Analytics and Advice for Leaders." Access the complete 2015 report at http://www.gallup.com/services/182138/state-american-manager.aspx.

4   David Grossman, "15 Employee Engagement Stats to Know in 2015," *The Grossman Group*, May 13, 2015, http://www.yourthoughtpartner.com/blog/15-employee-engagement-stats-to-know-in-2015.

5   See, for instance: Kenneth Nowack, "Toxic Bosses Could Be Putting Your Employees' Health at Risk," *Talent Management.com*, January 22, 2016, http://www.talentmgt.com/articles/7750-toxic-bosses-could-be-putting-your-employees-health-at-risk?utm_source=MyEmma&utm_medium=Email&utm_campaign=HR%20NB&utm_source=newsletter&utm_medium=email&utm_content=Toxic%20Bosses%20Could%20Be%20Putting%20Your%20Employees%27%20Health%20at%20Risk&utm_campaign=HR_NB_10071;

Travis Brandberry, "Nine Things Managers Do to Make Employees Quit," *Entrepreneur*, September 9, 2015, http://www.entrepreneur.com/article/249903;

Dina Gerdeman, "How to Demotivate Your Best Employees," *Harvard Business School/Working Knowledge*, April 8, 2013, http://hbswk.hbs.edu/item/how-to-demotivate-your-best-employees;

Sujan Patel, "9 Reasons to Switch Careers as Soon as Possible," *Entrepreneur.com*, November 9, 2015, http://www.entrepreneur.com/article/252537;

Leigh Branham, "7 Hidden Reasons Employees Leave," *ASAE/The Center for Association Leadership*, February 2005, http://www.asaecenter.org/Resources/EUArticle.cfm?ItemNumber=11514;

Jennifer Robinson, "Turning around Employee Turnover," *Gallup Business Journal*, May 8, 2008, http://www.gallup.com/

businessjournal/106912/turning-around-your-turnover-problem. aspx;

Susan Heathfield, "Top Ten Reasons Why Employees Quit Their Jobs, *About.com/Money*, August 22, 2015, http://humanresources. about.com/od/resigning-from-your-job/a/top-10-reasons-employees-quit-their-job.htm;

Christian Schappel, "Five Biggest Reasons Employees Quit Jobs Quickly," *HRMorning.com*, September 3, 2015, http://www.hrmorning.com/5-biggest-reasons-employees-quit-jobs-quickly/.

6   Laura Sydell, "Digital Pioneer Andrew Grove Led Intel's Shift from Chips to Microprocessors," *NPR.org/Morning Edition*, March 22, 2016, http://www.npr.org/2016/03/22/471389537/digital-pioneer-andrew-grove-led-intels-shift-from-chips-to-microprocessors.

7   "Managers: Your Strongest (or Weakest) Link in Driving Employee Engagement?" *Aon Hewitt*, 2011, http://www.aon.com/attachments/human-capital-consulting/Report_AonHewitt-2011-Euiropean-Employee-Engagement.pdf.

8   See Rob Asghar, "Incompetence Rains, Er (sic), Reigns: What the Peter Principle Means Today," *Forbes Leadership*, August 14, 2014, http://www.forbes.com/sites/robasghar/2014/08/14/incompetence-rains-er-reigns-what-the-peter-principle-means-today/.

9   Marcus Buckingham and Curt Coffman, "The Fourth Key: Find the Right Fit: The Blind, Breathless Climb," Ch. 5, *First, Break All the Rules* (New York: Simon & Schuster, 1999), 178-192.

10   Vineet Nayar, "Employees First, Customers Second," *Youtube.com/TEDx Talks*, June 9, 2015, https://www.youtube.com/watch?v=cCdu67s_C5E.

11   Susan Heathfield, "Top Ten Reasons Why Employees Quit Their Jobs," *About.com/Money*, August 22, 2015, http://humanresources.

about.com/od/resigning-from-your-job/a/top-10-reasons-employees-quit-their-job.htm.

12 Eean R. Crawford, et. al., "Linking Job Demands and Resources to Employee Engagement and Burnout: A Theoretical Extension and Meta-analytic Test," *Journal of Applied Psychology:* September 2010 (Abstract): http://psycnet.apa.org/index.cfm?fa=buy. optionToBuy&id=2010-18410-002.

13 Listed items adapted from: "Program and Management Forum," *12Manage.com,* or alternate ironic title, from Collins, *Good to Great,* "I'd like you to join me in doing the ordinary better".

14 Karen Kersting, "Personality Changes for Better with Age," *American Psychological Association/www.LifeScience.com,* August 6, 2003, http://www.apa.org/monitor/julaug03/personality. aspx, 34-7. See also: Staff, "Personality Set for Life by 1st Grade, Study Suggests," *LiveScience.com,* August 6, 2010, http://www. livescience.com/8432-personality-set-life-1st-grade-study-suggests. html.

15 Karen Franklin, "The Best Predictor of Future Behavior Is ... Past Behavior: Does the Popular Maxim Hold Water?" *Psychology Today,* January 3, 2013, https://www.psychologytoday.com/ blog/witness/201301/the-best-predictor-future-behavior-is-past-behavior, 70.

16 Judith A. Ouellette and Wendy Wood, "Habit and Intention in Everyday Life: The Multiple Processes by which Past Behavior Predicts Future Behavior," *American Psychological Association, Inc. Psychological Bulletin,* 1998, https://dornsife.usc.edu/assets/ sites/208/docs/Ouellette.Wood.1998.pdf, 24-1.

17 Lou Adler, "Don't be Fooled: Past Behavior Doesn't Predict Future Performance," *Linkedin,* August 4, 2014, https://www.linkedin. com/pulse/20140804015642-15454-don-t-be-fooled-past-behavior-doesn-t-predict-future-performance.

18 Barry Schwartz, "The Way We Think about Work Is Broken," *TED Conferences, LLC,* transcript posted September, 2015, http://www.ted.com/talks/barry_schwartz_the_way_we_think_about_work_is_broken/transcript?language=en.

19 Bill George, "Why Leaders Lose Their Way," *Harvard Business School,* June 6, 2011, http://hbswk.hbs.edu/item/why-leaders-lose-their-way.

20 Paul B. Brown, "The Best Way to Predict the Future," *INC,* August 29, 2014, http://www.inc.com/paul-b-brown/the-best-way-to-predict-the-future.html.

21 David Sturt, "The Easiest Thing You Can Do to Be a Great Boss," *Harvard Business Review,* November 9, 2015, https://hbr.org/2015/11/the-easiest-thing-you-can-do-to-be-a-great-boss.

22 See also Chapter 2, footnote 11. Brady Wilson presents case studies for "a brain-based" approach. His basics include manage energy, not engagement; build positive experience (see also, John Dewey); target the heart; dialogue; promote cognitive dissonance; assure joint accountability; and investigate beliefs. A brief article reviewing and summarizing Wilson's book, see Richard Regan, "It's about Energy, Not Engagement," *Govloop.com,* January 25, 2016, https://www.govloop.com/community/blog/energy-not-engagement/.

Additional places to dig deeper: the key study debunking any causal relationship to learning styles and improved learning outcomes, see Harold Pashler, et. al., *University of California,* 2008, http://psi.sagepub.com/content/9/3/105.abstract.

"Meta-Analysis Summary: Learning Styles," *Indiana Wesleyan University,* (undated), https://www.indwes.edu/cli/research/meta-analysis-summary---learning-styles.

See also: Cedar Riener and Daniel Willingham, "The Myth of Learning Styles," *www.changemag.org,* September-October, 2010, http://www.changemag.org/archives/back%20issues/september-october%202010/the-myth-of-learning-full.html.

Valerie Strauss, "Howard Gardner: 'Multiple Intelligences' Are Not 'Learning Styles,'" *Washington Post*, October 16, 2013, https://www.washingtonpost.com/news/answer-sheet/wp/2013/10/16/howard-gardner-multiple-intelligences-are-not-learning-styles/>.

Jeremy B. Teitelbaum, "Train for the Brain: What 25 Years of Brain Science Can Teach Us about Workplace Learning," *Training Industry Magazine/www.nxt.com*, Winter 2016, http://www.nxtbook.com/nxtbooks/trainingindustry/tiq_2016winter/index.php?startid=16#/16>.

Jenny Anderson, "Kinesthetic No More: You May Think You Learn Better in a Certain Way. You Actually Don't," *Quartz qz.com*, December 9, 2015, http://qz.com/568617/you-may-think-you-learn-better-in-a-certain-way-you-actually-dont/?utm_source=newsletter&utm_medium=email&utm_content=Read%20More&utm_campaign=HR_NB_100715.

23   Benjamin S. Bloom, ed., *Taxonomy of Educational Objectives. Handbook 1, Cognitive Domain, Vol. 1* (New York: Longman, 1956), 62-197.

24   Matt Donovan, "Incorporating Neuroscience into Effective Learning and Performance Improvement Initiatives," *Training Industry.com*, October 20, 2015, https://cdns3.trainingindustry.com/media/18842488/neuroscience_presentation_101915_final.pdf, Slides 12-15.

25   James Lavery, "Seek First to Understand, Then to be Understood," *Franklin Covey.com* (Blog), August 22, 2012, http://www.franklincovey.com/blog/seek-understand-understood.html.

26   Jim Collins, "Confront the Brutal Facts (Yet Never Lose Faith)," Ch. 4, in *Good to Great: Why Some Companies Make the Leap... and Other's Don't.* (New York: Harper Collins, 1st ed., 2001), 65.

27 Allen Toussaint, "You Will Not Lose" ("...not if you use your heart"), on *Southern Nights*, Reprise Records, produced by Marshall Sehorn and Allen Toussaint, MS2186, 1975, 33$^{1/3}$.

28 Gregory P. Smith, "Top Ten Reasons Why People Quite Their Jobs," *Attard Communications/Business Know-How*, 2013, http://www.businessknowhow.com/manage/whyquit.htm.

29 Mathilde Krim in Warren Bennis, "Mastering the Context," Ch. 1, in *On Becoming a Leader* (Philadelphia, PA: Basic Books, 20th Anniversary Edition, 2009), 31.

30 Daniel Goleman, Richard Boyatzis, and Annie McKee, "Primal Leadership," Ch. 1, and "Resonant Leadership, Ch. 2, *Primal Leadership: Unleashing the Power of Emotional Intelligence* (Harvard Business Review Press: Boston, Massachusets, 2013), 9-31.

31 Adapted from Michael Hyatt, "20 Questions to Ask Other Leaders, *Michaelhyatt.com*, June 19, 2009, http://michaelhyatt.com/20-questions-to-ask-other-leaders.html.

32 The Beatles, "All You Need Is Love," by John Lennon and Paul McCartney, on *Magical Mystery Tour*, Parlophone/Capitol, produced by George Martin, July 7, 1967.

33 The Arbinger Institute, "Beneath Behavior," Ch. 4, *The Anatomy of Peace: Resolving the Heart of Conflict* (Oakland: Berrett-Koehler, Expanded 2nd ed., 2015), 32.

34 Lawrence Kohlberg, "Post Conventional, Autonomous, Principled Level," in *The Philosophy of Moral Development: Moral Stages and the Idea of Justice* (University of Michigan: Harper & Row, 1st ed., 1981), 18.

35 Erik H. Erikson and Joan M. Erikson, "The Ninth Stage," in *The Life Cycle Completed: Extended Version* (New York: W. W. Norton, 1998), 112-113.

36 Carl R. Rogers, "Part 6, What Are the Implications for Living?" in *On Becoming a Person: A Therapist's View of Psychotherapy* (Boston: Houghton Mifflin, 1ˢᵗ ed., 1960), 332.

37 Michael Houseman and Dylan Minor, "Toxic Workers," Working Paper 16-057, *Harvard Business School/ Kellogg School of Management/Northwestern University*, November 2015, http://www.hbs.edu/faculty/Publication%20Files/16-057_d45c0b4f-fa19-49de-8f1b-4b12fe054fea.pdf.

38 Warren Bennis, "Understanding the Basics," Ch. 2, and "Forging the Future," Ch. 10, in *On Becoming a Leader* (Philadelphia, PA: Basic Books, 20ᵗʰ Anniversary Edition, 2009), 38/190, respectively.

39 David Dye, "Is Service Leadership Bulls—t?" *Engage Newsletter, trailblazelist@aweber.com*, December 16, 2015, on behalf of David M. Dye david@trailblazeinc.com.

40 Marcus Buckingham and Curt Coffman. "The Fourth Key: Find the Right Fit: The Art of Tough Love," Ch. 6, in *First, Break All the Rules* (New York: Simon & Schuster, 1999), 207-8. Buckingham's assertion suggests that effective use of soft skills does not imply that we are superficial about our actions. For instance, we do not visit with others because we believe this will position us better in obtaining a goal or building a relationship. We visit others with a purpose, their well-being and strategic goals in mind, not a selfish agenda. Other sources:

Jon Gordon, "Who's on the Bus," Ch. 16, and "Love Rules, Ch. 27, in *The Energy Bus* (Hoboken, New Jersey: John Wiley & Sons, 2007), 63/122, respectively.

James M. Kouses and Barry Z. Posner, "Leadership is Everyone's Business," Ch. 13, in *The Leadership Challenge* (San Francisco: John Wiley & Sons, 4ᵗʰ ed., 2007), 351.

John Mackey and Raj Sisodia, "Conscious Cultures," Ch. 13, in *Conscious Capitalism* (Boston, MA: Harvard Business Review Press, 2014), 225.

41   Steven R. Covey, "Public Victory: Paradigms of Interdependence," Part 3, in *The 7 Habits of Highly Effective People: Powerful Lessons in Personal Change* (New York: Perseus Books Group, 2000), 154.

42   Lincoln's March 4, 1861 Inaugural Address, **See** http://www. presidency.ucsb.edu/ws/?pid=25818 "..The mystic chords of memory, stretching from every battlefield and patriot grave to every living heart and hearthstone all over this broad land, will yet swell the chorus of the Union, when again touched, as surely they will be, by the better angels of our nature."

Additionally, Viktor Frankl's "The Meaning of Love," Part II, in *Man's Search for Meaning* (Boston: Beacon Press, 2006), 37, 111-12: "Love is the ultimate and highest goal to which man can aspire.... Love is the only way to grasp another human being in the innermost core of his personality. Furthermore, by his love, the **loving person enables the beloved person to actualize these potentialities**. By making him aware of what he can be and of what he should become, he makes these potentialities come true."

Chapter 11 "How Can I Help?"

Marquis de Vauvenargues, originally from *Reflexions et Maximes*.

1   Randall Beck and Jim Harter, "Mangers Account for 70% of the Variance in Employee Engagement," Gallup Business Journal/Gallup, Inc., April 21, 2015, http://www.gallup.com/ businessjournal/182792/managers-account-variance-employee-engagement.aspx.

1   Gallup, "The State of the American Manager: Analytics and Advice for Leaders," *Gallup.com*, 2015, http://www.gallup.com/ services/182138/state-american-manager.aspx>.

2   James M. Kouzes and Barry Z. Posner. "The Five Practices of Exemplary Leadership," Ch. 1, *The Leadership Challenge* (San Francisco: John Wiley & Sons, 4th ed., 2007), 3-26.

3   "Having a life outside of work doesn't detract from work success" but enhances it, from Kenneth Matos and Ellen Galinsky, "2014 National Study of Employees," *Families and work.org/ Families and Work Institute*, 2014, http://familiesandwork.org/ downloads/2014NationalStudyOfEmployers.pdf.

4   Sly and the Family Stone, "Family Affair," by Sly Stone, on *There's a Riot Goin' On*, Epic 5-10805, produced by Sly Stone, Nov. 6, 1971.

5   A sentiment, unverifiable to John Wesley; see Kevin Watson: https://vitalpiety.com/2013/04/29/wesley-didnt-say-it-do-all-the-good-you-can-by-all-the-means-you-can/.

Appendixes

Appendix A

CHECKLIST: HOW TO RUN AN UNPRODUCTIVE COMPANY

Appendix A: How to Run an Unproductive Company	
Personnel Issues	**Operational cont.**
o Absenteeism and tardiness.	o Communicates ineffectively.
o Duplicates efforts.	o Unhappy office vibe.
o Deficient preparation.	o Lacks risk analysis process.
o Absenteeism.	o Keeps employees fearful of losing jobs.
o Lacks interpersonal skills.	o Lacks system assessment process.
o Lacks focus and follow-through.	o Processes compromised by lack of trust.
o Reacts negatively to coaching.	o Missing connection to values and vision.
o Does not keep commitments.	o Ignores warning/concerns brought by others.
o Turns own mistakes into client's problem.	
o Poor hire.	**Management Issues**
o Holds Grudges..	o Sets unclear expectations.
	o Displays poor judgment.
	o Acta non verba (actions speak louder…).
Economic Issues	o Little collaboration (or create illusion).
o Deficient funds.	o Self-serving nature dominates.
o Executes poor accounting.	o Accomplishments… not recognized.
o Lacks budgeting and cost control.	o Does not check in with staff members.
o Ignores risk analysis.	o Lacks support staff or team ethic.
	o Takes credit for other people's work.
Operational Issues	o Carelessness about the staff.
o Makes assumptions without fact checking.	o Lacks focus and follow-through.
o No follow-up/through with customers.	o No faith or trust in others.
	o Employs power of intimidation.
o Operational mediocrity.	o Roadblocks between upper managers and employees.
o Lacks a succession plan.	
o Poor judgment.	o Acts differently with superiors than subordinates.
o Doesn't have an employee recognition program.	o Reacts negatively to criticism.
o Professional development opportunities available.	o Unable to deliver a straight answer.
	o Arrives late for appointments.
o Lacks strategic thinking.	o Unrelenting demand for perfection.
o Lacks planning.	o Turns mistakes into the client's problem.
	o Chastises socializing.
	o Blames others for failures.

Appendix B

LEADERSHIP INVENTORY

Characteristics/Self

- How have I evolved as a leader in the last five years?
- How do I feel about my own performance over the last year? Over the last three years? How often do I want my performance reviewed? Who else do I want to be aware of my progress/achievements?
- What insights have I gained about my talents and strengths from others outside of an insular circle?
- What am I doing to ensure continued growth and develop as a leader?
- What are the greatest lessons I learned as a leader– lessons that spur the profitable growth of your company or productivity from employees? (What lessons do I know I need to acquire?)
- What talents or strengths do I rely on most in my daily life as a leader? What do I telegraph?
- What are the most important decisions I make as a leader?
- What is one mistake I witness others making more frequently than others? What is the most dominant constructive behavior?
- What is the one behavior or trait that I have seen that has derailed other leaders?
- What are my expectations of myself? What do others expect of me? How do I make these expectations more synchronized and compatible?

- What are my priorities? How do I prioritize what I do best while ensuring that someone is accountable for what I cannot do? What are some things I have placed on the back burner?
- Can I name a person who has had a tremendous impact on me as a leader? Why and how did this person impact my life?
- What is one characteristic that I believe every leader should possess? What do I do to strengthen that asset in my behavior?
- What is the biggest challenge facing leaders today?
- What resources I would recommend to someone looking to gain insight into becoming a better leader?
- What advice would I give to someone going into a leadership position for the first time?
- Behaviors I wish to change? (e.g., not strategic enough; not good at networking); barriers? (e.g., lack of information, skills; just not social); supports (e.g., willingness to think with team support; find a friend for coaching).

Recognizing & Mentoring/Others

- What talents or qualities will I not live without from others? What does this tell me about myself? Are my behaviors consistent with these expectations of others?
- What makes me passionate working with colleagues and about my company? About my role or work? How can I use my passion to drive division, unit, and department improvement? How can I assist my colleagues in using their passion to drive growth?
- What are the real incentives for our most productive employees? How can I increase the emotional value of these incentives? Who are the most productive employees? What makes them stay and be more productive? What is

present in their emotional memory that propels them to even higher performance levels?

- Do I believe that people are valued and developed within our company's culture? What managers or departments are best at this? What managers or departments could do better? How do I find and respond to these needs?
- How can I build stronger emotional bonds with them?
- What is the best recognition I have ever received? What are my beliefs about recognition? How do I or how will I act in accordance among colleagues?
- How do I ensure that every workgroup has a caring culture and a manager who cares?
- Am I an open person who will listen to anyone, or am I seen as a person who has strong beliefs who is unwilling to listen to others? How open am I to the opinions of others, especially those who challenge or disagree with me?
- Who values me? Which people are my loving critics? How/Why did I get (or plan to get) to successive wins?
- How can I retain our most productive employees?

Challenges, Change & Culture

- What guidelines or promises should we make to each other to maintain trust?
- Am I considered an observer or someone willing to get in the trenches? Explain.
- Which is most important to my organization—mission, core values or vision?
- How do I or other leaders in my organization communicate the "core values" How do I encourage others in my organization to communicate the "core values?" Do I set aside specific times to cast vision to my employees and other leaders? How do I ensure my organization and its activities are aligned to what I "value?" How do I help a new employee understand the culture of our organization?

- What values or beliefs are important in creating sustainability?
- What are the greatest challenges I face? What are the challenges facing my team?
- How will positions within my area of expertise change within the next 3, 5 10 years? If I am close to retirement, and I helping others achieve their aspirations. Reflect on the answer for a few moments, and then ask two other people to share their responses with you.
- As an organization gets larger, there can be a tendency for the "institution" to dampen "inspiration." How would I keep this from happening?
- What are the first words that come to my mind that describe my company's culture? Does this vary between departments or divisions? Around the world?
- How do I define quality in my division, unit, and department? What drives quality at my company?
- What ideas have I read, seen, or heard about quality service or other concepts that I should consider implementing? Are employees given an vehicle to knowledge share? How/What?
- Think about a situation in which two or more people disagreed about something important to them. How would I help bring them together?
- What are some changes that leaders can make to keep destructive conflict to a minimum and encourage productive and creative conflict?
- Who are my greatest partners? Who helps me drive performance? Which is more likely to increase learning: a winning moment with reflection and recognition, or a classroom training experience? Which is more likely to aid in my development?
- Which groups in my company seem to have the most opportunities at work to learn and grow?

- How is creative thinking encouraged within my organization? Where do the great ideas come from in the organization?
- Can I explain the impact, if any, that social networking and web access/tools have made on my organization or in me personally?

Appendix C

On-Line Engagement Library

"...you can't evolve into what you won't explore."
–T. D. Jakes, *Instinct: The Power to Unleash Your Inborn Drive.*

~

The resources below are largely different from the footnotes in the book. These articles and websites below provide essential and representative engagement and recognition touchstones.

Note: The web addresses in this volume were functional at the time of the book's publication yet may have changed over time.

Coaching

- "High-Impact Performance Management: Maximizing Performance Coaching" by Stacia Garr, from Bersin by Deloitte: http://www.bersin.com/Practice/Detail.aspx?doc id=15021&mode=search&p=Talent-Management.
- Try Feed Forward Instead of Feedback" by Marshall Goldberg: http://www.marshallgoldsmithlibrary.com/cim/articles_display.php?aid=424.

Change

- "How to Rewire Your Brain for Change" by Keith Webb: http://keithwebb.com/rewire-your-brain-change/.

- "Leading Change: Why Transformational Efforts Fail" by John P. Kotter, from Harvard Business Review: http://www.srfmr.org/uploads/teaching_resource/1396 040272-211c50caa4635c59b/Leading%20Change.pdf.
- "The Little Book of Big Change" by Patty McManus, from Interaction Associates: http://interactionassociates. com/insights/publications/little-book-big-change?mkt_ tok=3RkMMJWWfF9wsRokv6zLZKXonjHpfsX56uko XKG0lMI%2F0ER3fOvrPUfGjI4ITsJ0aPyQAgobGp 5I5FELSLXYRbljt6wIWA%3D%3D#.VgwtTWYo7yN.
- "The Progress Principle" by Teresa Amabile: http:// progressprinciple.com/research.
- Related Suggested Change Books: *HBR's 10 Must Reads on Change Management* by Harvard Business Review, 2011; *Switch: How to Change Things When Change Is Hard* by Chip Heath.

Emotional Intelligence

- Consortium for Research on Emotional Intelligence in Organizations: http://www.eiconsortium.org/.
- "Emotional Intelligence" by Peter Salovey and John Mayer from Yale University/Baywood Publishing: http://www.unh.edu/emotional_intelligence/EIAssets/ EmotionalIntelligenceProper/EI1990%20Emotional%20 Intelligence.pdf.
- "Emotional Intelligence Theory: Highlighting and Developing Leadership Skills" from Educational Business Articles: http://www.educational-business-articles.com/emotional-intelligence-theory.html.
- "Howard Gardner: 'Multiple intelligences' Are Not 'Learning Styles" by Valerie Struass from *The Washington Post*: https://www.washingtonpost.com/blogs/

answer-sheet/wp/2013/10/16/howard-gardner-multiple-intelligences-are-not-learning-styles/

- "Primal Leadership: The Hidden Driver of Great Performance" by Daniel Goleman, et. al., from Harvard Business Review: https://hbr.org/2001/12/primal-leadership-the-hidden-driver-of-great-performance/ar/1.

- "The Corporate Person's Guide to Loosening Up" by Eduard Ezeanu, from People Skills Decoded: http://www.peopleskillsdecoded.com/corporate-person-guide-loosening-up/.

Core Engagement Thought Leaders and Websites

- Achievers / Engage: The Employee Engagement Blog: http://blog.achievers.com/.

- Employee Engagement Network: http://employeeengagement.com/engagement-resources/?utm_campaign=May%20Newsletter%20 2015&utm_source=Robly.com&utm_medium=email; http://employeeengagement.com/.

- Engage2Excel: http://www.engage2excel.com/resources/.

- Florida International University's Rewards and Recognition page: http://hr.fiu.edu/index.php?name=reward_recognition.

- Globoforce: "A Ten-Step Guide to Working More Human:" http://go.globoforce.com/Q315_WorkHuman_WP_LP.html?source=GFBlog.

- Derick Irvine: http://www.recognizethisblog.com/my-books/.

- Kevin Kruse: http://www.kevinkruse.com/about-kevin-kruse/.

- Kevin Sheridan: http://kevinsheridanllc.com/2015/09/wearing-employee-engagement-on-your-sleeve/.

- TINYnews: https://news.tinypulse.com/mission/.

- The Conference Board: https://www.conference-board.org/topics/subtopics.cfm?topicid=20&subtopicid=130.
- "Why Motivating People Doesn't Work and What Does: The New Science of Leading, Energizing, and Engaging" by Susan Fowler: http://motivationbook.susanfowler.com/wp-content/thesis/skins/mobile-first/images/sample_chapter.pdf.
- David Zinger: http://www.davidzinger.com/wp-content/uploads/Brief-Overeiw-of-the-Pyramid-of-Employee-Engagement.pdf.

For Managers and Leaders

- "4 Myths Most Bosses Believe about Employee Engagement" by Stephanie Vozza from *fastcompany.com*: http://www.fastcompany.com/3059482/your-most-productive-self/four-myths-most-bosses-believe-about-employee-engagement
- "4 Ways You Can Create Better Employee Engagement" by Bram Lowsky from Chief Executive Magazine: http://chiefexecutive.net/4-ways-you-can-create-better-employee-engagement/.
- "8 Secrets Employees Want Their Managers to Know Now" by Christian Schappel, from HR Morning.com: http://www.hrmorning.com/8-secrets-employees-want-their-managers-to-know-now/?pulb=1.
- "9 Employee Engagement Archetypes" from *thecontextofthings.com*: https://www.youtube.com/watch?v=9W4UVVHx370.
- "Employee Engagement Starts with You" by Byron O. Spruell: http://www.sbnonline.com/article/employee-engagement-starts-with-you/.
- "How to Engage Employees with Unfavorable Occupations by Ty Hall, from Profile International Workplace 101 Blog:

http://info.profilesinternational.com/profiles-employee-assessment-blog/bid/209009/how-to-engage-employees-with-unfavorable-occupations?source=Blog_Email_%5b How%20to%20Engage%20Employ%5d.

- "Leadership That Gets Results" by Daniel Goleman, from Harvard Business Review: http://az370354.vo.msecnd.net/socialhub/12-leadership thatgetsresults-140826195106-phpapp01.pdf.

- "Not Making Progress on Your Employee Engagement Initiative? 3 Keys for 'Moving the Needle'" from The Ken Blanchard Companies: http://www.kenblanchard.com/Leading-Research/ Ignite-Newsletter/September-2014.

- "Passion in Need of a Champion," by John Hagel III, from Deloitte HR Times Blog: http://hrtimesblog.com/2014/11/13/passion-in-need-of-a-champion/.

- Dan Rockwell: https://leadershipfreak.wordpress.com/.

- "Top 10 Reasons Why Employees Quit Their Job" by Susan M. Healthfield, from About Money: http://humanresources.about.com/od/resigning-from-your-job/a/top-10-reasons-employees-quit-their-job.htm.

- "The Tina Fey Guide to Management: 5 Practical Lessons from Ms. 'Bossypant'" by Renee Cocchi, Resourceful Manager: https://www.resourcefulmanager.com/tina-fey-quotes/.

- "The Best Interview Questions You Never Ask," Kristi Hedges, Forbes/ Forbes Women: http://www.forbes.com/sites/work-in-progress/2011/08/03/the-best-interview-questions-you-never-ask/.

- "The Engagement Gap: Why Executives and Employees Think Differently about Employee Engagement" by Brian Solis: https://www.linkedin.com/pulse/engagement-gap-why-executives-employees-think-employee-brian-solis.

- "The Hidden Drivers of Leader Engagement" from the Organizational Intelligence Institute: http://www.oi-institute.com/research-resources-reports-|intelligence-surveys.
- "The Manager's Employee Engagement Checklist" by Kevin Sheridan, from kevinsheridanllc.com: http://kevinsheridanllc.com/2016/05/managers-employee-engagement-checklist/.
- "The Seven Hidden Reasons Employees Leave" by Leigh Branham, from The Center for Association Leadership: http://www.asaecenter.org/Resources/EUArticle.cfm?ItemNumber=11514.
- "Why Middle Managers Are So Unhappy" Jack Zenger and Joseph Folkman, from Harvard Business Review: https://hbr.org/2014/11/why-middle-managers-are-so-unhappy.

Meetings (see also Teams)

- "Meetings: The Good, the Bad and the Ugly" from Knowledge@Wharton: http://knowledge.wharton.upenn.edu/article/meetings-the-good-the bad-and-the-ugly/.

Motivation

- "Recognizing Employees Is the Simplest Way to Improve Morale," by David Novak, from *hbr.org*: https://hbr.org/2016/05/recognizing-employees-is-the-simplest-way-to-improve-morale.
- "These Charts Reveal the Secrets to Motivation" by Max Nisen, from Business Insider: http://www.businessinsider.com/charts-about-performance-and-motivation-2013-3?op=1#ixzz377Ofn4W9.
- "What Motivates Employees? A New Look at Employee Engagement and Culture Risk" by Richard Barrett, from Barrett Values Centre: http://www.valuescentre.com/sites/

default/files/uploads/2013-08-05/What%20Motivates%20
Employees.pdf.

Positive Psychology

- Center for Positive Organizations: http://positiveorgs.bus.
  umich.edu/.
- "Ready to Quit Your Job? 3 Regrets to Avoid" by David
  Sturt and Todd Norstrom, from Forbes Leadership:
  http://www.forbes.com/sites/davidsturt/2015/06/18/
  ready-to-quit-your-job-3-regrets-to-avoid/.
- *The Energy Bus* by Jon Gordon: http://www.
  theenergybus.com/ and *The Positive Pledge*: http://www.
  thepositivepledge.com/.
- Potential Labs: http://potentialabs.com/launch-
  webinar?utm_campaign=Mailing+List&utm_source
  =hs_email&utm_medium=email&utm_content=23832
  186&_hsenc=p2ANqtz--edID8kSsn4_lFOrKnaF8KBtW
  PXWbwCcMTrwNZtc6PmQxKNZlGndYTFaQcgku09E
  MbsX1h2lx_-7t47szAxPKXBVRW3Q&_hsmi=23832186
- "The Science of Happiness" Berkeley MOOC: https://
  www.edx.org/course/science-happiness-uc-berkeleyx-
  gg101x-1#.VHjFer4rf8t.
- *The Happiness Advantage* (research) and *The Orange
  Frog (*research translated into a parable) by Shawn Achor:
  http://goodthinkinc.com/wp-content/uploads/2014/06/
  HA-bookclub-guide.R21-791x1024.jpg.

More on Recognition

- "5 Ways Leaders Rock Employee Recognition" by
  Meghan M. Biro, Forbes Leadership:
  http://www.forbes.com/sites/meghanbiro/2013/01/13/5-
  ways-leaders-rock-employee-recognition/.
- "24 Fast and Fun Ways to Recognize Employees" from
  BI Worldwide:

http://biworldwide.com.au/en/research-materials/thought-leadership/2014/24-ways-to-recognize-employees/.

- "A Paycheck Is Not Recognition for a Job Well Done" by Derek Irvine, from Compensation Café: http://www.compensationcafe.com/2015/03/a-paycheck-is-not-recognition-for-a-job-well-done.html.

- "If Money Can Buy Engagement, Should Happy Employees Earn Less?" by Tomas Chamorro-Premuzic, from Forbes Leadership: http://www.forbes.com/sites/tomaspremuzic/2014/08/08/if-money-can-buy-engagement-should-happy-employees-earn-less/.

- "New Research Unlocks the Secret of Employee Recognition" by Josh Bersin, from Forbes Leadership http://www.forbes.com/sites/joshbersin/2012/06/13/new-research-unlocks-the-secret-of-employee-recognition/.

- "The Five Elements of a 'Simply Irresistible' Organization" by Josh Bersin, Forbes Leadership: http://www.forbes.com/sites/joshbersin/2014/04/04/the-five-elements-of-a-simply-irresistible-organization/.

- "The 10 Differences Between Rewards and Recognition" by Roy Saunderson, from Incentive Magazine: http://www.incentivemag.com/Strategy/Ask-the-Experts/Roy-Saunderson/Top-10-Differences-Between-Rewards-and-Recognition/.

Research, Statistics, and Commentary

- "10 Things You Need to Know about Employee Engagement" by Don MacPherson, from Modern Survey: http://www.modernsurvey.com/blog/10-things-about-employee-engagement.

- "Building Workplace Trust: Trends and High Performance" by Andy Atkins, from Interaction

Associates: http://interactionassociates.com/sites/default/files/research_items/Trust%20Report_2014_15IA_0.pdf.

- Cornell University Digital Commons: http://digitalcommons.ilr.cornell.edu/.
- "Creating a Culture of Employee Engagement" from Modern Survey: http://www.modernsurvey.com/wp-content/uploads/2014/03/Creating-a-Culture-of-Employee-Engagement.pdf\.
- "Employee Voice and Silence" by Elizabeth W. Morrison, from Annual Review of Organizational Psychology and Organizational Behavior: http://www.annualreviews.org/doi/full/10.1146/annurev-orgpsych-031413-091328.
- Gallup State of the American Workplace: http://www.gallup.com/poll/181289/majority-employees-not-engaged-despite-gains-2014.aspx; Full report: http://www.gallup.com/services/178514/state-american-workplace.aspx.
- "The Collective Advantage" by Susan Ellingwood, from Gallup: http://www.gallup.com/businessjournal/787/collective-advantage.aspx.
- "Managers Account for 70% of Variance in Employee Engagement" by Randall Beck and Jim Harter, from Gallup: http://www.gallup.com/businessjournal/182792/managers-account-variance-employee-engagement.aspx.
- "Measuring the Benefits of Employee Engagement" by V. Kumar and Anita Panasari, from MIT Sloan Management Review: http://sloanreview.mit.edu/article/measuring-the-benefits-of-employee-engagement/?social_token=d741b90c8d91b20ec602a1eda889cac0&utm_source=twitter&utm_medium=social&utm_campaign=sm-direct.
- Pareto Principle and "The Pernicious Myth of the 80-20 Rule" by Corey Rosen, "from INC:

http://www.inc.com/corey-rosen/the-pernicious-myth-of-the-80-20-rule.html.

- "The Human Era @ Work: Findings" by Tony Schwartz, from The Energy Project and Harvard Business Review: http://documents.kenyon.edu/humanresources/ Whitepaper_Human_Era_at_Work.pdf.
- "The Power of Workplace Gratitude: A Brief Bibliography" by Darcy Jacobson, from Globoforce: http://www.globoforce.com/gfblog/2013/the-power-of-workplace-gratitude-a-brief-bibliography/.

Teams

- "Developing Your Team: Three Types of People (And Why You're the Problem)" by Kris Drum, from Fistful of Talent: http://fistfuloftalent.com/2013/11/developing-team-three-types-people-youre-problem.html.
- "How to Know if Your Team is High-Functioning" by Ben Olds, from Fistful of Talent: http://fistfuloftalent.com/2015/06/know-team-high-functioning.html.
- "Pixar Magic for the Rest of Use: Making Candor a Way of Life" by Patty McManus, from Interaction Associates: http://interactionassociates.com/insights/blog/pixar-magic-rest-us-making-candor-way-life?mkt_tok=3Rk MMJWWfF9wsRokuKXBZKXonjHpfsX56ukoX KG0lMI/0ER3fOvrPUfGjI4ITcR0aPyQAgobGp5I5 FELSLXYRbljt6wIWA%3D%3D#.VgmvoGYo7yN.
- "The Case against Teamwork" by Ty Hall, from Profiles International Workplace 101 Blog: http://info.profilesinternational.com/profiles-employee-assessment-blog/bid/209011/The-Case-against-Teamwor.
- "The New Science of Building Great Teams" by Alex "Sandy" Pentland, from the Harvard Business Review:

https://hbr.org/2012/04/the-new-science-of-building-great-teams/ar/1.

- From Psychology Today: https://www.psychologytoday.com/basics/teamwork.

Tools

- "50 No Cost/Low Cost Recognition Ideas" from the Office of Great Workplace Development, Executive Learning and Mentoring: http://www.michigan.gov/documents/firstgentleman/50_242400_7.pdf.
- Arbinger Institute: http://arbinger.com/whitepapers/.
- "Brainwashed: Seven Ways to Reinvent Yourself" by Seth Godin: http://www.sethgodin.com/sg/docs/brainwash.pdf.
- "Boosting Employee Engagement: 50 Ways to Motivate and Energize Your Workforce" by Gregory P. Smith, from *Chart Your Course*: http://www.chartcourse.com/confirmnavarticles/.
- "Can a Survey Tool Solve the Transparency to Trust Problem?" from *Waggl*: http://www.waggl.it/.
- "Disrupting a Tradition: The Only Engagement Number You Need to Know" by Tracey Smith, Human Capital Institute:
  http://www.hci.org/blog/disrupting-tradition-only-engagement-number-you-need-know.
- "Employee Engagement Surveys" by Kate Pritchard, from XpertHR: http://www.xperthr.co.uk/good-practice-manual/employee-engagement-surveys/112854/?cmpid=ILC|PROF|HRPIO-2013-110-XHR_free_content_links|ptod_article&sfid=701w0000000uNMa.
- "Employee Engagement Tips: 7 Ways to Show Employees They Matter" by David Zinger, from Halogen Talent Space Blog:
  http://www.halogensoftware.com/blog/employee-engagement-tips-7-ways-to-show-employees-they-mat

ter?utm_content=bufferef916&utm_medium=social
&utm_source=twitter.com&utm_campaign=buffer.

- "Engaging Millennial Employees: Recruit and Retain Top Talent with Cause" by Allison McGuire, from www. netowrkforgood.org/Quantum: http://learn.networkforgood.org/rs/networkforgood/ images/Network-for-Good-Millennial-Engagement.pdf

- "Engagement: 1 Idea, 3 Facts, 5 Tips" from the Center for Creative Leadership, Insights and Research: http://insights.ccl.org/articles/leading-effectively-article/ engagement-1-idea-3-facts-5-tips/?utm_source=Silverpop Mailing&utm_medium=email&utm_campaign=Leading %20Effectively%20-%20November%202014%20 %281%29.

- "Getting Engaged: Top Tips for an Engaged Workforce" from *Society for Industrial and organizational Psychology:* http://www.siop.org/WhitePapers/ EngagementFINAL.pdf.

- "Light a Fire: 7 Strategies for Developing Engaged, Inspired Employees" from Grovo: http://resources. grovo.com/light-a-fire/?gref=ACQ_Referral_Training Industry_LightAFire_LnD_EmployeeEngagement_ DedEmail_.

- "O Great One!" at https://www.whosyourogo.com.

- "Passion at Work: Cultivating Worker Passion as a Cornerstone of Talent Development" from CCL/Deloitte: http://d2mtr37y39tpbu.cloudfront.net/wp-content/ uploads/2014/10/DUP-825_Passion-at-work_100714.pdf.

- *People Development Magazine*: http://peopledevelopment magazine.com/.

- *People Artistry: http://www.peopleartistry.com/.*

- *Psychology Today* Tests: https://www.psychologytoday. com/tests.

- "Reflections for Enhancing your Own Employee Engagement" by Kevin Sheridan, from *kevinsheridanllc.com*: http://kevinsheridanllc.com/wp/wp-content/uploads/Kevin-Sheridan-Reflections-for-Enhancing-Your-Own-Employee-Engagement.pdf.
- "5 Retail Secrets that Will Give Your Employees a Boost" by Rich Henson, from *resourcefulmanager.com*: https://www.resourcefulmanager.com/boost-morale-staff/.
- "The Power of Full Engagement: Jim Loehr and Tony Schwartz" by Josh Kaufman: http://joshkaufman.net/power-of-full-engagement/.
- "20 Tips to Improve Employee Engagement and Performance" by Torben Rick, from Meliorate:
  http://www.torbenrick.eu/blog/performance-management/20-tips-to-improve-employee-engagement-and-performance/.
- "Understanding Generational Differences: The Key to Attracting, Motivating, and Retaining Your Workforce" by Sarah Vining, from The National Conference Center:
  http://www.conferencecenter.com/var/conferencecenter/storage/original/application/e92442bcf1d17de215f0271405395d6c.pdf.
- "Why You Should Ask New Employees What Most Shocks Them" by James Allen, from *The Wall Street Journal*:
  http://blogs.wsj.com/experts/2015/08/26/why-you-should-ask-new-employees-what-most-shocks-them/?utm_source=Bain-Insights-September-2015&utm_medium=Newsletter&utm_campaign=why-you-should-ask-new-employees-what-most-shocks-them.

Vendors, Additional Resources

- Aberdeen Group: http://aberdeen.com/research/8648/rb-employee-engagement-strategies/content.aspx.

- Adecco: type "engagement" into the article search box: http://blog.adeccousa.com/.
- AON Hewitt: "Beneath the Surface: Individual Engagement Volatility," http://respond.aonhewitt.com/ UK_2015FORM-Beneaththesurfacewhitepaper.
- Bamboo: "Top 3 Reasons Employees Quit Their Jobs (and Other Deal Breakers)," /HRMorning.com, http://www.hrmorning.com/top-3-reasons-employees-quit-their-jobs-and-other-deal-breakers/?pulb=1.
- Bersin by Deloitte: click on "Blogs," http://home.bersin.com/.
- Blackhawk Engagement Solutions: "The Happiness Study," http://www.bhengagement.com/services/employee/.
- Blanchard International: "The Big Problem with Employee Engagement," http://leaderchat.org/2014/11/10/the-big-problem-with-employee-engagement/.
- Dale Carnegie Training: "What Drives Employee Engagement and Why It Matters," https://www.dalecarnegie.com/assets/1/7/driveengagement_101612_wp.pdf.
- Deloitte University Press: "Passion at Work: Cultivating Worker Passion as a Cornerstone of Talent Development," http://dupress.com/articles/worker-passion-employee-behavior/.
- Entelechy: "Coaching for Talent Development and Employee Engagement": http://www.ipma-er.org/conference/2010/Presentations/Traut%20-%20Coaching%20for%20Talent%20and%20Emp%20Engagemt%20%20Handout.pdf.
- Everwise: "Why Employee Engagement is Keeping HR Executives Up at Night," from: https://www.geteverwise.com/human-resources/

mentoringmonth-why-employee-engagement-is-keeping-hr-executives-up-at-night/.

- Globoforce: http://www.globoforce.com/ (Globoforce Daniel Pink interview transcript: http://www.globoforce.com/resources/features/interview-with-daniel-h-pink/).
- Grovo: "The (New) Definition of Employee Engagement," http://blog.grovo.com/definition-employee-engagement/?utm_source=linkedIn&utm_medium=social&utm_campaign=SocialWarfare; see also, DeFranco Lenny, "Celebrate the 25th Birthday of Employee Engagement: A Look at the Life of HR's Most Important Millennial," 2015, http://blog.grovo.com/celebrate-25th-birthday-employee-engagement/.
- Hogan Assessment: "Why Engagement Matters," http://info.hoganassessments.com/why-engagement-matters.
- IBM Kenexa: "Engagement Levels in Global Decline," http://www.hreonline.com/pdfs/02012012Extra_Kenexa Report.pdf.
- IBM Canada: "A Successful Engagement Program: 10 Lessons from World-Class Organizations," https://www-950.ibm.com/events/wwe/grp/grp101.nsf/vLookupPDFs/A%20successful%20engagement%20program%20TO%20SHARE/$file/A%20successful%20engagement%20program%20TO%20SHARE.pdf
- ITA Group: https://www.itagroup.com/
- Juice: https://www.juiceinc.com/blog.
- Kinetix: The Boostrapper's Guide to Employee Engagement," http://employeeengagement.com/wp-content/uploads/2012/05/Kinetix-whitepaper-Its-Not-You-Its-Me-The-Bootstrapers-Guide-to-Employee-Engagement-Final_1.pdf.
- Maritz Motivational Solutions: "Recognize Achievements Not Just Anniversaries," http://www.maritz.com/~/media/Files/MaritzMotivationSolutions/White-Papers/Whit

ePaperRecognizeAchievementsNotJustAnniversaries-
updated-8172012Rev.pdf.
- NewWest Institute: http://www.newwestinstitute.com/
  winning_culture.html#cm.
- Officevibe: "10 Pillars of Employee Engagement,"
  https://officevibecdn.blob.core.windows.net/resources
  /v4/10-essential-pillars-of-employee-engagement.
  pdf; and "The 12 Things You Need for Successful
  Employee Recognition," https://www.officevibe.com/
  blog/12-things-successful-employee-recognition?
  utm_source=newsletter&utm_medium=email&utm_
  campaign=recognitiontips.
- Profiles International: "The Ultimate Guide to
  Employee Engagement," http://info.profilesinternational.
  com/email/email-the-ultimate-guide-to-employee-
  engagement/?utm_campaign=April+2015:+Ultimate+
  Guide+to+Employee+Engagement+Relaunch&utm_
  source=hs_email&utm_medium=email&utm_content=
  18506962&_hsenc=p2ANqtz-9achBDTbtEpHj9il3
  Oa7vexS8LX8PPWdI5DURhOFBH7QIYYMhID8to
  1PMGirthvm43Oz9n0W-oM-19Tbp9HNFRXZLv
  Pw&_hsmi=18506962; and "Employee Engagement in
  the Modern Workforce," http://info.profilesinternational.
  com/research-library/bid/207410/Employee-Engagement-
  in-the-Modern-Workforce
- Qualrics: "How to Ride a 10-Person Bicycle: Improving
  Employee Engagement in Real-Time," http://www.
  qualtrics.com/wp-content/uploads/2014/07/How-To-Ride-
  A-10-Person-Bicycle.pdf.
- Real Recognition Radio: http://rideau.com/radio.
- Silk Road: "The Ultimate Guide to Employee Engagement,"
  http://hr1.silkroad.com/tyb_ultimate-guide-employee-
  engagement; and http://hr1.silkroad.com/Employee-
  Engagement-Resources

- SkillSoft: "Discover 3 Ways You Can Engage and Retain Employees," http://learn.skillsoft.com/NA-FY16-TM-Pros-Training-Industry-Listicle-3-ways-engage-Register.html.
- Tharpe Robbins: "Recognition Tools," http://tharperobbins.com/learn/recognition-tools.
- Towers Watson: "The Global Workforce Study: Driving Engagement Through a Consumer-Like Experience," https://www.towerswatson.com/en-US/Insights/IC-Types/Survey-Research-Results/2014/08/the-2014-global-workforce-study.
- Weaving Influence: http://weavinginfluence.com/

Vendors, Gifts (please, note relative importance, see Ch. 6)

- Baudville (gift vendor): http://www.baudville.com/recognition-resource-center; also, "10 Ways to Revitalize Your Employee Recognition Program": http://www.baudville.com/10-Ways-to-Revitalize-Your-Employee-Recognition-Program/article-view/256.
- Bonusly: https://bonus.ly/employee-recognition-guide.
- Incentive Research Foundation (gift vendor): http://theirf.org/.
- Intelispend, (gift vendor): http://www.bhengagement.com/employee-rewards-recognition/.
- Kudos (gift vendor): http://kudosnow.com/en/blog.
- O. C. Tanner: http://octanner.com/.
- Officevibe: https://www.officevibe.com/
- Terrberry: http://www.terryberry.com/resourceslearn/tools.aspx

Video Primers

- *"Drive*: The Surprising Truth about What Motivates Us" from Daniel Pink: http://bkvids.blogspot.com/2014/08/

the-surprising-science-of-motivation.html?utm_source=
%2B%2B%2B%2B%2B%2B%2BJS+October+2%2c+
2014+Newsletter&utm_campaign=10/2/14+communique
&utm_medium=email.

- "Employee Engagement– Who's Sinking Your Boat?" from Bob Kelleher: https://www.youtube.com/watch?v=y4nwoZ02AJM.

- Employee Engagement Strategy" from Keven Kruse: https://www.youtube.com/watch?v=HNr4tE74xUE.

- "Flow, The Secret to Happiness" from Mihaly Csikszentimihalyi:: http://www.ted.com/talks/mihaly_csikszentmihalyi_on_flow

- "Informal Networks" from Informal Networks, Ltd.: https://www.youtube.com/watch?v=-GuIyTeZvG8&feature=player_embedded

- "One Minute Manager, On Change" from Ken Blanchard:: https://www.youtube.com/watch?v=ZRU9ERi-GtM.

- "Ten Leadership Theories in 5 Minutes" from Michael Zigarelli: https://www.youtube.com/watch?v=XKUPDUDOBVo.

- "The Employee Engagement Network's Video Collection": http://api.ning.com/files/Gp85O2XzVxjwN4lw3yPTCS9Wz9Q1JxV8im0tStUVOMr313njxlWWsEBBz0ZTp2J0DcyFtwLGlkJq3sbnkYeZ*wQ8yXUmaRzD/EENVideoListingsBook.pdf

- "The Happy Secret to Better Work" from Shawn Achor: http://www.ted.com/talks/shawn_achor_the_happy_secret_to_better_work?language=en.

- "Why Motivating Doesn't Work," webinar from Susan Fowler: https://attendee.gotowebinar.com/register/300000000009929555.

Appendix D

INTERACTIVE INDEX

You will not find any page numbers in this index!

In the final stages of production, as I pondered an index, Mortimer Alder's "How to Mark a Book" came to mind. Restated from the earlier introduction, Adler states,

> "There are two ways in which one can own a book. The first is the property right you establish by paying for it, just as you pay for clothes and furniture. But this act of purchase is only the prelude to possession. Full ownership comes only when you have made it a part of yourself, and the best way to make yourself a part of it is by writing in it. Reading, if it is active, is thinking..., [and] the marked book is usually the thought-through book. And that is exactly what reading a book should be: a conversation between you and the author."

To bridge the gap between writer and reader, I invite you to use these pages to pen your own notes and to add page numbers to the terms that best serve your personal contexts and needs! I would love to hear from you about your recognition and engagement challenges and victories. Please connect by sending your thoughts, criticisms, and suggestions to miholic@cox.net.

[Reader: Add page numbers and notes to suit your purpose(s); see rationale above]

A

Ability
Access
Accountable, Accountability
Acknowledge
Action
Active (Values)
Achievement(s)
Activities
Actualization
Advance, Advancement
Agenda(s)
Altruistic
Appreciate, Appreciation
Aspire, Aspiration
Assess, Assessment, Assessing
Assign, Assignment(s)
Authentic, Authenticity
Autonomous, Autonomy
Average
Award(s)
Authority, Authoritarianism

B

Belong, Belonging
Behavior, Behavioral
Belief(s)
Benefit(s)
Bored, Boredom

Disenfranchisement
Distributive
Dishonest
Dissonance
Distort, Distortion
Distrust
Dogmatic
Dreams
Drive, Driver
Dynamic(s)
Dysfunction(al)

E

Effect(s)
Effort(s)
Egalitarian
Ego
Emotion, Emotional
Empower, Empowerment
Empathize
Empathy
Enable, Enablement
Encourage, Encouragement
Energy
Entitlement
Entrepreneur, Entrepreneurial,
Entrepreneurship
Entrust
Enjoy
Equity
Esteem
Ethic, Ethics,
Ethical, Ethically

Evaluate, Evaluation
Excellence
Excite
Exclude, Exclusion
Expectations
Expert, Expertise
Extrinsic

F

Fair, Fairness
Faith
Fear, Fearful
Feedback
Feel
Fit
Flat (Hierarchy)
Flexible
Flow
Focus
Friend(s), Friendship(s)
Fuel
Fun
Function(al)

G

Genuine
Gift(s)
Give, Giving
Goals
Gossip(s)
Gratitude
Great(ness)

Grow, Growth
Guide(s) (d)

H

Habit(s)
Happy, Happiness
Heart
Hedgehog
Help, Helping
Hierarchy
Holacratic
Honest, Honestly,
How
Human
Humble
Humility

I

Ignite
Impact
Impartial, Impartially
Improvise,
Improvisation
Include, Inclusion,
Inclusive
Incompetence
Individual,
Individualized
Influence
Initiative
Innovation
Inspire, Inspiration

Input
Interdependence
Interview(s)
Intimacy
Intrinsic
Intuitive
Inventory
Involvement
Isolated, Isolation

J

Job
Joy
Journey
Judge, Judging
Just

K

Know-how

L

Label(s)
Learn, Learning
Learner(s)
Learning Styles
Leader(s), Leadership
Legacy
Lesson(s)
Leverage
Listen(s), Listening
Loop

Love
Loyal, Loyalty

M

Master, Mastery
Manager(s), Management
Message, Messaging
Mediocrity
Membership
Meaning,
Meaningful(ness)
Mentor(s), Mentoring
Meta-analysis
Metric(s)
Measure(s), Measurement
Micromanagement
Mind
Misjudging
Mission
Mistake(s)
Mistrust
Model, Modeling
Money
Moral(s)
Morale
Motivate, Motivation

N

Negative(s), Negativity
Network(s)
Neuroscience

O

Objective(s), Objectively
On-boarding
Opportunity(ies)
Organization
Ostracize
Other-centric
Outliers

P

Paranoia
Passion
Pay, Paycheck
Peace
Peer(s)
Perception(s)
Perfection(s)
Perform, Performers,
Performance
Persistence
Person/Personality(ies)
Personnel
Perspective(s)
Peter Principle
Plan(s), Planning
Point(s) of View
Positive
Power
Potential, Potentialities
Practice(s)
Principle(s)
Priority, Priorities

Problem Solving
Productivity
Profit
Progress, Progression
Psychological
Psychosocial
Purpose

Q

Question(s)
Q12
Quality

R

Reach
Recognize, Recognition
Reflect(ion)
Relationship(s)
Resource(s)
Respect(ed)
Responsibility
Retribution
Reward(s)
Risk(s)
Return(s) on Investment
Role(s)
Rule(s)

S

Sabotage
Safety

Salary
Satisfaction
Satisfy
Scaffold(ing)
Security
Self, Selfish,
Selfless, Selfishness
Self-actualization
Self-awareness
Self-esteem
Servant
Service
Silence
Share(s), Shared,
Sharing
Skeptical, Skepticism
Skill(s)
Social/Sociological
Spirit
Stakeholder, Stake-holding
Status
Status Quo
Staff, Staffing
Strategy, Strategies
Strength(s)
Story
Succession
Support, Supportive
Supervise, Supervisor(s)
Survey
SWOT
Synergy
System, Systematic

T

Talent(s)
Task(s), Task-oriented
Taxonomy
Teach, Teacher
Team(s)
TED
Thank You
Thrive
Time
Title(s)
Top-Down
Touch
Toxic
Train, Trainer
Transaction(al)
Transcend
Transform(ational)
Transparent,
Transparency
Trap(s)
Trust
Truth(s)
Turnover

U

Unconditional
Universal
V

Value(s)
Vision

Vincent Miholic, Ph.D.

Voice(s)
Vulnerable,
Vulnerability

W

Walking Dead
Well-being
Will (noun)
Win
Why (the)
Work
Work-life
Worker
Workplace

Z

Zen
Zombie

Appendix E

Sample Recognition Templates

The "awards," more properly recognition templates, below, are not intended to be comprehensive or complete, but provide fundamental starting points and basic background to aid success in using person to person recognition awards components, which are vastly different from impersonal cash incentives.

1. Informal Peer-to Peer Attitude Award

Process:

Ex. "ATTITUDE is Everything Award":

The *AIE* Award is an **informal,** impromptu and spontaneous recognition, based on the following "Level 5 Leadership" principles (see Collins) and other light-hearted, subjective criteria, such as:

- Brings a sense of humor
- Displays a sense of gratitude
- Exudes joy
- Talks about ideas
- Demonstrates transformational actions
- Puts people first
- Endeavors to learn more about others
- Works to flattening hierarchies
- Friendly with a purpose
- Volunteers a helping hand
- Instills greatness in others

The *AIE* Award Rules:

1. Award is a traveling trophy <u>cannot be held for more than two weeks</u>. The idea is to keep it dynamic and moving, the intent is to think beyond your immediate surroundings and "pay it forward."

2. Nominator gathers folks around (send meeting invite via email or calendar). And speaks on behalf of the recipient; announces the reason for the recognition.

3. The award cannot be returned to the person who gave it to you the last time around. (Can include a possible "steal" provision after three days to assure greater circulation and access).

4. Formal certificates do not accompany the trophy, but spirited recipients are invited to voluntarily chart "wins" on the recognition bulletin board, or post a annual running list of recipients.

Weakness: While better than an "employee of the month" award, some employees or departments can monopolize the award (commonly occurs where silos/disconnected departments exist). Some potential for favoritism has to be addressed by proper critiera and procedures.

2. Informal Peer-to Peer Attitude Award

"Shout Out" Recognition
Process:

Why Shout Outs? Recognition experts agree, being thanked is good not only for the receiver but for the giver. Acknowledgement of productive acts should be goal related, timely, and frequent.

Shout Outs emphasize <u>giving</u> and giving everyone a leadership role by recognizing each other.

What is a Shout Out? An internal means to recognize each other. Shout-outs must be professional in nature and meant to verbally recognize a teammate that you know performed a job in the right way or whose input produced an unexpected improvement. Shout Outs are positive compliments about achieving a specific result/goal and can be a way to let our teammates know the value of their performance input: help, problem solving, extra-effort, etc.; accomplishments outside of the office that would shine a positive light inside the office; things that the supervisor would highlight in an annual evaluation of the employee.

How to Shout Out? First, **personally recognize the individual** (either one-on-one or in unit meeting, fitting the employee's personality; some folks are more understated than others). Second, once you have already thanked and/or congratulated the teammate face to face, **everyone** is encouraged to submit the Shout Out as a public display of thanks, using ≤ 50 words, identifying from and to whom, and describing why. Then, submit/post your Shout Out to your internal newsletter/app/SharePoint/bulletin board to share with the entire office.

How Shout Outs Deviate from other peer to peer awards? Billboards of "the month's best salesperson" or other "employee of the month" placards are restricted to the person holding the award for the designated time. It also can become too predictable and sometimes feel like cronyism or favoritism if the criteria are not clear nor fairly applied. Shout Outs expand the immediacy and the opportunity to recognize each other for a wider variety of reasons. This allows more people to be performance stand outs with greater parity and for equally valid reasons. Experiment with what works best to foster effective cultural habits and good will!

3. Formal Peer-to Peer Performance Award

Process:

1. This is a **traveling trophy** which quarterly moves to new recipients. A certificate will also accompany the trophy, and history of recipients' names will be posted.

Weakness: Should not be tied to monetary awards. Managers or colleagues in a department do not understand the power of gratitude will be remiss to participate. Time to submit a nomination may be perceived as tedium and not worth the time.

2. **Nominations** can be submitted at any time to screening committee. See sample Peer Recognition Awards Nomination Form.
   - No more than a **maximum of 3 nominations** per nominator/quarter accepted.

   - A person/s may be nominated more than once (different nominators for different contributions).
   - If applicable (contribution impacts multiple areas), a person/s may be nominated by multiple nominators for the same contribution.
   - **Posting**: Once received, the nomination will immediately be posted on awards bulletin board in high traffic area. A copy of the nomination will be provided to the recipient.

3. **Deadline** for First recognition period nominations is _____ (2 weeks prior to evaluation of nominations – review committee should be peers, rather than formal managers/supervisors). Any nominations after deadline will roll-over to next quarter.

4. Award Announcement: An email recognizing all nominees will be sent after the deadline, prior to the award meeting, and ideally nominees should be recognized at an all hands on deck meeting. A review committee should consist of peers, rather than formal managers/supervisors will evaluate all nominations using advertised criteria to determine the final award recipient. The department director or designee will announce the award recipient.

Weakness: It's nearly impossible to avoid bias, but if the process and criteria are honestly employed, top candidates surface very quickly.

5.Nomination Form Contents/Peer Recognition Nomination Form

Nominee: Award recipients will be selected on the merits and strengths of the contribution(s) made towards the following goals. Choose all that apply.

() Innovation/Initiative – Recognizing leadership of, or outstanding participation in, a project or process improvement that aligns with our mission and/or streamlines our operations.

() Teamwork – To recognize outstanding commitment to teamwork by thinking creatively, removing internal boundaries, and communicating effectively.

() Outstanding Customer Service – To recognize excellent service that exceeds our customers' (internal or external) expectations.

( ) Commitment to Excellence – To recognize excellence in any endeavor that enhances the workplace and creates a positive work environment and culture.

Thank you for taking the time to recognize your peers. Please comment on why this employee is an excellent candidate to receive the award. Be as timely and specific as possible. Attach additional documentation if necessary. You may be contacted for more information.

Nominated by: _____**Date:** _____

6. Formal Peer-to Peer Performance Award/Evaluation Criteria:

_____

Evaluation Criteria for Formal Peer-to-Peer Performance Award. Check all that apply. ***Ex.* award name *INSPIRE*** [Integrity, Noteworthy, Smart, Productive, Innovative, Responsible, and Engaged]

1. **Number** of Nominations Received.

2. **Innovative**: impact, implemented and sustained over time, challenges/solution, cost savings.

3. **Initiative:** concept/strategy, management, budget, create value, takes initiative to improve skills and knowledge, seeks mentor for advice, guidance, feedback.

4. **Teamwork:** commitment to stakeholders, retention, life-span, engagement, social impact, calm and assured in stressful situations, integrates a sense of humor, creates a positive atmosphere, accepts and acts upon constructive criticism, serves as a positive role model, recognizes others either publically or privately.

5. Customer Service: expectations, circumstances, comparable services, convenience, accessibility, timeliness, reliability, thoroughness, prompt, knowledgeable, friendly, courteous.

6. Commitment to Excellence/Professionalism: consistently excelled in their positions, demonstrated integrity, demonstrated strong commitment to mission and values, exhibits high degree of camaraderie and professionalism, creates quality product.

7. Timeliness: works diligently to help complete critical work projects, wide array of work related competence, prioritizes workload in an efficient and timely fashion, completes tasks with little direction or supervision.

8. Issue Resolution: quickly troubleshoots and solves problems, communicates effectively, helps others in stressful situations.

Credits for Images

A generous thank you is extended to contributors to the public domain sites. A special thank you to Guy Sie for making the cover art available as a public domain image.

Public Domain Descriptions and Permissions: Unless otherwise identified, all graphics are original. **All graphics are public domain.**

Cover:
File: http://www.uhdwallpapers.org/2014/11/mechanical-gears-movement-watch-time.html. **File:** Mechanical. Gears. Movement. Watch. Time. Wallpaper **Photographer**: Guy Sie (Website). Flickr Portfolio June 16, 2012. License: Creative Commons Attribution-ShareAlike 2.0 Generic. Widescreen Desktop / Macbook (Retina): 2880x1800. **Free to Share** — copy and redistribute the material in any medium or format **Adapt** — remix, transform, and build upon the material for any purpose, even commercially. The licensor cannot revoke these freedoms as long as you follow the license terms are followed. **Attribution** —*photographer and the source.* link to the license, and indicate if changes were made in any reasonable manner, but not in any way that suggests the licensor endorses you or your use. **ShareAlike** — If you remix, transform, or build upon the material, you must distribute your contributions under the same license as the original. **No additional restrictions** — legal terms or technological measures that legally restrict others from doing anything the license permits not applied for this use.

File: Salvage: Are you helping? with salvage: LC-USZC2-1179https://www.loc.gov/item/98518981/ Photos, Prints, Drawings **Rights Advisory: No known restrictions on publication. Contributor Names**: Federal Art Project, sponsor. Created / Published: So. Calif.: Work Projects Administration, between 1941 and 1943]. Notes: Work Projects Administration Poster Collection (Library of Congress). **Call Number/ Physical Location**: POS - WPA - CA .01 .A58, no. 1 (C size) [P&P]. Repository: Library of Congress Prints and Photographs Division Washington, D.C. 20540 USA. Digital Id: cph 3b49079 http://hdl.loc.gov/loc.pnp/cph.3b49079. Library of Congress Catalog Number: 98518981. Reproduction Number: LC-USZC2-1179 (color film copy slide). Library of Congress Catalog Number Record:https://lccn.loc.gov/98518981. Online Public Access Catalog Record: https://catalog.loc.gov/vwebv/search?search Code=STNO&searchArg=98518981&searchType=1&recCount=10 Additional Metadata Formats:MARCXML Record, MODS Record, Dublin Core Record

Birds Graphics (by associated number):
Files:
1. http://digitalmedia.fws.gov/cdm/singleitem/collection/natdiglib/id/13100/ rec/26 **Title:** Snow Geese in Flight. **Alternative Title:** Chen caerulescens; **Rights:** Public Domain. **Contact:** nctcimages@fws.gov; **Creator:** Menke, Dave; **Description:** A flock of Snow Geese take flight in the DeSoto National Wildlife Refuge located in Missouri Valley, Iowa. **FWS Resource:** http://www.fws.gov/refuges/profiles/index.cfm?id=33510. **Publisher:** U.S. Fish and Wildlife Services. **Source:** NCTC Image Library. **Full resolution:** Snow-Geese-in-Flight-09016.jpg. **Date:** 2011-07-27 http://digitalmedia.fws.gov/FullRes/natdiglib/Snow-Geese-in-Flight-09016.jpg.

2. https://commons.wikimedia.org/wiki/File:PSM_V84_D218_Flocking_ habit_of_migratory_birds_fig6.jpg.

File: Flocking Fig. 6. This work is in the public domain in the United States because it was published (or registered with the U.S. Copyright Office) before January 1, 1923. File:PSM V84 D218. **Author:** H. K. Job. **Description:** Flock of Blue Geese in echolon formation, photographed at the Mississippi delta by the Rev. H.K. Job. Note the acute angle of the flock and that for each goose the view is unobscured in front and on the side, habit of migratory birds fig6.jpg; From Wikimedia Commons, the free media repository. **Date:** 1914. **Source:** C. C. Trowbridge: *On the origin of the flocking habit of migratory birds.* The Popular science monthly, Volume 84, p214. New York, Popular Science Pub. Co., March 1914. Online: archive.org.

3. http://www.pdpics.com/photo/6926-birds-formation/. **File:** Birds formation. 'Birds formation.' **Author**: Mukesh Patil_Public domain photo. Use this royalty free image in any project (commercial or personal). PDPics.com - Public Domain Picture. Pdpics.com is a repository of public domain pictures and photographs. Use freely in any

project. This photo was taken at 1:14am on Sunday 28th February 2016 **License :** Public domain images (CC0) **Size :** 3500px x 1733px **Uploaded :** 26-06-2013.

5. http://www.pdpics.com/photo/6807-birds/ **File:** Birds Download 'Birds' Public domain photo. Use this royalty free image in any project (commercial or personal). This photo was taken at 1:17am on Sunday 28th February 2016 \ \ Size : 3500px x 2218px Camera Used: License : Public domain images (CC0) **Uploaded:** 24-06-2013. **Author:** Mukesh Patil. PDPics.com - Public Domain Pictures Pdpics.com, free public domain pictures and photographs. Use freely in any project.

File: **adapted from Rogers Diffusion of Innovations Curve.** ideas. svg_https://commons.wikimedia.org/wiki/File:Diffusion_of_ideas.svg. From Wikimedia Commons, the free media repository *Public Domain.* worldwide. In some countries this may not be legally possible, *right to use this work for any purpose, without any conditions, unless such conditions are required by law.* **Description:** The diffusion of innovations according to Rogers (1962). With successive groups of consumers adopting the new technology (shown in blue), its market share (yellow) will eventually reach the saturation level. **Date:** 28 February 2012. Based on Rogers, E. (1962) Diffusion of innovations. Free Press, London, NY, USA. **File**: *Diffusion of ideas.svg* Size of this PNG preview of this SVG file: 800 × 600 pixels.

Compass: https://commons.wikimedia.org/wiki/. File: Gray_compass_rose. svg. File:Gray compass rose.svg. From Wikimedia Commons, the free media repository, *right to use this work for any purpose, without any conditions, unless such conditions are required by law.* **Description:** Français : Rose des vents pour carte. **Source:** Own work. **Author:** Vascer. 13:33, 27 August 2010 Size of this PNG preview of this SVG file: 162 × 197 pixels. The copyright holder of this work, release this work into the public domain. This applies worldwide.

Skinner Box: Composite of two images from wikimedia.org https:// commons.wikimedia.org/wiki/. **File**: Cubicle.png. **Author: HJ van Ree; Cubicle.png (142 × 127 pixels, file size: 6 KB, MIME type: image/png) Description:** English: cubicle. **Date:** 1 January 2010. **Source:** User:HJ van Ree. I, the copyright holder of this work, hereby publish it under the following licenses: You are free: to share – to copy, distribute and transmit the work, to remix – to adapt the work; Under the following conditions: attribution – You must attribute the work in the manner specified by the author or licensor (but not in any way that suggests that they endorse you or your use of the work. Share alike – If you alter, transform, or build upon this work, you may distribute the resulting work only under the same or similar license to this one. Permission is granted to copy, distribute and/or modify this document under the terms of the GNU Free Documentation License, Version 1.2 or any later version published by the Free Software Foundation; with no Invariant Sections, no Front-Cover Texts, and no Back-Cover Texts. A copy of the license is included in the section entitled *GNU Free Documentation License.*

File: https://commons.wikimedia.org/wiki/File:Skinner_box_scheme_01. png. **Author**: Andreasl. Skinner box scheme 01.png. From Wikimedia Commons, the free media repository. **Description:** Skinner box, a cage to perform behavioral experiments with animals. **Date:** 26 April 2007. **Source:** Adapted from **Image**: Boite skinner.jpg. Permission is granted to copy, distribute and/or modify this document under the terms of the GNU Free Documentation License, Version 1.2 or any later version published by the Free Software Foundation; with no Invariant Sections, no Front-Cover Texts, and no Back-Cover Texts. A copy of the license is included in the section entitled *GNU Free Documentation License.* This file is licensed under the Creative Commons Attribution-Share Alike 3.0 Unported license. Free: to share – to copy, distribute and transmit the work, to remix – to adapt the work. Under the following conditions: attribution - under the terms of the GNU Free Documentation License, Version 1.2 or any later version published by the Free Software Foundation; with no Invariant Sections, no Front-Cover Texts, and no Back-Cover Texts. A copy of the license is included in the section entitled *GNU Free Documentation License.*

Open Book Editions
A Berrett-Koehler Partner

Open Book Editions is a joint venture between Berrett-Koehler Publishers and Author Solutions, the market leader in self-publishing. There are many more aspiring authors who share Berrett-Koehler's mission than we can sustainably publish. To serve these authors, Open Book Editions offers a comprehensive self-publishing opportunity.

A Shared Mission

Open Book Editions welcomes authors who share the Berrett-Koehler mission—Creating a World That Works for All. We believe that to truly create a better world, action is needed at all levels—individual, organizational, and societal. At the individual level, our publications help people align their lives with their values and with their aspirations for a better world. At the organizational level, we promote progressive leadership and management practices, socially responsible approaches to business, and humane and effective organizations. At the societal level, we publish content that advances social and economic justice, shared prosperity, sustainability, and new solutions to national and global issues.

Open Book Editions represents a new way to further the BK mission and expand our community. We look forward to helping more authors challenge conventional thinking, introduce new ideas, and foster positive change.

For more information, see the Open Book Editions website:
http://www.iuniverse.com/Packages/OpenBookEditions.aspx

Join the BK Community! See exclusive author videos, join discussion groups, find out about upcoming events, read author blogs, and much more! http://bkcommunity.com/